MASCULINIST IMPULSES

MASCULINIST IMPULSES

TOOMER, HURSTON, BLACK WRITING,

AND MODERNITY

Nathan Grant

University of Missouri Press
Columbia and London

Library of Congress Cataloging-in-Publication Data

Grant, Nathan, 1957–
Masculinist impulses : Toomer, Hurston, Black writing, and
modernity / Nathan Grant.
p.   cm.
Includes bibliographical references and index.
ISBN 0-8262-1516-5 (alk. paper)
1. American fiction—African American authors—History and
criticism. 2. American fiction—20th century—History and criticism.
3. African Americans—Intellectual life—20th century. 4. Hurston,
Zora Neale—Characters—Men. 5. Modernism (Literature)—United
States. 6. Toomer, Jean, 1894–1967. Cane. 7. African American
men in literature. 8. Masculinity in literature. 9. Race in literature.
10. Men in literature. I. Title.
PS374.N4G73 2004
813'.5099286'08996073—dc22

♾ This paper meets the requirements of the
American National Standard for Permanence of Paper
for Printed Library Materials, Z39.48, 1984.

Text designer: Stephanie Foley
Jacket designer: Jennifer Cropp
Typesetter: Crane Composition, Inc.
Printer and binder: The Maple-Vail Book Manufacturing Group
Typeface: Times New Roman

The University of Missouri Press
acknowledges the generous contribution
provided by the Julian Park Fund of the
State University of New York at Buffalo
toward the publication of this book.

FOR SINIKKA

CONTENTS

Acknowledgments   ix

Abbreviations   xi

1. Introduction: Modernism and the Masculinist Impulse   1

2. Toomer's Male Prison and the Spectatorial Artist   20

3. Of Silent Strivings: *Cane*'s Mute and Dreaming Dictie   49

4. Hurston's Masculinist Critique of the South   92

5. Zora Neale Hurston and the Romance of the Supernature   117

6. Promised Lands: The New Jerusalem's Inner City and
   John Edgar Wideman's Philadelphia Story   145

7. When and Where We Enter: Closing the Gap in
   Morrison's *Beloved* and Naylor's *Mama Day*   182

Conclusion   211

Bibliography   217

Index   229

ACKNOWLEDGMENTS

I have often read, in such pages as these, the writer's expression that without the sincere, determined, and generous support of those named, the project with which the writer was engaged would not have been possible. I have always imagined that when one is in a position to write such words, one feels as fortunate as all the foregoing for such good colleagues and friends. But I have experienced something even rarer than this: I have had the unalloyed perception that I am far more fortunate than all the rest, and that no writer ever enjoyed a greater fund of goodwill, encouragement, ideas, and love. I should certainly like to thank Barbara Bono, who was there for me when I simply could not write; Victor Doyno, who kindly presented my work on the other side of the continent when I could not fly. David Schmid, who adroitly adjusted his innumerable time constraints to read for me; Carrie Bramen, Joseph Conte, Robert Daly, Ken Dauber, Masani Alexis DeVeaux, Stacy Hubbard, Shaun Irlam, Neil Schmitz, Mark Shechner, Jim Swan, and Susan Varney, who in their various ways, and all of those significantly, helped me move this process along.

Many thanks also to Barbara Foley and Arnold Rampersad for their incisive reads of early portions of the manuscript, and to Jim Hatch and Valerie Smith for reminding me of what was possible. Thanks as well to Lindsey Hair and Deidre Lynch, who offered sympathy when fortunes were low. And I would be irremediably remiss if I neglected to include Roberto Tejada for his wisdom and his great-souled generosity.

Where, indeed, is one without helpful graduate assistants? I warrant that he is hopelessly at sea, and without this group, I would surely have been without a most valuable resource. These wonderful students—Shelby Crosby, Tom Morgan, Lorna Perez, Peter Ramos, and Mary Visconti—fearlessly ferreted out information and volunteered their time, often at great sacrifice to their own projects, and always shared ideas with grace and aplomb.

The curators and staff of the Beinecke Rare Book and Manuscript Library at Yale University were wonderfully helpful in their assistance with the Jean Toomer Papers, an infinitely vast portion of the James Weldon Johnson Collection. Generous support for research came from the United University Professions Nuala McGann Drescher Affirmative Action Research Award.

The Frederick Douglass Center and the Rush Rhees Library at the University of Rochester were a pleasure to visit, and their librarians greatly assisted me in this project. So too did the staff of the George A. Smathers Libraries at the University of Florida at Gainesville, as I was able to work with materials there regarding the life and work of Zora Neale Hurston. Many thanks must also go to the very able staff of the Lockwood and Capen Libraries at the University of Buffalo, particularly for their very hard work and cheerful understanding of my incorrigible hoarding of overdue materials.

A final and wholly heartfelt thanks is long overdue to my life partner, my dearest Sinikka, who never flinched at my frustrations, not even when those frustrations became inanities. She has been a rock, a truly stabilizing influence in several turbulent periods when whole sections of the work were gutted for a "something better" that was as yet nonexistent. There were many of the best hours of our lives spent discussing anything *except* this book over wine and cheese, and her love, her generosity, and her gentle spirit become all my reasons for this effort.

ABBREVIATIONS

The following are abbreviations of the primary works often referred to in this text:

Along	*Along This Way*
Complete Stories	*The Complete Stories of Zora Neale Hurston*
DTR	*Dust Tracks on a Road*
Fire	*Philadelphia Fire*
Incidents	*Incidents in the Life of a Slave Girl*
Jonah	*Jonah's Gourd Vine*
Liberty	*Liberty or Death; or, Heaven's Infraction of the Fugitive Slave Law*
Moses	*Moses, Man of the Mountain*
Narrative	*Narrative of the Life of Frederick Douglass, an American Slave, Written by Himself* (1845)
Reason	*The Reason Why the Colored American Is Not in the Columbian Exposition*
Seraph	*Seraph on the Suwanee*
Souls	*The Souls of Black Folk*
Their Eyes	*Their Eyes Were Watching God*
TMH	*Tell My Horse*

MASCULINIST IMPULSES

1

INTRODUCTION

Modernism and the Masculinist Impulse

The preeminent African American autobiography of the nineteenth century, and the most widely influential text in the study of black autobiography today, is Frederick Douglass's 1845 *Narrative of the Life*. It sought, among other things, to solve the problem of being by rescuing from the situation of bondage the twin sensibilities of rage and defiance. For Douglass, this was crystallized, ultimately, in what some commentators have called his "cult of masculinity." His battle with the slavebreaker Edward Covey is "the turning-point" of not only his career as a slave but also the *Narrative*. In perhaps the most famous lines in the tradition of African American autobiography, Douglass sets the terms of his emergence into the realm of self-possessed consciousness: "You have seen how a man was made a slave; you shall see how a slave was made a man." This expression of defiance, which set the style for narratives following Douglass's, fashioned the desire beyond nonbeing: the writing of oneself into existence. But this was a project that seemed doomed to frustration. The first narratives known to emphasize the black male as subject—John Jea's, Henry Bibb's, and Douglass's—had begun to appear in the 1840s. Though David Walker's scathing *Appeal* of 1829 was already perhaps the most passionate effort of black men to gain both civil and social equality, they were generally forced to deny the rage they felt at their enslavement. Gaining wide acceptance among Southern whites was the viewpoint of Thomas R. Dew, and later George Fitzhugh, that Africans were by nature brutish and barbaric and that slavery was their only civilizing influence. In Richard Yarborough's

1

estimation, nineteenth-century African American thinkers had constructed a purposive masculinity as a countermeasure—one indeed
identical to normative white masculinity—in order to deflect claims
of inferiority that would surely materialize in the wake of expressions
of black anger: "[Douglass and other nineteenth-century African
American spokespersons] saw the crucial test of black fitness to be
whether or not black men were, in fact, what was conventionally
considered 'manly.' [The middle-class definitions of manliness they
used] contained the following crucial ingredients: nobility, intelligence, strength, articulateness, loyalty, virtue, rationality, courage,
self-control, courtliness, honesty, and physical attractiveness as defined in white Western European terms."[1]

Black men, however, had at best a tenuous hold on these definitions. At every juncture was the specter of the black male as beast, a
kind of raging, drunken Caliban who deserved his end of finally
being subdued by his white male betters. Since few of the elements
of middle-class manhood in Yarborough's litany could be attributed
to blackness, the function of class as a barrier to acquiring these elements consistently presented itself as a social issue for black intellectuals. How, they seemed to ask in unison, could one achieve
social equality without sacrificing a sense of racial loyalty? Even if
race were thinkable then as it is today—a social construction that for
its underpinning as essentialism loses rather than gains legitimacy—
how was it possible for blacks, as Terry Eagleton suggests, to preserve a sense of their humanity while ignoring precisely "the place
where . . . humanity is wounded and refused"? In trenchant remarks
that emphasize the difficulty in answering this question even today,
Houston Baker writes that Douglass, in reclaiming his past and in
making the transition from slave to Christian abolitionist, manages
to miss the importance of securing a textual black identity in the
process: "Even though the writer seems to have been certain . . .
how he was going to picture his development and how the emergent
self should appear to the reader, he seems to have suppressed the
fact that one cannot transcend existence in a universe where there is
only existence. One can realize one's humanity through 'speech and
concept,' but one cannot distinguish the uniqueness of the self if the

---

1. Richard Yarborough, "Race, Violence, and Manhood: The Masculine Ideal in
Frederick Douglass's *The Heroic Slave*," 167–68.

'avenue towards areas of the self' excludes rigorously individualizing definitions of a human, black identity." These "rigorously individualizing definitions" of identity envision a realizable humanity that is also a black one only when the background of slavery is considered: the fact of freedom is manifest in the autonomy of the body, which was an elusive freedom for both black men and women. Black men sought through a felt sense of maleness an economic autonomy of the body, which was registered by the ability to control one's own labor; as Baker points out elsewhere, the *Narrative* is heavily characterized by Douglass's efforts to create a consciousness of independent labor.[2] But the black male relationship to free labor was always met with a double irony. Though the black male did not own his manhood if he did not own his labor, the status of free labor, once attained, suggested an inexorable component of class consciousness, and its scarcity in slaveocracy left the black male the exponent of a legitimate rage—but a rage that would be used nevertheless to paint the black as beast.

Even the tempestuous fight with Edward Covey in the *Narrative*, then, is presumably muted in its more violent aspects: it seems reasonable to expect a fistfight that lasted two hours to indicate as its result a description of more violence than is available in the text. On the other hand, Douglass's restraint from an expression of rage actually functions as a masking: just as he wishes not to dilute Covey's status as monster by detailing his own anger, what is really at stake for Douglass is a strike for free labor, which will likely not be realized by his audience if he secures his freedom by fully unleashing his rage. Similarly, Douglass must be careful to diminish fears among his audience of the sexual side of the beast in discussing his relationship to his mistress and eventual tutor, Sophia Auld. There is often in the critical commentary an apt suggestion of a subliminal sexual bond between Douglass and Auld in this episode; as Douglass writes, "I was utterly astonished at her goodness. I scarcely knew how to behave towards her. She was entirely unlike any other white woman I had ever seen. I could not approach her as I was accustomed to approach other white ladies. . . . Her face was made of heavenly

2. Terry Eagleton, Frederic Jameson, and Edward Said, *Nationalism, Colonialism and Literature,* 24; Houston A. Baker, Jr., *The Journey Back: Issues in Black Literature and Criticism,* 38; Baker, *Blues, Ideology and Afro-American Literature: A Vernacular Theory,* 47–50.

smiles, and her voice of tranquil music" (*Narrative,* 36–37). But though this hint of sexuality may be one issue in the text, Douglass's real agenda is the promotion of a different sort of alliance. Douglass is a child of eight at this point in the *Narrative,* making sexuality difficult to imagine. At its horizon, however, is a valuation of maternity, which at various points is intertwined with the sexual; as an object of love in any case, Douglass apotheosizes Sophia Auld, making her a radiant paragon of virtue. This of course both complicates Douglass's relationship with his own mother, Harriet Bailey, about whom he seems so poignantly dismissive at the text's very opening, and reveals, correspondingly, black women's notorious absence throughout the text. David Leverenz remarks that Douglass's African American first wife, Anna Murray Douglass, seemed, given mention of her in the *Narrative,* "almost an afterthought," spending "the rest of her life as the stereotypic helpmeet to the public man of force." It continues to remain difficult at best to separate the private Douglass from the public one, or to gauge precisely the influence sexuality and race had on that aspect of the public Douglass that was also literary. While the near erasure of Anna Murray remains a problem in the text perhaps even regarding Douglass's commitment to black feminism, Leverenz remarks elsewhere that "[d]espite the various kinds of support given to Frederick as a child, by his grandmother as well as by Thomas and Sophia Auld, despite the continued mothering he received from his wife, and despite the intellectual and perhaps sexual solicitude proffered by a variety of women friends, Douglass argued vehemently and repeatedly for a vigorous self-reliance. Work and politics, not intimacy and emotional exploration, were the proper arenas for a man of force." Douglass's dismissal nevertheless invites us to consider, as Yarborough suggests, those forceful elements of Western manhood as being as difficult to attain for black men as were the cardinal virtues of the cult of womanhood for black women, thus giving rise to the single-mindedness with which black men tried to occupy this forbidden male niche. Ultimately the overdeterminations of slavery and white maleness as their engine are problematic in this vein, as Douglass, in enumerating Sophia's virtues, seeks to strike for the alliance of abolitionism with feminism: "She had never had a slave under her control previously to myself, and prior to her marriage she had been dependent upon her own industry for a living. She was by trade a weaver; and by constant application to her business, she had been in a good degree preserved from the blighting and dehumanizing effects of slavery" (*Narrative,* 36). The allegiance Douglass seeks between free black and white, male and female bodies soon collapses, however, as the return of Sophia's husband, Thomas, enforces the separation of not only sexual but also educational difference, as well as possible political affinity. At the irruption of Thomas Auld into the text, the scene might be imagined from young Frederick's perspective as he views the now vast and ever-widening distance between Sophia Auld and himself. Frustrated and suppressed by hegemonic denial, the African American's sense of masculine self-worth is thwarted even in the pages of what was its own liberating literature. But it is the black writer's negotiation through what James Olney suggests as being the white abolitionist-imposed appropriateness conditions of slave narrative that both the fight with Covey and the episode with Sophia Auld gain ground in the writer's approach to the modern. Free labor and transindividual, cross-racial relations were but small portions of the civil stature that Douglass and other black Americans understood as being the principal avenue to the nation's progress.[3]

Though with abolition came the end of physical violence as a means to freedom, the inadequately expressed rage of the previous era's injustices remained, and that was now coupled with the outrage of disenfranchisement. The Euroamerican middle class deepened its comfortable postwar entrenchment in a Victorian ethos and the self-consciousness that accompanied it; the growing awareness of social propriety among middle-class white Americans who subscribed to new prescriptions of taste carried with it an exclusionary attitude toward both whites of the lower classes and persons of color. Literary realism, as a reflection of these tastes, mirrored as well inclinations in American public policy against race. "[The work of] the realists," Kenneth Warren writes, ". . . assisted in the creation of a climate of opinion that undermined the North's capacity to resist Southern arguments against political equality for African Americans during the 1880s and 1890s through its conflicted participation in discussions about the American social order."[4] The more "radical realism" of the period was represented by the "plantation tradition," fiction and

---

3. James Olney, "'I Was Born': Slave Narratives, Their Status as Autobiography and as Literature," 153–54; Yarborough, "Race, Violence, and Manhood," 168; David Leverenz, *Manhood and the American Renaissance,* 128–29.

4. Kenneth W. Warren, *Black and White Strangers: Race and American Literary Realism,* 22.

poetry by writers such as Irwin Russell, Thomas Dixon, and Thomas Nelson Page, who created stereotypical black characters who abjured emancipation and yearned for the days of a legal protection through paternalism. The counterstatement to this climate appeared in the works of writers who were part of an emerging black middle class. The early black novel, called by Bernard Bell the "novel of reaction," sought to fight continuing prejudice, but it tended toward assimilationism in its characterization, promoting a class consciousness whose ideology is expressed in such forms as thrift, initiative, perseverance, and industry. While this formula represented a return to the white middle-class ingredients of proper manhood from which blacks had previously been excluded, it imbibed them while seldom critiquing them, fashioned a heroic status for black men often at the expense of the black masses, and also sometimes returned women to the cult of an oppressive middle-class, if protected, state. It appeared that such behavior by these characters anchored them forever in a social milieu that would always be hostile to their real interests of social equality and enfranchisement, and it also seemed that compromised forever would be qualities of black manhood once sought by earlier nineteenth-century African American commentators, particularly by Douglass, who was now nearing the end of his life.

But despite the fact that these characters can be considered in one sense heroic, the adherence of the novel of reaction to a Euroamerican ethos to which it presumably was reacting appears to have had serious consequences for black representation. The fact that repudiating the stereotypes forecast an apparently ineluctable repudiation of the black folk culture in which the distortions were first made caused novels such as Frances E. W. Harper's *Iola Leroy* (1892), Charles Chesnutt's *The Marrow of Tradition* (1899), and Pauline Hopkins's *Contending Forces* (1900) to be seen by many as creating characters without anchor in the larger African American milieu, characters who are inhuman because they are more than human; characters that are measured and constricted, with sensibilities that are governed rather by a rigid code of behavior to be accepted by whites than by standards of conduct that might otherwise emanate from their communities. Though Harper's *Iola Leroy* is generally acknowledged as one of the more forward-looking race-conscious novels of this era, its depiction of the laborer Tom Anderson has led one critic to declare that "whatever protest should be, it should [never] be, especially in an obviously futile way, a part of the very thing against which it purports to protest." The theme of proper social pairings for marriage also obtains in *Iola Leroy,* as well as does the idea that only a black elite can decide the proper course of action in securing rights for the freed masses. The black Belton Piedmont, in Sutton Griggs's *Imperium in Imperio* (1899), pays with his life for his steadfast and statesmanlike support and defense of the "Anglo-Saxon way of life" as the underground movement he leads plans to move against the U.S. government and the state of Texas. Despite the intensity and the savagery of racial discrimination experienced almost from birth, the political sensibilities of his adult life, because of his accomplishments, dissolve into a curious patriotism. At the end of Chesnutt's heavily ironic *Marrow,* the decision of the despised though moderate mulatto Dr. Miller to save a white child when his own child has been slain by his town's impulse toward antiblack violence is a decision which itself seems to deny any comprehension of natural anger. Caught between a responsibility to express the yearnings of all of the members of his race and the demands of emulation that exacted a loyalty to his class, the African American male of these novels now displays an inability to respond to the impulses of human rage. For some, however, African America of the late nineteenth century indeed gained more than it lost in casting itself in this emulatory mode. Bernard Bell sees the novel of reaction not only as a spirited challenge to the writing of the plantation tradition but even one he calls "salutary"; its renewing message was that black novelists in their conservatism "were above denying historical fact and psychological truth—however neurotic the parade of pretentious colored folk and their paternal white folks—in order to repudiate the stereotypes of Dixon and Page." As Dickson Bruce remarks, while the conservatism and genteel bearing of the works of early black writers "reveal a certain measure of uncertainty" with regard to the tension between the political weight of their productions and their middle-class aestheticism, the literature itself was "a measure of their optimism about possibilities for the future."[5]

But Peter Wollen suggests that as the twentieth century began, European high modernism, particularly in the realms of fashion and art, had sought to undo the fetters of nineteenth-century

5. Blyden Jackson, *A History of Afro-American Literature, 1746–1895,* 397; Bernard W. Bell, *The Afro-American Novel and Its Tradition,* 91; Dickson Bruce, *Black American Writing from the Nadir: The Evolution of a Literary Tradition, 1877–1915,* 32.

romanticism and had simplified its task through a kind of mechanistic reduction, by defining itself according to antinomies both classic and new to the age: "functional/decorative, useful/wasteful, natural/artificial, machine/body, masculine/feminine, west/east." The United States, still emerging as a world power, had more often reified these binarisms for utilitarian purposes—that is, as a function of a burgeoning imperialism. American literary modernism, taking its cues from across the Atlantic, had retained these European antinomies and added a few of its own: city/country, North/South, white/black. As Aldon Lynn Nielsen points out, the new Euroamerican literary sensibility, which thought itself transcendent of the old norms and mores that were generated by the era of realism, had in adopting these antinomies merely projected into the twentieth century realism's fundamental antagonisms. "High modernism's hopes to arrive at the thing itself," Nielsen writes, "freed from the encrustations of the language of romance, did not always succeed even in arriving at new ways of writing about the thing, especially if the 'object' under consideration was a living race. . . . Seldom in our literary history has blackness so occupied the imaginations of white artists as during the rise of modernism." Unlike the response that the novel of reaction gave to Euroamerican social interests, however, the modern black novel took advantage of discussions of pluralism, sociology, and the modern city that were then taking place. Not only were Pablo Picasso and Gertrude Stein imbibing African and Oceanic cultural forms in Europe, but broad changes were taking place in America as well, as black cultural forms were becoming increasingly more prominent. Nor could originary black folk culture be ignored, because the fact of the Great Migration to northern American cities became the lifeblood of the modern perspective. In New York, the principal modern City of Exiles, Harlem, as a city within this city, became the center of a vibrant African American culture with the arrival of great waves of Southern black folk, and the centrifugal result would have enduring cultural consequences for both the nation and the world. In Ann Douglas's apt remark, the 1920s became the decade "in which the Negroization of American culture became something like a recognized phenomenon."[6] This cross-fertilization of

6. Peter Wollen, "Fashion/Orientalism/The Body," 5–33; Aldon Lynn Nielsen, *Reading Race: White American Poets and the Racial Discourse in the Twentieth Century,* 49; Ann Douglas, *Terrible Honesty: Mongrel Manhattan in the 1920s,* 77.

American culture was sometimes troubled, however, even and especially at the level of the binarism. As much as white and black artists
became, in one of W. E. B. Du Bois's famous phrases, "co-workers
in the kingdom of culture," there were often at various psychological
and social levels many work-related injuries. For James de Jongh,
the approach to an assimilation of the bold new Harlem aesthetic by
white writers was quite normally reduced to a frustrated exoticism
or simplifications of political realities toward fantasies of otherness
and separateness. These writers "presumed Harlem, however foreign, to be a landscape that would readily surrender its patent moral,
cosmic, or teleological import. Any tensions in the Harlem environs
of these writers derived from the sensational contrast with the civilized white world; the only duality informing their ideas of Harlem
was the distinction of one's double, the alien other that puts one's
self in stark relief." As Euroamerican Adamism desired to create for
itself an original, generative, masculine spirit unbound from Europe,
its African American strain meant the recovery of a masculine black
spirit after its disengagement from the bonds of a repressed, if double, consciousness. If in what de Jongh calls "the cultural crucible"
of Harlem whites sometimes found the spirit of the "New Negro" a
difficult one with which to come quite to terms, blacks were as well
at variance with representations of the black self, as was suggested
by the series of questions and responses by black and white artists
and intellectuals begun in 1926 in Du Bois's *Crisis,* "The Negro in
Art: A Symposium." White and black authors felt the yawning chasm
of difference and recorded it in reactions as plaintive as Eugene
O'Neill's exhortation to black artists to begin representing themselves in the theater to Langston Hughes's impassioned statement on
behalf of black difference in "The Negro Artist and the Racial Mountain." But although this aestheticization of difference was being widely
articulated in intellectual forums, its genesis had deep roots; as
Nathan Huggins cautions, the ethos of the New Negro was always
confronted by the specter of the past. "Since the New/Old dichot-
omy is a mere convenience of mind," he writes, "the so-called Old
Negro was merely carried within the bosom of the New as a kind of
self-doubt, perhaps self-hate. How can one take up the promotion of
race (or nationality) through art without exposing this doubt?"[7]

7. James de Jongh, *Vicious Modernism,* 37; Nathan Irvin Huggins, *Harlem Renaissance,* 65.

Huggins describes a bald consciousness of class, the principal feature of this racial self-doubt that threatened at every moment to disrupt the New Negro's cultural experiment. The Old Negro, usually represented by a rustic and unlettered figuration, was an ineradicable element of New Negroness the New Negro wanted scrupulously to avoid. In *Imperium in Imperio,* Belton Piedmont confirms Huggins's view by conveying a doubleness of intention: "[L]et us pull the veil from before the eyes of the Anglo-Saxon that he may see the New Negro standing before him *humbly, but firmly demanding* every right granted him by his maker and wrested from him by man" (*Imperium,* 62, emphasis added). "The search for the personality of the New Negro necessitated the rediscovery of a heritage," Huggins writes, and although he speaks here of the urge of Renaissance intellectuals and writers to return spiritually and intellectually to Africa for cultural material, the more immediate and more crucial venue was the place where so much of it began—the agrarian African American South, as opposed to the industrialized North. For black cultural capital, then, it was ultimately necessary to return to the ground in contention between Booker Washington and the black Yankee Du Bois, the ground on which Frederick Douglass sought to forge with the ideals of freedom the values of masculinity.

Though the literary Harlem Renaissance is perhaps better known through its poetry than its prose, and that therefore Langston Hughes, often called "the poet of the masses," and Sterling Brown, "poet of the folk," will be remembered for their enduring characterizations of black life, the more thorough literary unearthing of African American masculinity would be the province of prose and its conventional use of formal realism (to be distinguished from literary realism as previously described), through which transvaluations between author and reader are more easily made than in other forms. The novel's multidimensional aspect, depicting not only character but also its specific movement through spatial and temporal environments, gives it a more largely contextual, depth-of-field advantage over other genres; as Ian Watt remarks, the movements of contemporary life find their expression in the novel "through a more largely referential use of language than is common in other literary forms." The persistence of narrative attests to the conveyance of human events as being even a fundamental necessity; noting that the fact of the story makes permeable the barriers of language, culture, and taste, Roland Barthes observes narrative's absolute necessity. "Caring nothing for the division between good and bad literature," he writes, "narrative is international, transhistorical, transcultural: it is simply there, like life itself."[8]

Of the Harlem Renaissance writers of prose, Jean Toomer and Zora Neale Hurston were virtually alone in returning to the South for material, and as a result bring to African American fiction the elements of agrarian black culture that not only augment this referential foregrounding of language but also employ it as an emblem of modernity in ways that were generally muted or avoided by many of the practitioners of the novel of reaction. They reveal as a result many elements of a distorted black male identity in their fiction, and complicate notions about black maleness whose expression had lain buried since the era of Douglass and earlier African American autobiography. For all its gains, the earlier black novel had obscured depictions of rural Southern black men and women, leaving to African American modernism the task of reconfiguring the fragmented representations of now contemporary black culture, fragments sundered by binarisms apparently peculiar to this new wave of African American artists: in the tension between North and South, between the representations of Du Bois and Washington, and between land and machine. The modernist forays of Toomer and Hurston into black representation, particularly black male representation, stand as signposts of progress in the interrogation of the condition of African American men rather than as simply necessary improvements over nineteenth-century depictions. If Victorian-era class consciousness was a barrier to black self-realization, then race and gender, given their mutual inextricability, were similarly implicated. The attention that Toomer and Hurston give not only to these elements but also to their imbrications highlights the issues that black men had as outraged, frustrated subjects with limited agency as well as the degree to which these limitations distorted both the visage in the mirror, at the level of race, and where gender was concerned, their relationships with those who would be their closest allies—black women.

Though it may suffice to say that the lives of Toomer and Hurston were simply forged by the forces of the new century that seemed to affect African Americans everywhere, it is interesting to note that

8. Ian Watt, *The Rise of the Novel,* 32; Roland Barthes, *Image, Music, Text,* 79.

elements of each author's background appear to resemble these features of their work. In Toomer's *Cane* black men appear to lose opportunities for redemption, and endure instances in which a bewildered, isolated soul—often resembling Toomer himself—is forced to make crucial choices and experience his consequences as failures in virtually every contingent moment. After his father, Nathan, deserted the family in 1895, the year following his birth, Jean grew up in the household of his grandfather, Pinckney Benton Stewart Pinchback, Louisiana's—and the country's—first black governor. Pinchback was a demanding, domineering sort who ruled absolutely the lives his family, including the writer and his mother, Nina Pinchback Toomer. Herein lies Toomer's ultimate dissatisfaction with not only issues of race but also his difficulty in finding a comfortable space in which to define his manhood. Toomer's preoccupations with his own physical strength, his sexual curiosities and tergiversations and his need for control of virtually every social situation, reflect the elements in *Cane* of men's physical strength and emotional power and their efforts to secure them—or their pathos in watching them ebb.

Toomer, who in *Cane* and some earlier works surveys this notion of manhood within a discussion of race, was ironically never quite comfortable with the African American strain that ran through him. As a descendant of P. B. S. Pinchback, he was connected to the Washington contingent of the "Colored 400," the light-complexioned black elite of which the white abolitionist Sarah Grimke lamented to Theodore Dwight Weld in 1837: "I mourn over the aristocracy that prevails over our colored bretheren. I cherished the hope that suffering had humbled them and prepared them to perform a glorious part in the reformation of our country, but the more I mingle with them the fainter are my hopes. They have as much caste among them as we have and despise the poor as much I fear as their pale bretheren. . . . I have given up going to any place of worship. I have tried all and they are all alike to me places of spiritual famine. My experience is the same in colored, as in white congregations." Such attitudes of caste and race pervaded the black elite, attitudes from which Toomer himself, despite Pinchback's apparent history of commitment to blacks during Reconstruction, could not have been insulated, and on many levels a distance from or simple dissatisfaction with Toomer's sense of self and an idealized self becomes apparent. An almost serendipitous circumstance of Toomer's young adulthood, that of a need of a family friend to have the young Toomer become temporary headmaster of an agricultural school in Georgia, led him to write several stories and poems about rural, Southern black life that eventually coalesced into *Cane.* But Cynthia Earl Kerman and Richard Eldridge strongly suggest that Toomer's creation of *Cane,* for his uneasy association with race, was never an anchor, but always a dangerous experiment: "In order to write *Cane,*" they write, "Jean Toomer had had to embrace a part of his background that had not been familiar to him. With pieces of the book now appearing in many places, it was inevitable that he would have to define his relationship with that background. Further, it is not surprising that the psychological movement which swung him so fully toward his heritage might complete its cycle in the opposite direction." As it was, Toomer, in publicizing the novel, never entirely appreciated being called "black" or "Negro." One of his complaints to Waldo Frank about Toomer's communications with Sherwood Anderson was that "Sherwood limits me to Negro. . . . As an approach . . . Negro is good. But try to tie me to one of my parts is surely to loose [*sic*] me." Such an attitude would certainly prefigure the foreclosure of an expansion of the literary race project; the sentiment easily resurfaced when Du Bois, Alain Locke, and others were urging Toomer to make an even more enduring literary statement of race than *Cane.*[9]

Almost immediately after the publication of *Cane,* however, Toomer abandoned writing. Disillusionment with the New York literary circle in which he had become involved and the need to enhance his spiritual life had overwhelmed him. He shortly gave himself entirely to the teachings of the Russian spiritualist Georges Gurdjieff, who in 1923, the year of publication of *Cane,* had opened his Institute for the Harmonious Study of Man in Fontainebleau, France. In Gurdjieffian philosophy, for a person to achieve wholeness of self, the three centers of self—intellect, emotion, and intuition—must work harmoniously, and only then can the self rise to a higher order of development. For Toomer, all art, all life, and every valuation of race and class had collapsed into Gurdjieff's teachings, known to the

9. Grimke to Theodore Dwight Weld, December 17, 1837, *Letters of Theodore Dwight Weld, Angelina Grimke Weld, and Sarah Grimke, 1822–1844,* 498; see also Willard H. Gatewood, *Aristocrats of Color: The Black Elite, 1880–1920,* 10. Cynthia Earl Kerman and Richard Eldridge, *The Lives of Jean Toomer: A Hunger for Wholeness,* 95, 111.

cognoscenti as The Work. But in a letter of introduction to one of Gurdjieff's chief American disciples, Toomer wrote that he needed help "to exist as a man."[10] Toomer's personal project for manhood, then, if it had ever been fully visualized, had apparently not been satisfactorily executed by the writing of *Cane,* although in that text aspects of manhood that seemed to have concerned him had been definitively wedded to considerations of race. That Toomer never again produced anything approaching the art of *Cane* and never again approached themes of race and masculinity in subsequent writings makes tempting the idea that "Kabnis," the last story in *Cane* (and also the story completed two days before his grandfather's death), represents Toomer's final sacrifice of both the senses of race and racially conceived masculinity in him. "Kabnis" is Toomer's perhaps preconsciously composed swan song, his final, devastating intrusion into—and extrusion from—the web of the text.

Considered the signal work of the Harlem Renaissance, *Cane* is the modernist projection of black life, expressing it not in terms of racial super-beings, as was the case with the early New Negro novel, but more fully in terms of life as truly lived, its drama being derived from fundamental, quotidian concerns, or even in spite of them. What appears, however, to be the unhappy set of circumstances forming Toomer's personal development also forms the inner matter of *Cane* as these elements, separate yet indistinct, seem foregrounded and backgrounded by turns. In this connection, Toomer in *Cane* more often shows us the fragmented black male while he shows us divisions of himself—elements he might never have had cause to put to print had he not, by mere chance, sojourned to Georgia in 1921.

Born in Notasulga, Alabama, in 1891, Zora Neale Hurston, though a graduate of New York's Barnard College, broadly accomplished as a novelist, anthropologist, and folklorist, and for her time the most-published African American woman, derived her personal and spiritual strength from Eatonville, Florida, where she was raised. It is this Southern repository of black culture to which she consistently returned for material, the key to her ability to see clearly the fundamental elements of rural African American life. As June Jordan writes, the people of Eatonville "expressed their own particular selves in a Family and Community setting that . . . fosters the natural, person-

10. Kerman and Eldridge, *Lives of Toomer,* 132.

postures of courting, jealousy, ambition, dream, sex, work, partying, sorrow, bitterness, celebration and fellowship." The Hurstons were one of the first families of Eatonville, the first town in the United States to be incorporated entirely through the efforts of African Americans. The Reverend John Hurston, Zora's father, was Eatonville's spiritual leader and moderator of the South Florida Baptist Association as well as a three-term mayor of Eatonville and the codifier of its laws. Like P. B. S. Pinchback, John Hurston was both strong-willed and persuasive, and was also a man who dealt in absolutes, ruling at home with an iron hand. Hurston's biographer Robert Hemenway describes John Hurston as having been "one of the strongest men in the village, two hundred pounds of hard muscle, known for his bravery, leadership, and powerful, poetical preaching."[11] Zora's mother, Lucy Hurston, like Nina Pinchback Toomer, courageously bore the pain caused by the man in her life and craftily challenged him as well. Often, however, Zora Hurston herself questions the consistency of family and community while leaving inviolate the values which emanate from them—a practice that seems to complicate Jordan's own particularizing of these elements among Eatonvillians. The following may suffice to illustrate: Lucy Hurston, on her deathbed, left instructions to her young daughter that reflected her apparent wish "to symbolically reject the folklore of her village." As she was dying, she asked that no one remove the pillow from her head, nor cover the clock or the mirror in the room. But the interests of the community—and those of John Hurston, as one of its leaders and guardians of its traditions—overrode those of a dead woman and a nine-year-old girl who later conveyed her immediate and lasting sense of failure. As Zora wrote in her autobiography, *Dust Tracks on a Road:* "Now, I know that I could not have had my way against the world. The world we lived in required those acts. Anything else would have been sacrilege, and no nine-year-old voice was going to thwart them. My father was with the mores. He had restrained me physically from outraging the ceremonies established for the dying. If there is any consciousness after death, I hope that Mama knows that I did my best. She must know how I have suffered for my failure" (*DTR,* 89).

11. June Jordan, "On Richard Wright and Zora Neale Hurston: Notes toward a Balancing of Love and Hatred," 6; Robert Hemenway, *Zora Neale Hurston: A Literary Biography,* 15.

This instance from Hurston's personal history has probable bearing on her characterization in her novels and stories of the community in moments of crisis. The townsfolk in her 1926 short story "Sweat" who at first not only lament Delia's abusive marriage to Sykes but also entertain notions of murdering him, turn almost imperceptibly to the issue of their own refreshment on the hot July day. The same community in *Their Eyes* that loved Janie as much as it loved Tea Cake lauds his beating of her, and is prepared to turn against her at the moment of his death. In this particular autobiographical instance, however, John Hurston is described as a man who bends to the will of outsiders rather than honor the wishes of his own wife. While Zora does not appear specifically to blame him, the simple sentence "My father was with the mores" seems to cast the will of the strong, dominant John Hurston as having been determined by forces that both surround him and have long preceded him. His wife now lost to him through death, she somehow seems far closer to him than when he ignored her dying wishes, and as a result, truly lost to both is a transindividualism, a means by which each could touch the other's better nature and perhaps in doing so, contribute to the health of the whole community. Such is often the case in Hurston's novels: while women in peril join the ranks of the damned, there is little support from a community oriented toward other mores, mores of dominance and domesticity, toward validating only speaking men and silent women. Paradoxically, however, Hurston's community is also more broadly and purposefully an insular one, with apparent possibilities for self-healing that are not to be found in the modern city. Though black folk culture can be exported to the North, as she suggests in "Characteristics of Negro Expression" (1934)—because of its potential as a commodity to white Americans—it would not do for that folk culture to be corrupted from without. Her thinking is similar in this regard to Toomer's notion that black folk culture, forged during slavery, is going slowly "to die on the modern desert," but for Hurston modernist folk culture can only embrace time by seeking to flourish where it is, particularly because of the elements of African American agrarian culture and its African source, each readable to the other. Powerful, final sanctions can be exacted against men who cause pain or impede the spiritual progress of women in any way, and Hurston demands that men somehow overcome themselves, that they become better than the communities that spawn them. Their penalty for failing to do so is retribution from the powerful pan-African forces of nature, which understood their real natures to be corrupted by sensibilities somewhat beyond their control, but in infinite and inscrutable wisdom chose to mark them as failed sons of the diaspora.

In the specific case of casting black masculinity, Toomer and Hurston have left a legacy of representation that many writers find crucially important today. Their critique of the modern, northern American city—Toomer through a palpable, if oblique appraisal, Hurston by constructing its absence—is taken up by contemporary African American writers. At the ground of African American masculinity, post-Migration and postmodern attitudes toward black life—that is, life in the northern city—with new perspectives on the South, particularly in the later work of John Edgar Wideman, Toni Morrison and Gloria Naylor, are remarkably incisive. In the chapter that discusses Wideman's *Reuben* and *Philadelphia Fire,* the theme of black manhood is one of recovery from the wasteland of despair as constructed by stifling political and social ambiguity. Wideman focuses on our missed opportunities to express responsibility for others, but painfully acknowledges the now near impossibility to transcend the rituals of the actual world in order to do this. His venues of Philadelphia and Pittsburgh are his laboratories for his critique; in *Reuben* the issue of recovery of black manhood is successful, but not without the frustration of battling the legal and social discourses that impede progress toward this end. In *Philadelphia Fire,* the quest is unsuccessful—but its failure is due not only to the fears of race but also through its influence on the abuses of political power and the ultimate class fantasies of American life that ensue. The quests in both texts are also somewhat personal ones, as the Toomeresque idea of the spectatorial artist, the personal investment of the postmodern author in the text, also becomes a feature of Wideman's project.

Contemporary black women's writing—as much as was the writing that came from the black women's Club movement at the end of the nineteenth century—is far less interested in denigrating black men and masculinity than in showing their errant natures. In Toni Morrison's *Beloved* and Gloria Naylor's *Mama Day,* there is an effort to resurrect black manhood by complicating his nature beyond his ordinary depictions, even those depictions that he had mistakenly chosen for himself. Though *Beloved* has been widely written about, and remains in enjoyment of a strong critical reception, little has been written about Paul D, its leading male character. Paul D's complications as a strong male figure in a text that presumably speaks principally to issues regarding black feminism interrogates some of the inner reaches of that feminism to aid in creating the discourse of a black masculinity responsive to feminism's political and social impetus. *Beloved*'s premodern setting—the antebellum and postbellum North—suggests postmodern possibilities for black maleness, perhaps in ways similar to Hurston's 1942 novel *Moses, Man of the Mountain,* that are available even before the advent of the modern city. At the same time, Sethe's and Paul D's search for transindividualism in their era is intriguingly transcendent over the negotiations through gender in Toomer's characters, frustrated as they often are by post-Migration and thus largely institutionalized restructurings of the racial compact.

Naylor's *Mama Day* and its focus on the relationship between George and Cocoa is fraught with the popular struggle between men and women that one can find anywhere in the products of today's media. But the text's deeper satisfactions come from an analysis of George's character as a man who, even unconsciously, seeks to come to terms with a masculinity that apparently has no provenance. George is an orphan who as an infant is rescued from the stack of newspapers on which he is found (his origins are made known to us in Naylor's preceding novel, *Bailey's Café*), which suggests implications of community but also of communitarian strife and discord that are both the products of culture and reported by it. The discord in the community he encounters—which, in the Sea Islands off the Carolina coast, is a world unto itself—and his singular and terrible sacrifice to save Cocoa and reconcile himself with her is only possible through his consistent reinvention of himself. George is mostly, and ironically, mediated by the world—but he is ultimately forced to create himself anew in every contingent moment.

Strong, decisive, elemental forces appeared also to drive Toomer and Hurston to a South fertile in human mystery. It is my hope to show that Toomer's and Hurston's uses of pan-African symbolism in the discovery of African American manhood make claims for modernism beyond those expected by many white aesthetes in the Harlem of the time; that is to say, that elements of blues structure, folk speech, and folk logic are rescued from the relegation to a benign primitivism by, among others, the Lost Generation writers, for the construction of a usable present. "When inanimate things ceased to commune with me like natural men," wrote Hurston in her autobiography, "other dreams came to live with me" (*DTR,* 78). Even Toomer, who persistently attempted to dissolve his racial consciousness into a sterile Americanism, could not avoid the black lyric whether sung or spoken; as he wrote to Sherwood Anderson, he could not ignore "the seed planted in *myself* down there."[12] In returning to ideations of black communitarianism, they rediscovered those facets of humanity once dissipated by the Euroamerican experience. Theirs is a rediscovery of constituents of a black masculinity that offer possibilities for reconfigurations of black manhood that black feminisms may find beneficial. It indeed appears that several contemporary black writers, both men and women, have already retraced Toomer's and Hurston's routes, again rediscovered these elements in our own time, and have mined them for the incisive effect of fashioning a new component to our national literature, one that speaks through another invisible, and thus endangered, minority. Also at the heart of this rediscovery is a literary vitalization of blues culture, the resurrection of the African mythic experience, and the recrudescence of the oppositional black text. None of these can truly be realized, however, without a recognition of their impact upon African American communities, of whose spirit they themselves are yet fragmentary though vital expressions.

12. Toomer to Sherwood Anderson, December 18, 1922, Box 1, Folder 1, JTP.

2

TOOMER'S MALE PRISON AND
THE SPECTATORIAL ARTIST

> My poor mother, she had stepped from one prison to an-
> other—and it was decreed that I share her lot, that her sit-
> uation be my situation, that I witness within two years the
> decline and final passing from this earth of she who had
> produced me.
>
> —Jean Toomer

In his teenage years, Jean Toomer sought bravely to face the responsibility of caring for his aging and infirm grandparents. As he later
records his lamentations about their waning health and strength, he
reflects upon the grandfather who had been such a powerful and enduring influence in not only his own life but also that of his uncles,
and particularly his mother. "My grandfather returned from New
York," Toomer writes. "He had resigned his post. The bad effects of
banquets had gotten into his legs and bunions. Suddenly he had felt
his age, and he couldn't carry on, as his job required trips all around
greater New York. So here he was, with us again, income stopped.
He held his chin up and was still the governor, but he brooded more
than usual and I could see how he felt. This was the last post he'd ever
have. In all ways his career was over, and he—a back number." Slowly,
the mighty Pinchback was falling, and the grandson who stood in his
shadow would now have to be his support. In Toomer's boyhood,
lighter moments between grandfather and grandson produced such
pastimes as Pinchback's playful bestowal of nicknames upon the boy;

it matured into a habit that Toomer the writer would later exercise in the creation of his characters. The naming of the self, however, was a much more serious matter: as young Eugene Pinchback Toomer later became Jean Toomer, author, and still later reverted to Nathan Jean Toomer in middle age, he in the first case ousted the fact of the grandfather, and in the second, reinscribed the lost father. But even before this passionate renaming, the teenager, perhaps with his grandfather's slow decline in mind, began an acute focus on his own body, which became a "source of shame" to him. He became a disciple of Bernarr Macfadden, the fitness maven and showman whose magazine *Physical Culture* and voluminous *Encyclopedia of Physical Culture* consisted of various diets, exercises, and unusual moral and sexual philosophies that became famous at the turn of the century. The young Toomer thoroughly imbibed the Macfadden philosophy, changing his body and increasing his sense of his manliness in the bargain:

> I had built up a certain strength of will over my body. I could *make* it do things. The bodies of the other boys simply moved of themselves. True, my own sight at the time was focused not on my increased will but on my increased muscles. None the less the will was there to be called upon and to serve the future in unexpected ways. I dare say the gain of it balanced the undue strains I had put upon myself. I also dare say, indeed I'm sure of it, that the gain of this will even compensated for the idiocies and the excesses of this, my first neophytism.[1]

But by the spring of 1921 Toomer, now having served a decade of duty to his grandparents, had become so exhausted that it became necessary to escape, to have at least a brief respite from the overwhelming task of doing virtually everything for two people who could do no more for themselves. The week he had taken from the Pinchback home in Washington to Harpers Ferry probably seemed to have provided enough rest, but when the subsequent opportunity for true adventure materialized upon his return, he seized it immediately. Linton S. Ingraham, the principal of the Sparta Industrial and Agricultural School in Sparta, Georgia, and a friend of P. B. S. Pinchback, called at the Pinchback home on his way north in an effort to raise funds for the school. He would need a substitute principal

1. "Book X," Box 11, Folders 347 and 362, JTP.

while in Boston, and Toomer, seeking adventure and desperate for release from the crushingly enervating task of looking after his grandparents and maintaining the home, eagerly accepted the job. He could not have known then that this decision was itself a placement at the crossroads—that, in the land of rural black folk, unadulterated by the demands of life in the city, his success as a writer would be forged. In a letter to his friend, the author Waldo Frank, he described the new milieu: "There, for the first time I really saw the Negro, not as a ps[eu]do-urbanized peasant, strong with the tang of fields and soil. It was there that I first heard the folk-songs rolling up the valley at twilight, heard them as spontaneous and native utterances. They filled me with gold, and tints of an eternal purple. Love? Man they gave birth to a whole new life." In this place Toomer would for the first time confront his African heritage. He had stayed in Sparta for only two months, but while there he would become deeply connected to its residents. "No picture of a Southern person is complete without its bit of Negro-determined psychology,"[2] wrote Toomer in his letter to Frank, and that part of the picture of Toomer which was *Cane* would embrace some of the most elemental concerns of black life: religion, the harvest, the "Sorrow Songs" as Du Bois had called them, men, and women.

Although several of the poems and stories in *Cane* had appeared separately in *The Crisis* and in several of the "little magazines" of early literary modernism in 1922, it was the essential nature of things characterizing black life in rural Georgia that held the tales and poems together as *Cane* the following year. Toomer was concerned throughout, however, that that essence could easily be corrupted by the influence of a growing industrialism in America; that authentic black life would not survive the pervasive and altogether seductive influence of the newly mechanized North:

> The Negro of the folk-song has all but passed away; the Negro of the emotional church is fading. A hundred years from now these Negroes, if they exist at all will live in art. . . . The supreme fact of mechanical civilization is that you become part of it, or get sloughed off (under). Negroes have no culture to resist it with (and if they had, their position would be identical to

2. Toomer to Waldo Frank, March 24, 1922, reprinted in Kerman and Eldridge, *Lives of Toomer,* 87.

that of the Indians), hence industrialism the more readily transforms them. A few generations from now, the Negro will still be dark, and a portion of his psychology will spring from this fact, but in all else he will be a conformist to the general outlines of American civilization, or of American chaos.

He continues his lament by turning to the stories in *Cane* and the effort they make to capture this ephemeral beauty. "In my own stuff," he writes, "in those pieces that come nearest to the old Negro, to the spirit saturate with folk-song: Karintha and Fern, the dominant emotion is a sadness derived from a sense of fading, from a knowledge of my futility to check solution."[3] This remark has an intriguing double sense that renders subtly Toomer's constructions of black men. In "Karintha" and "Fern," stories in which women are both exploited and hardened, the "sadness derived from a sense of fading" includes the distorted way in which men and women relate to each other. While Toomer's women become enduring symbols of beauty, his men are that beauty's most consistent, if unwitting, corruptors. Throughout most of *Cane,* black women are damaged by men whose often unregenerate nature is partly derivative of their devaluation by a system that has shown the benefits of democracy only to a white elect. At various points, however, in a sympathetic evaluation of the dilemmas of these men, Toomer offers himself as narrator as a model of effeteness, seemingly as if his carefully nourished stamina has suddenly failed him. With perhaps the vague awareness of how to acquit himself responsibly, manfully, and in an awareness that includes his own felt racial ambiguities, he casts himself as being similarly ill-equipped to face a New Negro's new challenges.

Toomer sets the stage for his own participation in this drama with adumbrations of the kind of man he wishes to examine. "Karintha" is the story of a young girl who was "a growing thing ripened too soon"; a beautiful child, the men of her village, both young and old, find her beauty the object of their fantasy. As she grows older, young men want to possess her, and finally, a yield to passion brings forth a child, which she murders at its birth by burning it in a nearby sawmill. Karintha's liaison is not named, but his very namelessness identifies the provenance of her tragedy: the insistence of men in the

3. Toomer to Waldo Frank, ca. October 1922, reprinted in Kerman and Eldridge, *Lives of Toomer,* 98.

wanton, willful destruction of beauty. It is in this connection that Houston Baker writes that "the natural compulsion of man to corrupt the beautiful" informs "the frustrating encounters" of the first part of *Cane*. It is unnecessary to know the names of Karintha's previous lovers, or Fern's, or the names of the fathers of Becky's sons. Deeper than this compulsion is the reason for it, and this seems to constitute the most salient element of frustration. Black men, in their pursuit of the destruction of beauty, appear less purely to will that corruption than to be manipulated or coerced into embracing it. What is violent in them—what appears to constitute any act of violence toward which they may be led—is codified by the violence done them as the property of others. Echoing Justice Roger Taney's infamous majority opinion in the Dred Scott decision, Baker writes that "good and evil waged an equal contest in a South that contained its own natural harmonies but considered blacks as chattels personal, having no rights that a white man need respect."[4]

This constructed indifference to human rights is a process that Toomer himself intimates, in his letter to Waldo Frank quoted previously, is still at work if Negroes "have had no culture" with which to resist the rapacity of industrialism, that culture having been vitiated by the institution of slavery itself. The very *un*naturalness of slavery—the blind chaos of a disenfranchising economics, of industry, and of unfree labor—forced an unnatural development of African America with a result that is itself naturally chaotic, vengeful, and self-destructive. To this end, the men in "Karintha" and in most of the first part of *Cane* are shadowy, even amorphous figures, without identity, without conscience or sensibility. Their development has been fragmented, splintered by both the heritage of slavery and the urgencies of a new, industrializing twentieth-century America that can find no place for them. The dehumanizing effects of slavery behind and the lure of the Northern metropolitan milieu before had distorted those elements of African American culture which at one time could have fortified African American manhood. Now these elements appear only as signposts to his defeat, portions of a self to which he is now not admitted, or of which he often is not even aware. In "Karintha," for example, there is this recurring lyrical description of her:

4. Baker, *Afro-American Poetics: Revisions of Harlem and the Black Aesthetic*, 20–21.

> Her skin is like dusk on the eastern horizon,
> O cant you see it, cant you see it,
> Her skin is like dusk on the eastern horizon
> When the sun goes down.

This is physical beauty as described in the mode of the Spiritual, and not only does its lyric appear as the story's chief irony in Karintha's destruction, but it acquires another irony in its form. As an element of black culture ignored by those who would destroy Karintha, it exists quite apart from the considerations of the men in the story. Who is the vocalist, and who is the listener? The form belies the violence that is itself so much a part of the tale. The sense of ephemerality of Karintha's beauty exists either in itself only or also in the souls of those who would have none of the degradation, of this slow demise of African American culture which characterizes *Cane*. Even Karintha's transgression—the incineration of her infant child—seeks amelioration in this particular lyrical form. "Someone," Toomer tells us, "made a song":

> Smoke is on the hills. Rise up.
> Smoke is on the hills, O rise
> And take my soul to Jesus. (2)

The song was not sung, or written, but "made," made of the African urge to fashion meaning in human history and in the Americas, and against a Christianity powerless to prevent this horror. The preacher who says that Karintha is "as innocently lovely as a November cotton flower" is alone in moral rectitude; he thus draws our attention to one of the poems following, "November Cotton Flower," in which the flower appears suddenly, naturally, and beautifully, despite all of the chaos of a destructive nature surrounding it.

Toomer's strongest indictment is not of Karintha or perhaps even of the men who want and even have her. On their behalf and hers, Toomer finds the root cause of Karintha's tragedy to be economics: "Homes in Georgia are most often built on the two-room plan. In one you cook and eat, in the other you sleep, and there love goes on. Karintha had seen or heard, perhaps she had felt her parents loving. One could but imitate one's parents, for to follow them was the way of God" (1). The efficacy of mere function—here, the spare home, useful only in its utilitarian function as shelter, pares down values by eliminating privacy and attenuating innocence. In *The Souls of Black Folk,* Du Bois describes the homes of African Americans in rural Georgia at the turn of the century: "The size and arrangements of a people's homes are no unfair index of their condition. . . . All over the land is the one-room cabin. . . . It is nearly always old and bare, built of rough boards and neither plastered nor ceiled" (*Souls,* 165). Baker, in citing both Du Bois and a similar description of work-camp cabins in the 1920s, writes: "The scant diachronic modification in 'size and arrangements' allows them . . . to stand as *signs* of the continuing impoverishment of blacks in the United States." The small boy who, in playing "home" with Karintha, would not be afraid to do her bidding is similarly situated, his home having shaped for him, as Karintha's home fashioned for her, the limited and limiting child's sense of love as an hour or so at play. The sawmill, which has always been a part of her life in this valley, is darkly attractive as it too destroys innocence: Karintha's newborn child. Susan L. Blake writes that the stories are ostensibly *about* the women, but "the real interest—the interest developed throughout the book—is in the men who labor to possess them."[5] The interest in the men in "Karintha," then, lay in the fact that while Karintha, like Fern in her story, retains the essential and indomitable soul, the men who will sacrifice for Karintha at the end of the story do so not because of love, but out of the same rapaciousness that occasioned men's sexual domination of her; they have already been trapped in cyclical, overdetermined roles of dominance. "These are the young men," Toomer writes, "who thought that all they had to do was count time" (2). But their bewilderment at Karintha's indifference to them secures their domination by her. Karintha's single abhorrent act has further destroyed her innocence, but the predatory nature of her male pursuers betrays their unrelieved and unholy allegiance to all machines, including the one machine that figures so prominently in the story, the sawmill whose fires consume Karintha's child. Toomer advances his view of the rapine of technology with not only his ending in "Karintha" but also the following poem "Reapers," where the unconscious slaughter of the rat in the field is made all the more heinous by its lack of human in-

---

5. Baker, *Blues, Ideology,* 30; Susan L. Blake, "The Spectatorial Artist and the Structure of *Cane,*" 196.

volvement in its performance by a thresher. The black reapers—themselves ambiguous symbols of death for their blackness, and thus their grimness—are yet men without machines, who place their hones "in their hip-pockets as a thing that's done, / and start their silent swinging, one by one," representing the time-honored way of working the land. There is conveyed a sense of ritualized togetherness in the rhythmic swinging of the scythes that is opposed to the isolated and isolating operation of a machine, which results in the rat's death. Karintha's choice similarly represents this horror of the rat's death in that her only available answer to the machinery of economics is the dreaded and totalizing economy of the machine itself.

The tale "Karintha," however, has a career that precedes the coalescence of *Cane*. Its first appearance was in *Natalie Mann,* a play that Toomer wrote in 1922 though it was rejected for production. Frank had read the text, and rendered comments revealing that perhaps Toomer's ideas outstripped true dramaturgy:

> My first impression is that the central drama of Natalie, Merilh, Mertis, Law, etc is smothered by the form of the other stuff . . . the teaparties, the talk of the incidental. Then it occurs to me that the trouble is not with the density and amount of this milieu but with the deadness of the texture. If all this were living, the drama would live in it in its correct relation. The thing, therefore, needs rewriting rather than reconstructing. The life is not permeated into the whole thing. In individual scenes, there is a very beautiful colorful glow of life . . . as the lovescene of Natalie and Merilh, the two cabaret scenes . . . the gorgeous symbolism of the dance with Etty, and the lovely poem that M. recites in NY.

Frank is conveying his general dissatisfaction with scenes of middle-class life so overwrought as to make stilted some of the characters, particularly Therman Law, Merilh's close friend, and Mertis Newbolt, a friend of Natalie's but an intrusive busybody. While the work does fail as a play, the irony remains that the world of aristocratic black Washington was a world Toomer knew. Deeper than its overall aesthetic value, then, is *Natalie Mann*'s commentary on the interiority of race. The "lovely poem" to which Frank refers is "Karintha." Shortly after the appearance of "Karintha" in *Cane,* John McClure, editor of the "little magazine" *The Double Dealer,* was able to inform Sherwood Anderson as to Toomer's literary strengths and weaknesses, citing the tale as his best:

> As for JT, I am thoroughly convinced that as a piece of litera-
> ture, of durable writing, Karintha is afar superior to Kabnis. I
> do not think that T can't write short stories. I merely think that
> his finest work so far is lyrical and that if he ever does supreme
> work it must be in a lyrical manner. In my opinion he cannot
> handle dialect. He can do a certain sort of realistic story better
> than most and can rise to prominence in realism if he wishes to.
> But the lyrical expression of his own moods he can accomplish,
> in his own fashion, better probably than nearly anyone. He can
> be an unusually good short story writer or a supremely fine lyri-
> cal rhapsodist as he pleases. He should mould his stories into
> lyrical rhapsodies rather than attempt to present them realisti-
> cally. . . . If he follows that African urge, and rhapsodizes, he
> will be a commanding and solitary figure.[6]

The protagonist, writer Nathan Merilh, composes the tale; Dar-win J. Turner suggests that Nathan opposes "Karintha" symbolically to Natalie, the woman with whom he has fallen in love.[7] Merilh and Natalie, though among the members of Washington's fair-skinned, moneyed African American elite, are not of it. Merilh—a name for Toomer's alter ego, as Nathan was Toomer's father's first name—feels himself to be above the pettiness of bourgeois black society. Merilh is substantively more than the average man, having mastered the nu-ances of art, literature, and music, and he has transcended even this achievement by somehow reconciling both his white and black back-grounds. He is proudest, we are told, of the portraits in his study—one of Tolstoy, and the other of a powerful but nameless black man (which is interestingly reminiscent of the portrait of Toussaint L'Ouverture that hangs in the study of Walters, the dashing James Forten–like character in Frank J. Webb's 1857 novel *The Garies and Their Friends*). While Merilh is her "instrument of achievement," Natalie, whom Toomer describes in the dramatis personae as being "a personality who achieves herself," is a young woman who by

6. Frank to Jean Toomer, March 25, 1922, Box 3, Folder 83, JTP; McClure to Sherwood Anderson, January 29, 1924, Box 1, Folder 7, JTP.

7. Darwin T. Turner, ed., *The Wayward and the Seeking: A Collection of Writings by Jean Toomer,* 237.

scant degrees is able to liberate herself from the stifling milieu of the black elite. The final scene of the play, in her face-to-face confrontation with saloon owner Etty Beal in which there is not hostility at Merilh's collapse but mutual recognition, reveals a woman who, by embracing the aspects of race and historicity, is presumably liberated from the entrapments of class and unrestricted by its residual elements.

These elements are but parts of Toomer's universe of opposites, whose principal poles are man and woman. Although the clearest delineation of their types as opposites in any of Toomer's work is to be found in the expressionistic drama *The Sacred Factory* (written in 1927), his overall conviction about the sexes is that man, as an ideal type, embodied thought and reason whereas woman, again ideally, was possessed of emotion, which for Toomer was the more functional and therefore more desirable of the two. Unlike *The Sacred Factory,* however, the issue of race functions at the ground of every psychic and social consideration in *Natalie Mann.* Of all the artifacts in his study, Merilh is proudest of his portraits of Tolstoy and the powerful-looking but nameless black man. Merilh must face the very suppression of this identity, as must Toomer (though neither ever quite does), for in the consideration of all recollections of art and culture that the name Tolstoy will generate, the elision of the black man's identity signifies the repression of the larger representative discourse of blackness. This element appears to have repercussions later in the play, as Merilh and Natalie prepare to entertain some artist-friends one evening in their New York apartment. Merilh gives Natalie an idea of just who will be in the house: "Yep, young America shall gather under this roof tonight," Merilh exclaims, "Jews and Germans and Irish and Russians and Latin, God Almighty's Anglo-Saxon, and Niggers! Wheeee!" "Young America" was the name of that group of modernist aesthetes with whom Toomer associated, which included Sherwood Anderson, Randolph Bourne (who died in 1918), Gorham Munson, Paul Rosenfeld, Van Wyck Brooks, and Toomer's close friend and *Cane's* impresario, Waldo Frank. As Robert Crunden chronicles their rise in the young twentieth century, "these critics actually agreed on little beyond the religion of art that most of them practiced" (*Body,* 7), which suggests, particularly as regards Toomer's participation, that race and ethnicity were among those things regularly in contention. Charles Scruggs, however, in recounting the group's coalescence, remarks upon a liminal nuance that likely gave this participation its contours:

> Two things which first linked the group (which included James Oppenheim and Paul Rosenfeld, both Jewish Americans, as was Waldo Frank) were their sense of being outsiders and their belief that modernity was creating a new American culture; of course, these were related concerns, because their hope was that this new culture would be open to them in ways the old one had not been.
> . . . Much as he might have wished to do so, Toomer's racial identity kept him from reading "Young America" with an innocent eye. The distance between JT writing *Cane* and the white intellectuals . . . seems to emerge unbidden and unwillingly— their work and companionship had been his source of inspiration, yet *Cane* might be seen as an almost continuous critique of their ideas, of their unconsidered assumptions about American culture.[8]

More than Merilh's youthful exuberance and exultation in his ironic remark are at work in the play: his last designation, an epithet, is made even more conspicuous by the emphasis of the genitive in the preceding entry ("God Almighty's Anglo-Saxon"), as the proximity of these two recalls the two portraits in Merilh's study. The procession of the acceptably identified others similarly emphasizes the degradation invoked by "Niggers," but no emphasis is in this instance more thorough or more succinct than that given by the fact that Merilh's use of the epithet is also entirely self-referential. Kimberly Benston writes that the entire body of African American literature is replete with descriptions of the process of first unnaming blackness, as in seeking to vitiate the received term "nigger" (or even Negro), and then *renaming* blackness, thus forging and fixing its authentication:

> Allotting to black people the brand of "nigger" indicates a desire to void the possibility of meaning within the "blackened" shell of selfhood, thereby reducing substance to the repetitive

---

8. Turner, Introduction to *Cane, xiv; Wayward and Seeking,* 303; Charles Scruggs, "The Photographic Print, the Literary Negative: Alfred Stieglitz and Jean Toomer," 61–89.

echo of a catachresis. "Nigger" is a mechanism of control by contraction; it subsumes the complexities of human experience into a tractable sign while manifesting an essential inability to *see* (to grasp, to apprehend) the signified. If Toomer's white characters speak perplexedly of "nigger" as a quality (see "Blood-Burning Moon"), their translation of slur into modality is only the obverse of an original reification by slander.[9]

In "Blood-Burning Moon," the story of a lynching in *Cane,* the use of the term by whites is fixed as a negation before the obliteration of the body begins. But in *Natalie Mann,* where violence is absent, an odd similarity occurs to serve the subversion of blackness: while Merilh's irony in using the term is understood as a felt quality, he as a black man is never quite involved in the work of the trickster, never actively engaged in the crucial effort at unnaming. He rather remains imprisoned by the name, its modality conferred by default upon the likeness of the African in his study. Turner's suggestion that Merilh's literary creation is contrasted to Natalie to the effect of further developing her human potentialities seems to mask the likelihood that in the late stages of Natalie's developing consciousness, at which time Merilh unveils his writing, Karintha is more like Natalie than Merilh may think, and that the true opposition is between Karintha and Merilh, as Karintha revels in her youthful, unfettered spirit, and Merilh is bound by the unconscious desire to erase his blackness. The fact of declaring an unnameable subject marked by unnameability is an element in Toomer utilized by later black writers, often in the service of displaying a political, social, or genderized coming-of-age, with the most outstanding example perhaps being Ralph Ellison's 1952 novel *Invisible Man.* But the elision of a racial self, powerful for its attendant suggestion of sacrifice, is one of the earliest manifestations of Toomer's career in his writing as what Gorham Munson called "the spectatorial artist," a figure to which I would like to return shortly. At least as important in the early portion of part one of *Cane* is modernity's most oppressive and insistent force, the machine.

The deadly machine reappears in "Becky," as the symbol both of modern progress and African American flight in the twentieth

9. Kimberly W. Benston, "'I Yam What I Am': Naming and Unnaming in Afro-American Literature," 3–11.

century, the train, summarily disposes of those who would trans-
gress Southern racial and sexual codes. Toomer continues displaying
shadowy representations of men, but adds foregroundings of other
types for contrast, with the inclusion of himself in a first-person
guise. Becky is doubly beyond the nurturing and healing aspect of
community because of her interracial liaisons and the children they
have produced. Blacks and whites shun her with equal conviction,
yet there are those in each group who supply her surreptitiously with
goods from town. They want her dead, but only secretly, as guilt
forces them to harbor the wish for her demise in their thoughts and
their prayers. The black men who fathered her sons (we are invited to
wonder what lone black man could remain or return for either blessed
event in the circumstance of Becky's whiteness, as the boys are born
five years apart) remain nameless to the town and to us, doubtless
protected by Becky. As well, her sons' names are not known to us. As
the miscegenated, they bear the stigma of double-outsidedness that
suggests a difficulty in their naming. The double-outsidedness that
Becky herself endures makes it difficult for us to understand and appreciate the interiors of her consciousness, altered many times as
they must have been during all of the years her sons had been growing up. The boys have become violent and even lethal, their youth
and strength having been nourished by the passions and the guilt of
men, both black and white, and like their fathers they desert Becky,
displaying their hatred for her as well, and displaying also the self-
hatred she must feel, which is mirrored by her self-seclusion. That
they would curse both the blacks and whites of the town, that they
would engage in wanton killing as an expression of their anger, is indicative of their cursing the mixture of those bloods in themselves,
thus engaging in a reflexive damnation; they are lost not to the machine, but to a conspiracy in which they themselves participate: society's toxic banalities, the everyday world's ritualistic scorn.

Old David Georgia is one of those who would not have Becky
starve; he brings her more goods more often than anyone else. He is
also the only benefactor who does not hide his gift-giving, which attests to his being the least abashed at his own charity. As the community's sage, he is vaguely reminiscent of the biblical David and
reappears as Toomer's elegiac male figure in "Blood-Burning Moon,"
as he stands next to the stove which boils the syrupy, sweet-smelling
cane that is itself an activity which is slowly fading before the new,
modern, mechanized future. But in "Becky" perhaps the most inter-

esting figures are Barlo, who appears with the most clarity later in "Esther," and also in Toomer himself, who intrudes as first-person narrator to unmask his own effeteness—to expose his "futility to check solution." Barlo the preacher teams with Toomer the first-person narrator as both encounter Becky's fallen cabin on the way back to town from church. Barlo is here effete because he is fearful; the phrase "Pines whisper (shout) to Jesus" is the Spiritual or elegiac current running throughout the tale, and the fact of evil characterizing them is that they are at once the pines of which Becky's cabin is made and those which, ground up, served as the mound of kindling on which Karintha's infant was cremated. Barlo's brand of contingent, convenient Christianity is unable to answer the evil that may be riding astride Becky's ghost. Within the space of only two stories and two poems, then, there is a great crying out for redemption that Barlo cannot mediate, and in this he is linked to the effete Christianity of "Karintha," which cannot prevent the murder of her infant. But even more intriguing is the fact that Toomer's presence in the tale is similarly insufficient to mediate this anguish.

Susan Blake, in further discussing *Cane*'s structure, uses Gorham Munson's idea of the spectatorial artist to describe the artist who intrudes upon his own imaginative portrayals so as to give form to experience. Blake astutely locates the ironic commentary that occurs at the end of "Becky," "Carma," and "Fern" about the limits of knowledge, which applies to Toomer, who appears as first-person narrator in each of these stories, as well as to the other characters in these stories.[10] This commentary also comes nearer to the second stage of Toomer's lament for the passing of black folk culture discussed earlier. The futility he experiences at his inability to halt this devolution is deeply connected to his personal history. This notion also allows the inclusion among these three tales of another story in part two of *Cane,* "Avey," wherein Toomer again figures as first-person narrator. In this connection, Toomer, as spectatorial artist, unites these stories and, with his first-person presence, explains the insufficiency that Toomer himself may have felt as an African American male. Ambiguities of masculine power and influence in *Cane* are sometimes impelled less by the movement of a culture's emergence from a slaveocracy than they are controlled by Toomer's exploration of his own temperament, in a powerfully psychosexual fashion, within the narrative.

10. Blake, "Spectatorial Artist," 196, 198.

Toomer's trip to Sparta, though made ostensibly to help Ingraham, was in another way a severe and serious quest which may have had its impact in the issue of naming that supports the structure of *Natalie Mann*. Though Toomer could scarcely have known his father, he understood that Nathan Toomer was a planter in Georgia, somewhere between Macon and Augusta. As Turner states, this may have accorded well with Jean, who had already romanticized his father as being a Southern aristocrat. But this notion of Toomer's father may already have been compromised by the Pinchbacks' suspicion of Nathan as an opportunist who married Nina because he thought that her wealth would fund his indulgence of excess, and deserted her when he learned that her father closely controlled the family's finances. Turner writes that "the loss of [Toomer's] father may have motivated his attraction to various father figures in his life." From various townsfolk, Jean is able to piece together a picture of this missing father, though it is not quite a complete one. The romanticization of Nathan Toomer begins to collapse as Jean learns that his father may have been a farmer, not a planter—and the more he ponders the difference between these designations, the more they elude him. In photographs he had seen of Nathan, Jean recalls a man with quite fair skin and a noble, even foreboding, countenance. Now, in a conversation Toomer is having in a barbershop during a haircut, he takes the opportunity to discover the answer to a question that had probably troubled him greatly over the years:

> Was Nathan Toomer a white or a colored man? I asked the man who thus far had done all the talking. The man shrugged and said: "He stayed at the white hotel and did business with white men." Now a second man spoke up: "He paid attention to a colored woman." Then a third man said one of those things that are never said in the South, yet sometimes are said: "The white boss of this town is called a nigger behind his back, by his enemies. They say he has some Negro blood. What do you make of that?" No one wanted to make anything of that. Not a single word was spoken thereafter. Every man in the shop felt that too much had been said as it was.

Nina Pinchback Toomer, Jean's mother, was shadowed by her relationship with Toomer's father, a relationship that proved very unpopular with the Pinchback family. A letter she writes to Nathan in 1897 rejects his offers of love and support after his long absence and seeks permanently to sever ties between them. "I will be glad to have any aid you may see fit to furnish for [Jean's] support which is his lawful right," she writes, "but I shall not seek or expect it. I will endeavor as best I can to raise and educate our boy, if God spares our lives, in such a manner to make him a useful and honorable man. . . . [E]very dollar I have and all I may be able to earn, if need be, will be devoted to that purpose." Jean learned of this letter in his twenties, and with the knowledge of another similar letter to his father from his uncle Bismarck Pinchback, they render a figure for the young man of his father that is "altogether unpalatable . . . the picture they give . . . is one of unrelieved waywardness, deceit, and irresponsibility. And this puts it mildly." Though Nina charges Nathan in the letter with taking her "from a comfortable home and kind and loving parents," for a very long period she endured the humiliations and dominance of her father. Never having trusted Nathan or approved of the alliance with him, the redoubtable Pinchback may even have forced Nina to divorce him.[11] In looking at the several versions of Toomer's autobiographies, almost wherever he begins to discuss his mother Nina at length, he digresses with more about Pinchback or his influence on her. It shortly becomes apparent over the course of these drafts that Pinchback is so dominant a force that he manages to insinuate himself into Jean's writing long after his death, imposing himself where his daughter should be.

In returning to Toomer's letter to Waldo Frank, it is again interesting to note that he laments the ability to halt the ephemerality of the folk Negro as represented by women like Karintha and Fern because of his sense of his own effeteness. His presence as first-person narrator directs "Fern"; he appears later in part two as the patient-but-suffering, would-be confidant of the orphan-woman, Avey, herself a Karintha-figure in an urban setting. In "Becky" he is the bewildered witness of a tragic event; in "Carma," he is the fairly sophisticated but somewhat smug onlooker of "this cruelest melodrama." In each case he is the somewhat hesitant, reluctant quester whose awareness of a particular woman's dilemma is often just behind the veil that separates perception from reality. In these stories

---

11. Nina Pinchback Toomer to Nathan Toomer, July 8, 1897, Box 8, Folder 262; "Incredible Journey," Box 18, Folder 487, JTP.

are perhaps expressions of some of the unresolved strivings he had against Nina. One version of his autobiography recalls the long childhood illness that separated him from his playmates, but the illness was itself a means of both manipulating his mother and of coming to terms with his parents' divorce:

> My illness had been the climax of the long train of my experiences with mother, experiences which started in that very first year when I was bathed in the pain and struggle and suffering caused by father's going away and the divorce and her return to the Bacon Street house, which continued and increased as I grew up and loved her and resisted her loving anyone else. The wonder is, I suppose, that the psychic strain had not made me sick more often, had not come to a head before. This was perhaps because I was sturdy and healthy in other ways. As the doctors would say, my exceptional constitution had enabled me to accommodate and withstand the tension—until the crisis in mother's life produced a crisis in mine. . . . My illness had been a means of securing through sickness what I unconsciously feared I would not be able to secure in any other way, namely, the complete concerned attention of my mother. Many times in life I have seen the human psyche behave in just this manner. It will resort to both sudden and chronic illness in order to gratify a wish which is threatened with defeat. . . . Indeed I once experienced just this in so acute a degree that I seriously questioned if it were not the invalids who rule the world.

These episodes of Jean's manipulation of his mother would later include those for attention he sought when she wanted to escape for a period Pinchback's domineering behavior and incessant humiliations. When possibilities at new love for Nina became apparent, Jean would become an obstacle: "One day mother asked me how I would like to have a father," he writes. "I made a face and tried to forget it. As I would now say, I gulped it quickly into my subconsciousness and put up my front." But at least as much as Nina's absences are troubling for him, he is aware of the degree to which the fact of her complexion also has issue for his development. He is at least peripherally aware in these autobiographical fragments of 1930 of the relationship between Nina's complexion and that of girls in whom he took romantic interest—and the impact of that relationship upon him:

But to return to Dorothy [Hanvey, a childhood friend]. One other thing she did was to stamp me with, to indelibly impress upon me, her image. It was the image of a fair girl. My mother was dark. Already her picture, also fixed permanently, lay within me. And so the two, dark and fair, existed side by side, to govern my taste throughout life.

And in truth, often enough I have found myself now strongly drawn towards the one, again towards the other. And sometimes I have been in situations involving a choice between them, situations which, in a sense, were repetitions of my childhood circumstance.

Still again—for this matter of attraction is, in reality, far more complex than our formulae suggest—I have liked girls and women who were neither dark nor fair but in-between—such a one, for example, as Bernice Carson.

Blonde and brunette—two physical types, two kinds of women with whom a man can be in love. But in life nothing is only physical. There is also the symbolical. White and black. West and East. North and south. Light and darkness. Day and night. In general, the great contrasts. The pairs of opposites. And I, together with all other Is, am the reconciler.[12]

This Oedipal manifestation of Toomer's may also shed light upon the appearance in *Cane* and elsewhere of fair-complexioned black women, as well as it more immediately reflects the figural antinomies that were features of a modernist sensibility itself. Judith Berzon notes that for Toomer as well as for many other writers, "there is the challenge of exploring the psychological and sociological dimensions of mulatto characters who seek to create a third caste in what is essentially a two-caste system. For some black writers, [these characters] are utilized to attack the aping of white bourgeois values and to praise the values and life-style of the black 'folk.'" With respect to the African American men in *Cane,* this third caste composed mostly of women, whose presence is most pronounced in part two, is also one branch of Toomer's imaginative bifurcation. A darker black womanhood can represent the rich dark earth of the country while a feminized whiteness stands for the shining city; the black man in *Cane* is generally suspended between these, as is the case in "Seventh

12. "Earth-Being," 2nd draft (Book III, chaps. 17–19): Box 12, Folder 387, JTP.

Street," for example, or "Bona and Paul," or "Kabnis." As Patricia Chase suggests, Toomer projects these possibilities not solely as symbols of race, but by presenting the divided consciousnesses of all of *Cane*'s women, he renders them as antithetical, polarized opposites between which *he* may stand:

> If Toomer poses a question through one woman, he often answers that same question, or makes his statement through another. If Carma, in her ferocity and natural drive, does not understand her responsibility for her actions and their consequences, then Louisa most clearly does. If Karintha and Fern are the existential questions, of being or nonbeing, of identity versus nonentity, then Avey is the statement of survival through acceptance and indifference. If Becky is reality in the face of absurdity, then Esther is absurdity in the face of reality. If Dorris mirrors the question of finding life sustenance in the North, then Muriel is the answer.

Just as important as the faceless (and feckless) men in "Karintha" is the thinly cloaked narrator of "Becky," "Carma," "Fern," and "Avey." At the end of "Becky," the cabin in which she lives is referred to by Toomer as "the Becky cabin," suggesting that she possesses neither her dwelling nor anything else in her life. Similarly, Nina, a grown woman, even after the departure of Toomer's father, could not claim her autonomy. In the autobiographical sketches, the young Toomer is always toward his mother the sensitive, caring being whose only shortcoming is his inability to ease her pain because of his youth, as can perhaps be seen in a comparison of this concluding portion of "Becky" with the autobiographical excerpt from Toomer's recollection of Nina's treatment for an illness, which follows:

> Goose-flesh came on my skin though there still was neither chill nor wind. Eyes left their sockets for the cabin. Ears burned and throbbed. Uncanny eclipse! fear closed my mind. We were just about to pass . . . Pines shout to Jesus! . . . . the ground trembled as a ghost train rumbled by. The chimney fell into the cabin. Its thud was like a hollow report, ages having passed since it went off. Barlo and I were pulled out of our seats. Dragged to the door that had swung open. Through the dust we saw the bricks in a mound upon the floor. Becky, if

she was there, lay under them. I thought I heard a groan.
Barlo, mumbling something, threw his Bible on the pile. (No
one has ever touched it.) Somehow we got away. My buggy
was still on the road. The last thing that I remember was whipping old Dan like fury; I remember nothing after that—that is,
until I reached town and folks crowded round to get the true
word of it.

One day, grandmother and the whole house seemed ner-
vous. Two doctors came and arranged a long table in the middle of the room. I was told they were going to do something to
mother, and then she'd feel better and get well. I wanted to
see. I saw them lift her from bed and place her on the table.
She groaned a little. I squirmed and wanted to yell that they
should leave her alone. The doctor was very gentle and kind
and spoke to her as if she were a little girl. They fussed about
her. I began smelling a peculiar odor. And then, suddenly, I
heard her voice. It was hers, and yet it wasn't. It sounded
small and weak and far off. "Not yet. Not yet." Later I understood that she was telling them not to operate until the anes-
thetic had had its effect. She was letting then know she was
not yet under it. Again her voice, "Not yet." But it was weaker
and even farther off. It gave me a sinking feeling and terribly
frightened me. The doctor discovered me concealed near the
door and put me out. I went away and thought very seriously
about everything.[13]

In each instance the narrator struggles to master a disquieting
situation. He fails, however, in each case, succumbing to a kind of
helplessness. Though in the autobiographical excerpt a child is
being escorted from the scene by adults, it is a child's helplessness
that is mirrored in the terrified behaviors of Barlo and the narrator in
the "Becky" excerpt. In both the fictional and the autobiographical
cases, the sense of the nightmarish rules: there is the uneasy approach to the scene followed immediately by the intervening voice
of an inscrutable female presence, but rather than its having what
might be thought of as a calming effect, the voice serves instead as

13. Box 12, Folder 380, JTP; Patricia Chase, "The Women in *Cane*," 389–90;
Judith R. Berzon, *Neither White nor Black: The Mulatto Character in American
Fiction,* 13.

an impediment to calm; moreover, the voice has an immediate proximity to a situs of trepidation and apparent incommensurability. In the first case this is the moment of the collapse of Becky's cabin; in the second, it is Nina's being transported by the doctors from bed to table. In both cases, this situs is the place that Toomer cannot approach, even though he can in each case perhaps discern a helpless groan. In both cases he remains voiceless, and it is this instance which makes manifest his effeteness. In Carma's story, her disappearance into the canebrake signals her distress, for she must find a way to deceive her jealous husband, Bane; the narrator, while watching the scene, hears the gunshot in the canebrake, which is Carma's cry of desperation. Carma's tale, however, is qualified by the narrator, becoming the "tale as I have told it" at the story's end, which suggests an inability he has always had to understand her dilemma as posed by her unique composition ("Carma . . . strong as any man . . ."). In "Fern," the location of conflict—a sexual conflict, characterized by his unconscious holding of Fern in the cane field—is broken suddenly by Fern's wild, convulsive utterances—*her* helpless groan. "And then she sang, brokenly," the Toomeresque narrator relates in "Fern." "A Jewish cantor singing with a broken voice. A child's voice, uncertain, or an old man's" (17). Though here the narrator is cast as being from the North, thus presuming the worldliness that region has to offer, he is nevertheless ignorant of the intricacies of the South. He cannot fathom the layered complexity of Fern's heritage, the subtle interrelationships and tempestuous contests for primacy among her senses of blackness, Jewishness, whiteness, and Christianity.

The extended groan—the cry for help—is once again far off, unseen and indistinct, as in the description of Nina's preparation for surgery. Fern becomes like the others, ineffable, irretrievable: "Dusk hid her; I could only hear her song" (17). As well, Avey, for whom nothing can be done while she slumbers deeply in the shadow of the Capitol Building, becomes the reincarnation of the inaccessible, indomitable Karintha, as Toomer the narrator spots Avey with another man on "one evening in early June, just at the time when dusk is most lovely on the eastern horizon" (45). In this connection Toomer mirrors any one of the men in "Karintha" who "will die not having found it out" (2), who will die not having understood the world, because of their own lack of sophistication, in terms of the humane treatment of others. The narrator in "Avey" is any of the men in "Karintha" writ large. At the final consciousness of his effeteness, long after his ardor diminishes at the sight of the sleeping Avey, the narrator recalls the childhood behavior he described at the beginning of the story. He wants to whittle at the boxes of young trees, something he did with his childhood friends, something that expressed the "deep hidden purpose," the sexual storm and stress of adolescence. This image, at once regressive and aggressively sexual, locks this Toomeresque narrator into his effeteness and forces his angry and frustrated epithet upon Avey. "Orphan-woman" she is and remains— not only because she has lost crucial bonds with her parents, as did Nina—but also because he must abandon her, and because of a strength absent in himself give her over to the ravages of the wide world.

In this construction of a vital African American male identification, then, another reading can be given to the idea of the spectatorial artist, and also to its definition by Gorham Munson: "But an artist who feels that his gifts entail a grave responsibility, who wishes to fight on the side of life abundant rather than for life deficient, must pause and seek the answers to certain questions. What is the function of man? What are the potentials of man and what may he become? What is experience and what is knowledge? What is the world?"[14] A need to challenge the gradually increasing distance created by the narrator between himself and a female subject begins in its own way to answer some of these questions, if Toomer truly believed in man and woman as potential creators of a harmonious, integrated whole. The very problem for Toomer of fashioning black male identifications appears to begin here, for the mapping of this distance involves, as Toomer knew, the unmasking of the spectatorial artist to reveal the participating artist, and however effete they reveal themselves to be, men of action are far preferable to men of inaction. The irruptions of the Toomeresque voice into the text are the means of this unmasking, as they seek to close the gaps in which they appear by revealing the author's willingness to sacrifice himself to the type of man he delineates, making clear the urgency of his condition by disallowing his omission.

In "Esther," the fifth tale in *Cane,* Barlo receives a clearer repre-

---

14. Gorham Munson, "The Significance of Jean Toomer," 262–63.

sentation than he did in "Becky." Esther, a tragic mulatta in her own right, is nominally rejected, or held at arm's length, by both black and white society, though she perhaps enjoys a bit more respect from blacks; her father is the main storekeeper and the most prominent black man in town. Her perceived ostracism from mulatto society and her frustrated effort to retain a uniquely black identity lead her to make a sexual superman of Barlo—now known to us as King Barlo. At age nine, she is oblivious to both the white and black men of the town—but one day, she sees Barlo, "a clean-muscled, magnificent, black-skinned Negro" (20); she notices him almost for the first time as he drops to his knees in a trance at a spot called, for its value as a communal spitting place, the Spittoon. The white men who are spitting there are oblivious to Barlo's presence, and thus continue spitting, covering his face with tobacco juice as his vision, deemed by the black townsfolk to be decisive to African American life, comes to him. At this moment Barlo becomes Esther's sexual, social, and spiritual savior. In Esther's confused state, a dreamy, delusional aloofness, she believes that sexual union with Barlo will help her win the respect and security she longs for from the townsfolk. But Barlo is a pariah, and both white and black preachers conspire how best to be rid of him and his seductive messages couched in a blues that regularly lures their parishioners away. As Barbara Bowen contends, Barlo's perfect blues stanza is his conscious affirmation of his and the listening group's Africaneity. "More important . . . ," she writes, "than Barlo's sense of continuity with the past is the implicit promise of a future. The crowd hears his vision of the past as a vision of the future; they turn his story of oppression into a prophecy of regeneration." After the trance Barlo leaves town, and there ensue strange, mystical goings-on, such as the drawing by the Negress of the black madonna on the courthouse wall—an instance that also figures in "Fern." Barlo has rendered the story of the African's loss of power through bondage in his kneeling trance; the trance and its accompanying vision constitute Barlo's manifestation of *magara,* the Yoruba life-force, the communal sense of power whose most powerful expression in African American culture is through blues.[15] His return to town after many years proves a political perfidy in him,

15. Barbara E. Bowen, "Untroubled Voice: Call-and-Response in *Cane,*" 12–18; Janheinz Jahn, *Neo-African Literature: A History of Black Writing,* 170ff.

however, since he returns wealthy after having made his fortune in the cotton trade—an activity which, even after slavery, exacts its toll in the labor and the health of black men such as Tom Burwell, from the next and final tale in part one, "Blood-Burning Moon." "Esther" uses for some of its effect the biblical tale of the same name, a story of personal and national identity, to highlight the tragedy and confusion of race in the twentieth-century South. The biblical Esther's uncle Mordecai warns the young girl not to reveal her identity as a Jew just as the father of Toomer's Esther admonishes her to avoid color-consciousness by forgetting her station as a rich, near white Negro woman. Toomer's Esther here learns "the difference between the business and the social worlds" (24) just as the biblical Esther learns the difference between gaining the political advantage of being at court and what it means to shield her Jewish identity in order to do so. The implications of the biblical Esther's actions have interesting consequences for Fern in her tale, whose conflict with Christianity as a Jewish woman is exemplified by her habit of resting her head against a nail that sticks out from a beam on her front porch as she sits there: either instance might seem to invite self-immolation. In *Cane,* the baby in Esther's dream is paradoxically an emblem of sin, for although Barlo appears to her to be messianic, it is a sin for her to deify Barlo by her imagining having come by it immaculately. The fat Negro women and the scrawny white women of the dream— each stereotypic of lower social position—are ludicrous in their sexuality because while Barlo has had them all, only Esther can, because she feels she must, take the issue of Barlo's virility into herself. She thinks herself, finally, to be the only one deserving of this issue because of her higher station. But Barlo is the perennial trickster, the incomplete holy man, the preacher/prophet who quailed before the high spiritual seriousness of Becky's death, and who can be spat upon by white men while rendering the solemn task of unifying his similarly situated brothers and sisters. Barlo himself knows how tainted he is, but he is unaware that Esther is looking for a transcendental experience, an immaculate conception of her own. Her confused quest for identity parallels the failed spiritual quest of Fern, but more crucially exposed in both tales is the failure of black men to reinvent the self and assume supportive masculine agency.

In this connection, Toomer's effeteness as an independent and effective masculine agent is highlighted as Barlo's presence in "Esther" recalls his pairing with the Toomeresque narrator in "Becky"; Toomer is again linked to ineffectuality through the biblical Book of Esther to "Fern," wherein her conflicts of religion and race render him a failed deliverer, an effete Moses. If the spectatorial artist in the voice of this Toomeresque narrator is an unfinished savior, then the remark that "God has left the Moses-people for the nigger" in "Carma" is also a remark of resignation which again reveals his effeteness in "Esther" by continuing his ironic unmasking. As this narrator relates in "Fern," "I felt that things unseen to men were tangibly immediate. It would not have surprised me had I had a vision. People have them in Georgia more often than you would suppose. A black woman once saw the mother of Christ and drew her in charcoal on the courthouse wall . . . when one is on the soil of one's ancestors, most anything can come to one" (17). This is also the same strange occurrence among those others that come as a result of Barlo's trance in "Esther," which describes Barlo's power while continuing the description of the Toomeresque narrator's outsidedness. If it is understood that the action of the drawing in "Fern" coincides with its description as having been the result of Barlo's magic in "Esther," then we can locate the narrator's announced lack of vision alongside Barlo's apparent charlatanry—a location that figures again in "Becky" as we recall having witnessed the preacher Barlo's timidity before the death mound and Toomer's confused effort accurately to relate the occurrence—to tell "the true word of it." Among the other occurrences in Esther's tale is Fern's spiritual convulsion in the canebrake, at which Toomer as narrator fails both as a sexual partner and as a friend who can give solace or offer counsel in a human bond. Striving with elements of women's spirituality across the tales, then, are the difficulties and self-deceptions of African American men who remain underdeveloped, incomplete, and fragmented.

In "Blood-Burning Moon," however, there appears a male figure who seems unbelievably able to meet even the fear so strongly fundamental to Southern black life. Tom Burwell is the strongest representation of black maleness in this first part of *Cane,* both for the expression of that strength and for the supreme sacrifice he makes, though even the thought of expressing that strength dooms him from the outset; the black Madonna of both "Fern" and "Esther," though absent in this tale, nevertheless foreshadows Tom's sacrifice as her single dimension on the courthouse wall is the sign of the distant, in-

accessible mother. The tale begins with the description of two mi-
lieux—factory town, wherein the hulk of a pre–Civil War cotton factory stands, and a hill clearing on the edge of the forest nearby,
which slopes upward from the town. The factory is almost more than
metaphor for the life of the town as situated in this tale: its floorboards are rotting from years of lack of care, but its "skeleton stone
walls," its "solid hand-hewn beams of oak" are testimony to the fact
that even though the system of slavery has ended, the spirit of dominance which supported it remains. Further representing that spirit is
Bob Stone, the white-supremacist heir of factory town and of much
of the surrounding land. Both Tom Burwell and Bob Stone are vying
for the love of Louisa, the black woman who works on the Stone estate and with whom young Bob Stone has been having an ongoing
affair.

As in "Karintha" and the other stories in part one, economics
again plays a crucial role. Not only does the factory-as-relic recall
the oppression and the privation of slavery, but also Tom Burwell's
circumstance reveals the degree to which his particular economic
situation determines his destiny. He is a humble sharecropper on
Stone land, in love with Louisa, but hopelessly trapped in a vicious
cycle: he is unable to court her regularly because he works so hard.
He works hard because his lot as sharecropper demands it; he works
harder because he vainly seeks a more secure future for Louisa and
for himself. Bob Stone, on the other hand, who less loves Louisa
than fetishizes her racially, has his pleasure of her with a leisure
born of dominance: "He saw Louisa bent over that hearth. He went
in as a master should and took her. Direct, honest, bold. None of this
sneaking that he had to go through now. The contrast was repulsive
to him. His family had lost ground. Hell no, his family still owned
the niggers, practically. Damned if they did, or he wouldnt have to
duck around so" (31). Not only is Bob Stone's dishonesty to be contrasted with Tom's honesty (Tom confesses to Louisa that he has
known other women), but the honesty of Tom's labor is contrasted to
what may be seen as being Barlo's perfidy in the preceding tale,
"Esther." In "Blood-Burning Moon," Tom proves a linkage between
these two tales by telling Louisa how much cotton he had picked on
that day, and that he had come close to beating Barlo in doing so.
This admission revives for us a fact already established in "Esther,"
that Barlo is "the best cotton picker in the county, in the state, in the

whole world, for that matter" (23). But Barlo had also left town only to return rich from having made his money on the backs of men like Tom in this sharecropping age. Barlo's stature as a redemptive figure, then, is drawn into even closer question in "Blood-Burning Moon" than that which is forced upon his value as prophet during his revelation in "Esther." Tom, by contrast, fights to claim his right to manhood both by fighting Bob Stone and by seeking a future by dint of his own labor—however futile an enterprise this may prove. Tom in this sense becomes Moses-like, at least for the effort, in sharp contrast to Barlo's status as a failed deliverer, a trait whose earliest manifestation was seen in "Becky," as he fearfully tossed the Bible on Becky's death mound.

Tom Burwell lives in factory town, but he is clearly not of it: he sits on a hill above the town with the benevolent, griot-like Old David Georgia who first appeared in "Becky," Will Manning, and some of Manning's friends. This is Toomer's Southern version of the New Jerusalem, the paradise on the hill that is an emblem of African American writing as it serves as something of an oasis in the midst of violent racial tension. The men are boiling cane syrup, tending to their industry in the time-honored way. A young boy whips at a mule who turns the cane grinder by going around it as another draws the syrup from the grinder to take it for boiling. The scent of cane that not only fills the forest but also descends into factory town symbolizes a kind of innocence, a slower and perhaps even more meditative way of life. Tom meets his fate as he leaves this peaceful, idyllic scene whose quiet is suddenly shattered by Will Manning's remarks about Louisa and Bob Stone. He descends the hill into factory town, with defiant purpose mixed with foreboding, and begins his poignant last courting of Louisa. Tom, unlike other black men of his time in his situation, is unwilling—perhaps, as Toomer's designated warrior figure, even unable—to choose flight, which would be considered a reasonable, even wise course of action against Southern justice. But Tom makes no distinction between Bob Stone and any black man he would fight to have Louisa. It would be at least harrowing to witness a fight between Tom, who would cut Stone "jes like I cut a nigger" (30) and Barlo, who, as we are told in "Esther," is the "best man with his fists . . . with a razor" (25). But the fact of the South for a Tom Burwell engaged in a fight with a Bob Stone makes Tom seem almost otherworldly and unreal rather than warriorlike.

Tom the warrior, however, and Barlo the trickster are in fact two sides of the same coin.

Though Tom is called "Big Boy" by the townsfolk, Barlo actually appears to be more commanding physically. As he describes the African in his trance in "Esther," "he was big an black an powerful . . . —but his head was caught up in the clouds." The African was "gazin at th heavens, heart filled up with th Lord" (21). Barlo is in one sense describing himself; as he rises from his kneeling position, he seeks consubstantiation with an essence he creates: "He is immense. To the people he assumes the outlines of his visioned African" (21). Some "little white-ant biddies" come to chain the feet of the immense African of Barlo's vision and lead him into bondage. On the other hand, Barlo is also describing Tom, who endures the African's fate for slashing Bob Stone's throat. In this recognition, the impressions of the two men begin to shift: the imminence of Tom's Christlike sacrifice now makes him appear huge. Upon the very moment of Bob Stone's naming of his assailant, "white men like ants upon a forage rushed about. Except for the taut hum of their moving, all was silent. Shotguns, revolvers, rope, kerosene, torches" (34). It is Barlo in an odd representation of John the Baptist who has prefigured Tom's sacrifice and crucifixion. If the mechanized spirit of a new century had corrupted the men Karintha knew, and killed Becky—if Esther was deceived by Barlo's manipulation of local economies—then Tom shows himself to be more thoroughly, if futilely, engaged in the struggle against the now-new, now-defunct machinery of capital, the fuel for both the old order and the new order of things; accordingly, the form of immolation for the "Old Negro" is retained for Tom's "New Negro" outrage. While he must pit his labor against this machinery in the hopeless effort to secure his freedom, the same machinery consumes itself in order to consume his life. Tom is crucified, burned at the old prewar cotton factory, the bygone standard of slavery. It is now a hulk of symbolic oppression, with its "skeleton stone walls" and rotting floorboards; it is a macabre reflection of the fact that the structure of white supremacy remains. Its "solid, hand-hewn beams of oak" represent the strong inner skeleton, the spirit of the old South as reflected in Bob Stone and others like him. Tom's eyes are described by Toomer as being rigid and fixed, much like Barlo's when he is in his trance. But while Barlo's gesture of arms outstretched in entering this state in "Esther" mocks the divine posture, Tom's crucifixion is real. Presaging his sacrifice is the charcoal portrait of the Madonna on the courthouse wall, the drawing seen both in "Esther" and in "Fern" with the strange attendant remark of the narrator, "when one is on the soil of one's ancestors, most anything can come to one." This visionary drawing on the courthouse wall is its own announcement of protest against that body of law that obstructs the uniquely American freedom that Toomer sought to express on behalf of all men and women, and its first appearance in "Fern" suggests a desire for a messianic resolution of that dilemma of Fern's that is at once interfaith and cross-racial, a desire for a redeemer much like, perhaps, the self-proclaimed "reconciler" of the racial and other divergences found in Dorothy Hanvey, Nina Pinchback, and the other women of Toomer's autobiographical fragments.

Through his crucifixion, Tom Burwell has taken upon himself Barlo's treachery, as well as Bane's hysteria, Fern's forced virginity, and the murderous rage of Becky's sons. If the hill from which Tom descended to meet his fate is the best part of the culture Toomer felt was fading from view, Tom's death crystallizes for us that culture's reason for being and the shape of the form in which it survives. The fact of the Migration, whose reasons were those for which Tom died—the twin dangers of racism and a suffocating economy—would bring millions of blacks to Toomer's arid northern desert. The spectatorial artist, who had already sacrificed himself to the ranks of the fallen, is perhaps the most crucial figure of the redemptive reach as he bears witness both to it and to the world to come.

3

OF SILENT STRIVINGS

Cane's Mute and Dreaming "Dictie"

Part two of *Cane* experiences an initial shift in venue from rural Georgia to Washington, D.C., both the nation's capital and the mid-point between the rural South and the industrialized North. Here Toomer develops his "dictie" theme, the idea that urbanized blacks, having lost (or discarded) their folk spirit, speak and behave in a way imitative of their white counterparts, a way which seeks to forge a sameness via the medium of class. In part one, the generalized voice-lessness of women complemented the misuse of men's voices: Becky's only plea for salvation is a distant groan before death, while Barlo's mumbled funeral sermon and the Toomeresque narrator's effort to give "the true word of it" determine the final scene; despite the world of words locked in her, Fern's convulsive stammering in the cane field is unable to produce understanding, and the words of promise from black men that Karintha hears are words actually de-noting pride and possession. *Cane*'s stories after "Seventh Street"— "Avey," "Theater," "Box Seat," "Bona and Paul," which takes place in Chicago, and "Kabnis," which returns to Georgia—yield a conscious-ness about self and language that is manifest at each male subject's limited awareness of the ethos of the machine. "Seventh Street" be-gins part two not with the words of men or women, but with a change in rhythm:

> Money burns in the pocket, pocket hurts,
> Bootleggers in silken shirts,

Ballooned, zooming Cadillacs,
Whizzing, whizzing down the streetcar tracks. (39)

This lyric strain has a jazz rhythm, and jazz to Toomer was the harbinger of death for original, Southern black folk culture. As James de Jongh claims, unlike Langston Hughes, whose apotheosis of jazz rhythm "specified his transcendent apprehension of the expansiveness of human possibility . . . with the particular texture of the black condition [as] perceived through the prism of the blues," Toomer was certain that the inevitability of blues culture would provide only the constriction of this possibility. "The folk-spirit was walking in to die on the modern desert," wrote Toomer,[1] and this romantic visualization of a beautiful death became the perfect opposition to the birth of a complex, garish new order. The lyric that heads and concludes "Seventh Street" contrasts the lyric that opens and haunts "Karintha" as its rougher tone competes with the more meditative, languishing mood of the earlier Southern section. If, in the entirety of *Cane,* the poems that interlace the stories can be thought of as modernist epigrams to them, perhaps in answer to the last previous great work to have European cultural sensibilities in tension with the black text, W. E. B. Du Bois's *The Souls of Black Folk,* then "Seventh Street" makes this tension doubly palpable as its epigram shapes its prosaic matter at either end.

"Seventh Street" resumes the quest for and examination of values that ended dramatically in part one with Tom Burwell's lynching. Toomer suggests that what helped create black Washington was lynching's depredations upon the black South. "Who set you flowing?" is a recurring apostrophe that generates the ancillary question "Why?" and suggests a return to Tom's murder in "Blood-Burning Moon" through "a blood-red smoke" swirling "up where the buzzards fly in heaven." It also heralds the last vestige of the black peasant, as there is also in the sense of black migration in "Seventh Street" a return to the uniquely Southern rhythm of agrarian labor as captured in the work song, "Stale soggy wood of Washington. Wedges rust in soggy wood . . . Split it! In two! Again! Shred it!" (39) It is a rhythm that also recalls the rhythm of "Cotton Song" in part one: "Come, brother, come. Lets lift it; / Come now, hewit! roll away!" (11) As Southern labor and Northern class consciousness are united in this complexity

1. *Wayward and Seeking,* 123; de Jongh, *Vicious Modernism,* 25.

of rhythm and landscape, the valuation of black labor, South or North, is compromised; Seventh Street, as "a bastard of Prohibition and the War," heralds both the onset of World War I and the signing of the Volstead Act in 1919. The war saw the exodus of blacks from civil service employment, while Prohibition saw illicit gain by some, though there more importantly began the consistent identification by media and police of urban blacks with crime, particularly rape—a condition that would seem in another vein to make the sexual shredding of Washington's whited wood ironic and dangerous. Although blacks would acquit themselves heroically during the war, segregation in federal employment, begun in the presidency of William Howard Taft and expanded in 1913 under the auspices of the Wilson administration, caused "stirrings of anger among Washington's Negroes over the suddenly more 'Southern' outlook of their lives."[2] Such bastardy changes the rhythm of black song, as the heightened sexuality of song that is reflected in "Seventh Street" returns a distorted reading of an already dangerous black Southern vitality, one that now becomes deeply attenuated in this new venue of the black masculine.

Farah Jasmine Griffin, in her insightful study of the literature of the Migration, writes that Toomer's Washington is "a white woman, a stale and stagnant being entered forcefully by the black male migrant blood." She observes the significance "that Toomer's migrants are defined as masculine," but the migrants of *Cane's* part two show a discernible loss of virility after "Seventh Street." Though black labor was not solely masculine, as Trudier Harris details, lynching was overwhelmingly so, and as the wasting of the body came with unskilled labor, ultimate danger lay in the specter of white womanhood.[3] Toomer's Washington, particularly his Seventh Street, changes at the behest of maleness: its powerful and insistent imagery of penetration, its "loafer air, jazz songs and love, thrusting unconscious rhythms, black reddish blood into the white and whitewashed wood of Washington" signify a bold sense of black culture with a threat of potency for a new urbanity. Just as "Seventh Street" imagines and inaugurates a modernism made manifest in its rapid generation of

2. Arthur I. Waskow, "The 1919 Race Riots: A Study in the Connection between Conflict and Violence," 24.

3. Farah Jasmine Griffin, *"Who Set You Flowin'?" The African-American Migration Narrative,* 65; Trudier Harris, *Exorcising Blackness: Historical and Literary Lynching and Burning Rituals,* 7.

Manichean opposites, however, the men of *Cane*'s second part who walk this metonymic boulevard seem to suffer from forms of impotence, from a kind of generalized inadequacy that speaks to not only sexlessness but also aimlessness. Seventh Street, though soaked with a vital black blood, is a restricted thoroughfare, its gates closed by the same jazz impulse that began it; it is probably not surprising that Toomer's men in parts two and three are barred from satisfying sexual relationships, or that these same men show a significant lack in other settings. Rhobert is doomed to bearing the weight of property and pretension; Dan Moore is unemployed and neurotic; John's employment depends on the debasement of black women for gain; Paul Johnson and the Toomeresque narrator of "Avey" are a pair of confused students; and Ralph Kabnis, in his return to the South in part three, is conveyed back to bondage through his emasculating fear of lynching.

These individual dislocations metaphorize the sense of black fragmentation endured by all African Americans in the young twentieth century, and also signaled the erosion of the black elite, a class to which Toomer belonged. Toomer focuses in part two principally upon the Washington of the black middle and working classes, and on a Chicago engaged, in "Bona and Paul," in a genteel questioning of alterity. This focus recalls the Washington and Chicago that were the sites of two of the country's worst urban race riots in what James Weldon Johnson called the "Red Summer" of 1919 (*Along*, 351). The immediate reason for the Washington conflict—the ordinary association of blacks with crime—was a burden that blacks of all classes could share, and it is precisely this shared condition that allows Toomer's critique of class valorization. As Barbara Foley indicates, Toomer's two articles in the socialist *New York Call* in June and August of 1919 viewed the race riots with "proletarian didacticism" and "from an explicitly Marxist standpoint." But as Charles Scruggs's suggestion of Toomer's parallax view of "Young America" appears to make evident, Marxism would also be a perspective through which Toomer would be working out difficult personal issues of race as well as those of class; additionally, he almost certainly would have read and been influenced by a July article in the *Call* discussing the more local issue of white jealousy at growing black prosperity in Washington and its significant role in stirring discord.[4]

4. Barbara Foley, "Jean Toomer's Washington and the Politics of Class: From 'Blue Veins' to Seventh-street Rebels," 289–321; Scruggs, "Stieglitz and Toomer," 68, 69, 80; Waskow, "The 1919 Race Riots," 25.

Toomer's "dictie" lives here, at this capital not only of the nation but also of black duality that is only sometimes the duality of double consciousness. To have this duality more often means to be bifurcated along a different modernist continuum: not only are city and country and whiteness and blackness generated here, but so are divisions along lines of class and race that were not as much in evidence in part one. Black blood, alloyed by lynching and the inequalities of labor and stamped on Washington's starched white femaleness, could produce for Toomer only an effete maleness, a maleness governed by a mute domesticity on the one hand and a generalized social confusion on the other, and not by an integrity useful in communitarian struggles and to other black men as a space of resistance. Toomer, in a way very similar to his constructed points of incommensurability, sees this opportunity for alterity in the modernist realm as dangerous stasis—the folk-spirit walking in to die on the modern desert. While the new music of the Jazz Age is the evidence of Seventh Street's sins, the Spirituals function as a dirge for Rhobert, the narrator of "Avey," and Kabnis. The "monument of hewn oak, carved in nigger-heads" (41) in mock tribute to Rhobert (who in his bondage to property also experiences a kind of social and psychological lynching) may also be the totem to the "nigger God" of "Seventh Street," the god who in his own effeteness, much like Barlo's in part one, sees the crushed and crushing life of blacks as only a desultory thing, and in response does not invoke himself as the Word, but can only "duck his head in shame and call for the Judgment Day" (39). Charles Scruggs and Lee Vandemarr's remark that "secrecy and miscegenation are the major themes in the first section of *Cane*" makes interesting the fact that both "Rhobert" and "Seventh Street" are nondialogic pieces, tableaux for Toomer's ideational movement from South to North, and thus the silent settings for both the difficult birth of the dictie and the various voices heard toward the end of *Cane*.[5]

Avey is a reincarnation of Karintha, as she is at one point seen by the narrator on "one evening in early June, just as the dusk is most lovely on the eastern horizon" (45). This is an interesting revival for the Toomeresque narrator, because in presenting the Washington version of his opening tale, a tale whose men were muted

5. Charles Scruggs and Lee Vandemarr, *Jean Toomer and the Terrors of American History*, 23.

but nevertheless nefarious, he again sacrifices his first-person voice to an ethic of African American manhood. Like Karintha, Avey has given herself over to prostitution, and exists at the whims and for the lusts of men. This time, no old men follow in her wake, but young boys do instead, and these are brought into sharper focus than the men in "Karintha" because of the now fuller view of their degradation by the Northern impulse toward the machine. The boys are even named this time, but for the most part, they remain fundamentally unidentifiable, or identifiable only with the nicknames of adolescents: Doc, Ned, Bubs, and the story's nameless narrator refuse the idea that Avey's actions reveal not a capitulation to masculine control, but rather her considerable manipulation of both sex and economics. The boys are the victims of arrested development in every sense, and sacrificers of Avey's blossoming youth to their adolescent prurience. Ned, the oldest and most experienced of this group, does not seem to get very much past the felt maturity, however specious, of wearing long pants for the first time. Even the Toomeresque narrator is guilty of allowing a typically adolescent solecism to creep into the speech of a presumably educated man: "Us fellers were seated on the curb before an apartment house where she had gone in" (42), thus betraying with his voice another distortion of development, as represented by his own halting movement between the agrarian South he has locked in his heart and the sophisticated North to which he ardently aspires.

Just as in "Karintha," wherein the persistence of the sawmill results in the slow wasting of the landscape and ultimately in the consumption of Karintha's newborn child, and just as young men counted time faster in anticipation of a sexual opportunity that could only be ruinous to the maturing girl, the boys in "Avey" represent yet another phase of ecological disaster in *Cane*. In order to appease their sexual urges, they whittle away at the boxes of saplings that line a street in town: "I like to think now that there was a hidden purpose in the way we hacked them with our knives. I like to feel that something deep in me responded to the trees, the young trees that whinnied like colts impatient to be let free . . ." (42). This measure of waste in the story shows as much disrespect for the natural as exists in "Karintha," but this time men are full agents as destroyers. The disrespect for the feelings and lives of women, although quite evident in "Karintha" and throughout most of the rest of part one, is never stated as bluntly, or with as much reference to dirt and uncleanliness, as in this instance: "There was nothing [Ned] didnt know when it came to women. He dilated on the emotional needs of girls. Said they werent much different from men in that respect. And concluded with the solemn avowal: 'It does em good.' None of us liked Ned much. We all talked dirt; but it was the way he said it. And then too, a couple of the fellers had sisters and had caught Ned playing with them. But there was no disputing the superiority of his smutty wisdom" (42).

The descriptions of illicit sexual activity of any sort in part one follows an economy that does not manifest itself with any references to soiling or dirtying. In this tale, however, as in much of part two, sex as thwarted or controlled by the machine invites the idea of the opprobrious permanence of stain. Conversely, as the narrator engages in a crisp reminiscence about his Southland, there is within that recollection a mood of refreshment and renewal: "And when the wind is from the South, soil of my homeland falls like a fertile shower upon the lean streets of the city" (46). This fertility recalls "Seventh Street" and the black blood that overcomes the new urban landscape. Immanent in these recollections of Ned and black blood is a more mature re-membering of the fertility of Southern soil through black labor, a sensibility that an intended sexual union with Avey would symbolize. But because the African American's movement to northern climes is itself fraught with ambiguities of place and identity, the answer to the urges for this ironic cleanliness and purification are now somehow insufficient. These ambiguities are made complementary to an urge toward moral cleanliness as the narrator takes great pains to inform his friend the policeman that he has not brought Avey to the park with him for sex. This configuration of sexual opportunity as waiting for a sanctioning authority appears again at the end of "Bona and Paul," wherein the black doorman is called upon by Paul to somehow bless his intended union with the white Bona Hale. Here, as in "Avey," the figure of authority, a *uniformed* presence, is sought out and beckoned to the scene of sexual chance. In his autobiography "Earth-Being," Toomer relates instances of his early childhood in which he craved autonomy and generally resisted authority. His rage and resistance would increase with increases in supervision, making him rebellious and intolerable:

> The way to handle me was to show me the thing, say you thought
> I should do it, and state with conviction that you believed I

> would. Then go away—leaving me entirely on my own, and
> with the feeling that you recognized my ability both to see that
> the thing should be done and to do it without anyone com-
> manding or watching over me. If you did so leave me, you
> could be sure I would do my utmost not to fail your high esti-
> mate of me. But let me feel that you thought I was incapable, or
> that I needed a policeman, and I'd try my best to make you wish
> you had ten of them to help control me.[6]

Both in "Avey" and in "Bona and Paul" the policeman is the signifier
of the generalized impotence of the principal male characters. In
"Box Seat," the crossing cop who leads Dan Moore's stricken old
man away remains the check on black possibility, and though here
the policeman does not immediately appear to represent a sexual
prohibition, he in fact does by securing a historical one. Without the
old man's wisdom, Dan cannot re-create his song, a song that nevertheless has its sexual and familial implications, as the houses that
Dan tried to sing to are "shy girls" (56). The rage indicated at the
surveillance of young Eugene Toomer's doings surfaces in the confused adolescent in "Avey." Its narrator engages the policeman he
had befriended over many nights of visiting the park alone: "I tell
him I come to find the truth that people bury in their hearts. I tell
him that I do not come there with a girl to do the thing he's paid to
watch out for. I look deep in his eyes when I say these things, and he
believes me" (46). But on this night, as the policeman passes, the
narrator, gazing at the sleeping Avey, begins to "visualize certain
possibilities" as an "immediate and urgent passion" engulfs him. He
will not fulfill this passion, as one of its impediments is this hovering
constable. The policeman is the modernist brake on the narrator's
sexual drive, a signification of guilt about sex that has even its racial
and class bases; the narrator imagines and utilizes a moral whole-
someness without which he believes the policeman would not be-
lieve him, beguiled as he himself is by both fair skin and social
aspiration. The narrator also imagines his escapade with Avey as a
continuance of the fertilization of the urban landscape by the surge
of black Southern folk, but this image is corrupted by the shame of
black Southern labor and the black blood shed by lynching. Avey's
general indolence is a more severe impediment for the narrator, now
frustrated as he is by her slumber.

6. *Wayward and Seeking,* 64.

The narrator is going to become a "college feller," one of the different kinds of men who would have wooed Karintha and failed, but the critical feature of his presence in "Avey" is the loss of his soul as he embraces the ideology of success, emulates perceived superiors, and confuses these with devotion. The conversation he engages in with the policeman and the "energetic Swedes" he tries to imitate during his summers in Wisconsin contribute to his idea of the moral, successful (read white) American, and Avey, who for the narrator is delicate and bovine by turns, is now diminished for her demonstrated lack of ambition. Then again, the women of Wisconsin become the true cows, lacking the sensuality that Avey only exudes, a condition that once again fuels the narrator's ardor. In Foucault's remarks on leisure and sexuality, he writes that " . . . the first figure to be invested by the deployment of sexuality . . . was the 'idle' woman. She inhabited the outer edge of the 'world,' in which she always had to appear as a value, and of the family, where she was assigned a new destiny charged with conjugal and parental obligations"; the female body thus became the object of conservatism and social control.[7] To the narrator, Avey is the potential mother of the "underground races" that Dan Moore imagines just below him in "Box Seat," but the narrator's chagrin that he cannot consummate his desire renders Avey's face "pale . . . she did not have the gray crimson-splashed beauty of the dawn" (47). Avey's idleness, however, is her own resistance against the control of her sexuality by the narrator's bourgeois conventions, and his confusion only reveals his lack of sympathy for her. He is again a fixed distance away from the woman in distress, unable to lend his humanity: "I gave her one burning kiss. Then she laid me in her lap as if I were a child. Helpless. I got sore when she started to hum a lullaby. She wouldnt let me go. I talked. I knew damned well that I could beat her at that. Her eyes were soft and misty, the curves of her lips were wistful, and her smile seemed indulgent of the irrelevance of my remarks. I gave up at last and let her love me, silently, in her own way" (44).

The narrator responds inadequately to Avey's humming of the lullaby, just as he fails to respond to Becky's moan from beneath the mound, or to Fern's convulsive cries at the edge of the canebrake, or, in the instance from his autobiographical writings, to his mother's fearful groan from the operating table as she is being prepared for a

7. Michel Foucault, *The History of Sexuality,* vol. 1, 120–21.

mysterious surgery. In "Avey," the arresting moment of weakness is bracketed by the material emblems of industry and progress: "A railroad track runs up the valley and curves out of sight where part of the mountain rock had to be blasted away to make room for it. The engines of this valley have a whistle, the echoes of which sound like iterated gasps and sobs. I always think of them as crude music from the soul of Avey" (44). A "crude music" played in this way points up an ironic contrast to the narrations of part one. Unlike Fern, whose convulsions provoke in that narrator the feeling that "some fine unnamed thing" should be done for her, the intervening elements between the narrator and Avey are gasps and sobs as generated by the machine. The narrator's desire to hear the Spiritual "Deep River" after associations made with the descent of Rhobert is a call for a spiritual death for Avey for her idleness. His fragmentation is expressed as regression: his passion, both awakened and frustrated by Avey's deepening sleep on the lawn, revives his adolescent, masturbatory urge: "My body grew numb. I shivered. I coughed. I wanted to get up and whittle at the boxes of young trees" (46). Avey becomes an "orphan-woman" to the narrator as the rejection of the mother in the lover again occurs, and the narrator's paternalistic voice is both amplified and undone in the echo of technology.

By a kind of literal foreshadowing in "Theater," we are led to the class conflict between John, a choreographer and the brother of the theater's manager, and Dorris, his best dancer. Toomer begins by reviving the scene of the city that begins part one: "Life of nigger alleys, of pool rooms and restaurants and near-beer saloons soaks into the walls of Howard Theater and sets them throbbing jazz songs. Black-skinned, they dance and shout above the tick and trill of white-walled buildings" (50). This is "Seventh Street" redux, where black life swings on a jazz edge, taunting and titillating the whiteness that surrounds it. John, who begins the day's rehearsal, opens up the theater to have revealed to us his true nature by light: "Light streaks down upon him from a window high above. One half his face is orange in it. One half his face is in shadow. The soft glow of the house rushes to, and compacts about, the shaft of light. John's mind coincides with the shaft of light. Thoughts rush to, and compact about it" (50). This mixed half represents in one instance a consciousness divided between an African American rootedness in folk-speech and folklore, sensuous and agrarian, and in the other, the distant Euroamerican stance of the patrician, who deigns to inferiors only griev-ously. The other side of John's face, draped in shadow, is a void (a/void), steadily increased by John himself, that exists between his own subordination of passion deemed African, to high reason, con-sidered to have a European foundation. That his mind coincides with the light that shines on his face, and that all his thoughts adhere to it, reveal his racial perfidy; it is a light whose intensity is fueled by John's definition of it as European Other. Jean Wagner writes of Paul Laurence Dunbar that Dunbar interpreted "the public's refusal to recognize his standard English poems as superior to his dialect poems to be a rejection of the 'white man' in him—since his poems in stan-dard English must be regarded as a projection of his 'will to white-ness' and a compensation for his feeling of inferiority" (*Black Poets,* 110). The manuscript John reaches for during the dream sequence recalls this remark, in that it represents a form of rejection of Dorris. Intriguingly, Wagner's softer assessment of Toomer's poetry invites comparison with his remarks on Dunbar while enhancing the con-sideration of Toomer as the interrogating, spectatorial artist: "[I]t cannot be said that Toomer lacked identification with his people, since his own voluntary return to the people enabled him to discover that the elements at war within his own consciousness were also those dividing his people within theirs. But one cannot say that he made himself entirely one with the destiny of his people, for they had no choice but to assume the burden of slavery along with the burden of daily life, while Toomer had striven for an awareness of his inner division, not in order to accept it, but to transcend it" (*Black Poets,* 271). Sexuality drives this division both in Toomer's life and in that of his male characters; in "Theater," the vitality of the house and the line of dancing women awaken John's desire while he strug-gles to separate the two realms of intellect and passion. Into the space between these comes Dorris, herself hidden by the shadows of a set. It is this representative shadow, the wide chasm between John's vaguely felt blackness and his will to whiteness, which Dorris must negotiate to find John's love.

In John's mind, the dancers are little more than beasts: "Soon the director will herd you, my full-lipped, distant beauties, and tame you, and blunt your sharp thrusts in loosely suggestive movements, appropriate to Broadway. (O dance!) Soon the audience will paint your dusk faces white, and call you beautiful" (50). He thinks of the

front line of women as "dancing ponies" (51), a sexualized and racialized description akin to that of the cow that Avey becomes when she
is compared to Wisconsin's "energetic Swedes." John believes the
Great White Way (properly so called) must not be unduly shocked
by the women's exotic movement to the taut sensuality of African
rhythm, which suggests the urge of the capitalist to modulate sexuality in the modern moment: to exploit through the bestial but also to
preserve propriety behind the mask of morality. Dorris pits her sensuality against his valuations of intellect, but she is able to cast John's
pretentiousness in perspective. Her question, "Whats a manager's
brother, anyhow?" allows her in one sense to entertain genuine con-
ceptions of love when she thinks about him. In the dream montage,
John conceives Dorris in his own image as he advances toward her
with a "collar and tie colorful and flaring," indicating his willingness
to adopt Africanesque style if only through fantasy. Though Dorris's
singing is characterized by Toomer as being "of canebrake loves and
mangrove feastings" (53), thus commingling a flavor of Africa with
the experience of the American South, John is a dissembler, seeking
to escape the South even in his dream. The manuscript he reaches
for in the dream is a text whose actuality appears to have been compromised by the conflict between his intellectual fantasies and his
status at the Howard Theater ("Whats a manager's brother, anyhow?");
he reveals to himself and embraces his class-bound aversion to folk
expression, itself the modernist difference that challenges standard
and familiar forms.[8] John is irretrievably lost to his already divided
consciousness, having sought to transcend not only Dorris but also
the environ of which she is a part, the vernacular blackness he does
not trust. The metonymic valuation of John's sense of his cultural
space is the end of his dream, as "[T]hey are in a room. John knows
nothing of it. Only, that the flesh and blood of Dorris are its walls.
Singing walls. Lights, soft, as if they shine through clear pink fin-
gers. Soft lights, and warm" (53). The walls of the theater and of so
much of Washington through which black life flows are identified
with Dorris herself; he realizes them only through the lighting
whose softness is determined by a corporeal whiteness, the hand of

8. For the contest between standard English and its variants, see Michael North,
The Dialect of Modernism: Race, Language and Twentieth-Century Literature; also
see Raymond Williams, *The Politics of Modernism: Against the New Conformists,*
chap. 4.

the cerebrating Other whose pull on John leaves Dorris far behind. In losing her dance in John's dream, Dorris realizes that she can never negotiate that void as represented by that shadow which now covers the whole of John's face. This circumscribed area of darkness has a double nature as it also emphasizes John's determination to deracinate.

Though the entirety of *Cane* is woven with music, there is a much greater emphasis on song in part two. The explicitness of song is somewhat muted in "Avey," as the Spiritual "Deep River" is not sung but whose melody is wished for, and the whistle of the train sounds like "iterated gasps and sobs" from Avey's soul. The bumper chord that ends John's dream in "Theater" is similar to that which begins the minstrelsy scene in the second part of "Box Seat," suggesting a crossing pattern of performance between the two, and even the sharing of a parallel universe: in "Theater," beautiful, long-legged women dance on the stage, their gyrations given an even more heightened sexuality by John; while in "Box Seat," the comparative unattractiveness of a pair of dwarfs who fight on the stage reflects a grotesqueness extended through the medium of sexuality by the dwarf Mr. Barry's song to Muriel. The image in "Theater" is also a grotesquerie, as the dancing women are again, as received by John, little more than animals. The women are eroticized as exotic beasts, constituting a Manichean duality based on desire in conflict and complicit with aversion. This duality spawns a host of other dualities, as it generates black/white, and male/female as well. Toomer's taste for the menagerie extends also to "Box Seat," where each of the patrons' seats "is a bolt that shoots into a slot and is locked there" (61). Minstrelsy's doubly racialized history among its audiences projects the aspirations that inhere in John's shadowy "blackface" into an exploitative whiteness in "Theater," while Muriel's class conflict in "Box Seat" renders her oddly appreciative of the low humor onstage. These ideas of race and sexuality as performance as arranged by Toomer become sharply magnified in consideration of the fact that Dan's deluded *dis*engagement from the onstage action enables his more broadly aggressive presence in the text. While he may appear insane, he has actually attained a level of sanity that sends him away from pretentiousness—but also away from communion with his "underground races." What is most important, however, is that Toomer shows in this crossing how black consumption of white-constituted forms of blackness reinforce and rearticulate other representational dislocations in black culture. As Michael North suggests, black audiences and performers rarely experienced the opportunity to reappropriate the black performative presence, being indeed many removes from such opportunity. "Minstrel shows," North writes, "allowed white audiences to have it both ways, to mock tradition, aristocracy, European culture by comparing them to something earthier, more natural, more 'American,' while simultaneously distancing all these qualities in a figure to which even the commonest white audience could condescend." Black audiences in consumption of the same product consistently begged the question of who was masking.[9]

Something of this idea is again captured in Toomer's play *Natalie Mann,* wherein Nathan Merilh's ethnic nomenclature curiously characterizes black representation in "Young America." These remain "niggers" in an even playful way to Merilh, because their African *American* sense of self is overdetermined. Natalie's representation of self—her proof that she has "achieved" herself—is her recasting of herself in primordial, African terms. The folk spirit's fatal advance is a matter of grave importance to Toomer, but it is not solely a romantic speculation upon the growing black migrations of the late nineteenth and early twentieth centuries. It is also a larger testament of his youth, because in this sentence he implicates himself and figures his place in what was for him the shifting sand of Euroamerican modernism. He did not always share the optimism and bright promise shared by many of the white modernists by whom he was surrounded, haunted as he was by a sense of blackness whose elite bearing was many times removed from the folk setting he discovered in Sparta in 1921. As Charles Scruggs suggests, while a poem like the much later "The Blue Meridian" (1936) would perhaps in its Whitmanesque sweep omit Southern folk spirit, Toomer "showed in *Cane* that the demonic forces that had shaped America's past might also determine its future."[10]

As regards the representation of the black masculine spirit in part two, Toomer appears to suggest that the failure of the folk spirit to embrace modernity during the Migration involved the failure of

9. North, *Dialect,* 81; see also Robert Toll, *Blacking Up: The Minstrel Show in Nineteenth-Century America.*

10. Scruggs, "Stieglitz and Toomer," 62.

black male entelechy to carry that spirit as revealed in song to Northern environs. Song in *Cane* becomes metonymic rather than metaphoric, and such a distinction suggests that the reification of both terms in this construction, song and spirit, allows the waning folk spirit to be considered liminally, that is, as a tangible, realizable, eminently recoverable element dependent not solely on memory, because memory is contained in it. Ronald Radano notes that Du Bois's chapter on the "Sorrow Songs" in *The Souls of Black Folk* sought this very concretization in black song as a means of overcoming the power of the metaphoric "Veil" that existed between black and white. "Rather than simply inverting racial logic," Radano writes, Du Bois "celebrates the difference made real in black experience, while simultaneously exposing that realness as a discursive fiction that can be transcended." In *Cane,* which already looks back to *Souls* in terms of efforts toward this transcendence, black difference also becomes the real that can be transcended, but success here depends on a fleeting sense, among other things, of masculine determination. Du Bois reconstitutes black song for the articulation of its constituent parts in the modern, and for the completion of the circle whose first link began with the double consciousness of a black elect. This articulation is for Du Bois the black real transcended, for the fractured nature of black song is in its acknowledgment of its pathos, its grave acceptance of its incomplete and inevitable binarisms: "Mother and child are sung, but seldom father; fugitive and weary wanderer call for pity and affection, but there is little of wooing and wedding; the rocks and the mountains are well known, but home is unknown" (*Souls,* 542).[11]

Cane's modernist portrayal of black life depends on the spaces, silences, and disparate rhythms of song to render the pathos of contemporary life that "The Sorrow Songs" anticipates. In "Bona and Paul," Paul's reverie in Chicago about Southern life appears to reproduce this Du Boisian sensibility: "Paul follows the sun to a pine-matted hillock in Georgia. He sees the slanting roofs and gray unpainted cabins tinted lavender. A Negress chants a lullaby beneath the mate eyes of a southern planter. Her breasts are ample for the suckling of a song. She weans it, and sends it, curiously weaving, among lush melodies of cane and corn" (71). Song-as-spirit fashions

11. Ronald M. Radano, "Soul Texts and the Blackness of Folk," 71–95.

the space in which Paul and the Du Boisian "real" move and have their being, but a crucial element in each is the proximity of the father. In Du Bois, he is the black father who otherwise would share toil and travail, but is absent because of the technology of slavery; in Toomer, Paul's daydream configures the mother-and-child scene—a Nativity scene!—under the shadowy planter's "mate eyes." Toomer replaces Du Bois's absent black father with a nefarious white one, but it is perhaps the mannerist pose of this father in Paul's reverie that helps provide, with the conjunction of Du Bois, a deeper listening. While even an absence of maleness is preferable to a dominating, glowering presence, Toomer in "Bona and Paul" renders a frequently recurring truth of the South in characterizing miscegenation.

Toomer's use of white maleness in this signifying redaction of "The Sorrow Songs" is a trope that not only shapes and gives dimension to Paul as artist (Paul as bearer of the song is "curiously weaving") but also calls into scrutiny (via this same weaving) Toomer's own varied racial background and its several resonances throughout *Cane.* The white father in Paul's daydream, when juxtaposed to Du Bois's absent one, represents the idea of the "changing same," Amiri Baraka's term for the interplay between tradition and the individual talent in African American music. It is utilized by Houston Baker in his discussion of the "mastery of form" and the "deformation of mastery," wherein *form* becomes "a family of concepts . . . figures, assumptions and presuppositions that a group of people (even one as extensive and populous as a nation) holds to be a valued repository of spirit. . . . the form most apt for carrying forward such notions is a *mask.*"[12] The father is a cultural icon that is widely and always already valued. White and absent by turns, the Toomeresque white father and the Du Boisian void seek to inscribe blackness in the interstice, but cannot. Paul's masking among his friends and in the Crimson Gardens is evidentiary of this struggle, a struggle that mirrors Toomer's fervent quest for a settled racial identity—but Paul's confusion (and the confusion of all the miscegenated men in part two) is a gentle corrective to Du Bois, reflecting not double consciousness but again the subtextual "site of incommensurability" that reverberates throughout *Cane.*

Hortense Spillers writes that "the African American male has

12. Baker, *Modernism and the Harlem Renaissance,* 17 (original emphasis).

been touched . . . by the *mother, handed* by her in ways that he cannot escape, and in ways that the white American male is allowed to
temporize by a fatherly reprieve . . . the black American male embodies the *only* American community of males which has had the
specific occasion to learn *who* the female is within itself, the infant
child who bears the life against the could-be fateful gamble, against
the odds of pulverization and murder, including her own" ("Mama's,"
80; original emphasis). The travail of black mothers should be the
conduit through which black sons acquire an understanding that is at
once both sexual and political, and impediments to this mean a confusion that could lead, at the least, to spiritual demise. The saga of
slavery, as captured by "The Sorrow Songs," never transcends the
tragedy of the absent father, for as the expression of black life that
will imbue a talented black elite, the songs themselves become the
essence of black folk art. "The Sorrow Songs" remains Du Bois's magnificent final effort to render dignity to the voices behind the Veil
through the sui generis expression of cultural fact, but it acknowledges its own tremendous difficulty in coming full circle to *Souls'*
opening chapter to call for committed responsibility among the talented elite in its joining the fervent yet dignified cry of the oppressed.
(In this instance a new relevance to Toomer's use of the semicircles
between the sections of *Cane* may have surfaced: his personal quest
may have been based at least partly on Du Boisian terms he found
incomplete.) The absence of the black father in the Sorrow Song
thus enters the Du Boisian text as a *form,* as an artifact of black suffering, an aesthetic underpinning of black cultural spontaneity. It is
ultimately to be given its static, nuanced perspective in history as
double consciousness itself is finally overcome when the black becomes "a co-worker in the kingdom of culture" (*Souls,* 365).

As Shamoon Zamir suggests, double consciousness as a social
and psychic ideal is its own statement of middle-class resistance but
never becomes more than this, as it endures the collapse "of its own
progressive ideals in the late nineteenth century, in the aftermath of
failed Reconstruction and under the gaze of a white America." Rather
than what would be Hortense Spillers's analysis as construed along
lines of class rather than gender, "Of Our Spiritual Strivings," the
opening chapter of *Souls* that reveals the famous passage on the Du
Boisian divided self, "is intended as a psychology of the Talented
Tenth in crisis, not of the 'black folk' as a homogenized collectivity"

(*Dark Voices,* 116). Toomer well understood this philosophical difficulty as well as its hold on 1920s Progressivist thinking, and in parts
two and three of *Cane* sought a "deformation of mastery"—sought
to undo the form and thus release the song from under the proprietary impulse of a black elite. Scruggs and Vandemarr recall the effort
exerted by Toomer to value working-class thought in the paternalism
of Progressivist reform: "[I]t was implicit in Du Bois's concept of
the Talented Tenth and 'uplift,' and it beadeviled the radical intellectuals. . . . When Jean Toomer recalled his observation of the
working-class audience in Chicago, his distance as an onlooker admitted the difference of class which literary radicals more frequently
tried to ignore. That distance would become central to the narrative
of *Cane,* where the representation of race, class and gender difference shifts unpredictably between characters and narrators. And
Toomer's stories would powerfully represent these differences as a
mystery not only of alienation, but of empathy."[13] In parts two and
three, however, aspects of the would-be elite remain intact in an effort to demonstrate that its new misfortunes with racism affect all
people of color; for African Americans, class values are permeable,
specious, and unable to withstand the depredations of the expanding
modern desert.

Toomer's response to Du Bois—his program for *Cane*—is another aspect of the changing same, another redaction of double consciousness. Once appropriated from the talented elite, the song is
reassigned to the shaping of the voice of resistance. Rather than vitiate the educated elite entirely, however, Toomer gives the song to
those whose struggles represent the indifference of racism to education; they thus participate in the process of becoming the undiffer-
entiated yet spiritually broken masses of a new urbanity. In this
connection, the stories of part two all have in common their unique
archetypal connection to the figures of Ariel and Caliban in Shakespeare's last and most musical play, *The Tempest,* which is not a simple trading of one aspect of high art for another, or a furtive return to
elements of European high culture. It is rather a contrast in styles of
oppression: in Ariel, there is the indentured servant who, in bargain-
ing with the master, can silently arrange his progress toward a free
future; in Caliban, his condition as slave necessitates his employ-

---

13. Scruggs and Vandemarr, *Terrors,* 47–48.

ment of not every artifice to secure his freedom, but demands the use of his voice as a weapon. Toomer's affinity with Shakespeare is here an aesthetic expression of the broken wail of the oppressed *within* the confines of high culture, itself a masterly deformation of class fantasies that releases elements of subjectivity, language, and sexuality—three buoys endlessly receding from the horizon of the black masculine. The real horror of Caliban's great crime is not, with respect to the play's element of fantasy, his having simply been born to the witch Sycorax and her mate, a black devil; that horror is rather more deeply expressed by what this fantastical representation means in a racialized sphere. Though Caliban has been serviceable since Shakespeare's time as the symbol of the colonized, enslaved Other, the unwilling possessor of the master's voice, he is not simply the "black beast" of either the master/slave model or completely named by Prospero's ambiguous reference to him, "this thing of darkness" (V.i.275). He is also, because of these, representative of the fear of the inscription of the black male body upon white female sexuality.[14]

Ariel is the servant of Prospero who is all too eager to do his master's bidding, and most of his entrances are performed with a blithe Hegelian subservience:

> All hail, great master, grave sir, hail! I come
> To answer thy best pleasure; be't to fly,
> To swim, to dive into the fire, to ride
> On the curl of clouds. To thy strong bidding, task
> Ariel, and all his quality. (I.ii.189–93)

Ariel has been saved from imprisonment in a cloven pine by Prospero after having been put there by Sycorax, the mother of Caliban. When Ariel petitions for an end to his indenture, Prospero rebukes him for his ingratitude and reminds him of the birth of Caliban via Prospero's objectification of Sycorax: she is referred to as being a "blue-ey'd hag" (I.ii.269), which thus makes Caliban himself the "freckled whelp . . . not honor'd with / A human shape" (I.ii. 283–84), thus erecting not only a difference in both class and consciousness between Ariel and Caliban but also one that devalues the mother (here, for her sexual choice). In Ariel's case, the syrupy, fawning

14. See Jose Fernandez Retamar, "Caliban"; see also *The Tempest*, I.ii.345–62.

attention he gives to Prospero is based on Prospero's promise to free him after he helps foil the plot by Prospero's brother Antonio to usurp the throne.[15] In the excerpt above, and elsewhere, as a spirit of fire or cloaked to invisibility while playing the lyre in keeping surveillance over those whom Prospero believes prepared to take his throne, Ariel protects his master's interest and his own by masking. He is of course interested in his freedom, but ultimately depends upon his master's whim, denying his own subjectivity in the bargain. Caliban, on the other hand, is the beast who, also enslaved by Prospero, aggressively seeks his freedom by attempting to steal Prospero's magic. For Caliban, Prospero's magical worth is the language that he has been taught, a language by which Caliban remains enslaved. He yearns to hurl curses against Prospero for having him bound in this discursive prison-house: "You taught me language, and my profit on't / Is, I know how to curse. The red-plague rid you / For learning me your language!" (I.ii.362–65) In the tradition of every enslaved person who has demanded access to consciousness, Caliban, even when at great personal risk, feels the need to imprecate against Prospero: "His spirits hear me, and yet I needs must curse" (II.ii.3–4). Even more than this, however, is the importance to the play of the dream, for in the dreamlike state, Caliban is unfettered from Prospero's tongue and can embrace his own lyric:

> Be not afeard, the isle is full of noises,
> Sometimes a thousand twangling instruments
> Will hum about mine ears; and sometime voices,
> That if I then had wak'd after long sleep,
> Will make me sleep again, and then in dreaming,
> The clouds methought would open, and show riches
> Ready to drop upon me, that when I wak'd
> I cried to dream again. (III.ii.135–43)

15. "Brother mine" was an endearment exchanged between Toomer and Waldo Frank in several of their letters. The friendship ended after Toomer's affair with Frank's wife, Margaret Naumberg, which invites speculation along these lines from *The Tempest,* where Prospero forgives his usurping brother Antonio:

> You, brother mine, that [entertain'd] ambition,
> Expell'd remorse and nature, whom, with Sebastian
> (Whose inward pinches therefore are most strong),
> Would here have kill'd your king, I do forgive thee,
> Unnatural though thou art. (V.i.75–79)

"To dream the fantastic is to dream the dream of the Other," says Henry Louis Gates, writing here about the signifying function in chiastic reversals of power relationships. Although throughout his career Caliban falls just short of approaching such a reversal, it may be even heroic that he voices his rage beyond the boundaries of the dream. In "Box Seat," Dan Moore approximates the voice of Caliban as he inveighs against Muriel's class-bound shame; in "Theater," however, John's acquiescence to class consciousness casts him in an even more subservient role, that of Ariel. John's dream proves to be his most inaccessible moment of feeling toward Dorris. In the next instance of wakefulness, any opportunity he may have had to give voice to this feeling had already been surrendered. Again in "Box Seat," Dan locates his Tiresian apparition in the old man who may have known Walt Whitman. While he rails against Muriel's pretentiousness, he sees the access to a racial truth lost in the suddenness of the old man's illness. In similar fashion, Caliban fails in his bid to defeat Prospero, for in seeking to recapture his voice by engaging the fantasy, he shares with his dreaming brothers in *Cane* the tragic dynamic of the dream in the Freudian principle of *Nachträglichkeit,* ingeniously described by Eric Lott as "revealing its anxieties even as it devises its censors."[16]

The failure of the music in *Cane* is equally shared by black aspirants to American middle-class culture who seek insulation from the discord of difference, and those who, realizing their situation, inveigh futilely against "having the doors of Opportunity closed roughly" in their faces. They are as well marvelously ill-equipped to answer adequately the distorted binarisms of black song's "eloquent omissions and silences," enervated as they are by exertion of the "dogged strength alone [that] keeps [the Negro] from being torn asunder" (*Souls,* 365). In Toomer's reassignment of the "dictie" sensibility there is a similar yet different subjective positioning with respect to Du Bois, a dualism that generates its own host of other Manichean ambiguities. Toomer, himself a member of the talented elite, understood too well the difficulty it encountered in seeking to speak decisively for the masses, fractured as they were by the seductions of the modern. Ariel and Caliban, then, represent the combined failure in *Cane* of black masculinity to represent itself on the modern stage. In

16. Henry Louis Gates, *The Signifying Monkey,* 59; Eric Lott, *Love and Theft: Blackface Minstrelsy and the American Working Class,* 27.

"Avey," the Toomeresque narrator retains the mark of Ariel by maintaining the distance between himself and Avey; similarly, Dan in "Box Seat" is rendered unable to connect with history and a hope for the future. Paul Johnson in "Bona and Paul" expresses an effeteness of aspiration, a racial shame in embracing the white woman. Interestingly, each of these stories employs the figure of the policeman, the sexual sentinel who is made to determine that the principal male characters *cannot* be trusted to complete the assigned task—the sacred task of cultural transmission. Whereas in "Theater" the blood of black men (and women) had already permeated the walls of Washington, John immerses himself in exploitation and isolates himself from black possibility as conveyed by Dorris. In "Box Seat," however, is an expression of the voice of Caliban, however fractured and futile the voice may be. "Both Theatre and Box-Seat . . . spring from a complex civilization," Toomer wrote to Waldo Frank, "and are directed to it."[17] This complexity depends partly on the stories' interiority and exteriority of voice, the fundamental difference between Ariel and Caliban. "And Kabnis is *me,*" he concludes to Frank, discussing the work in which both the Arielesque and Calibanesque voices are fatally united, the result being the dramatic sacrifice of the spectatorial artist and the confirmation of the frustration of the modern black masculine voice.

From John in "Of the Coming of John," the penultimate chapter in *Souls,* to Bles in *The Quest of the Silver Fleece* (1911) to Matthew Towns in *Dark Princess* (1928), the Du Boisian black hero "display[s] a vagueness and hesitation in dealing with the world, [and] a susceptibility to manipulation because of this lack of confidence . . . [he] has the mark of saintliness in him, a nostalgia for asceticism, a yearning for Puritan self-control, against which the passionate black body steadily rebels." It is the doubt and reticence of this Ariel that composes Toomer's "modern desert." While Du Bois's "man of action" sometimes hesitates action as he waits for the shifting gears of his double consciousness, Toomer's searching male is Negro "only in the boldness of his *expression*"—only in the effort to transcend Ariel and appropriate Caliban. But the Calibanesque sensibility is only rarely appropriated in part two, for it is just as rarely expressed. *Cane's*

17. Toomer to Waldo Frank, n.d., reprinted in Kerman and Eldridge, *Lives of Toomer,* 98.

men of part one luxuriate in the idea of the body, for through its appropriation in slavery and in the inhumanity of the postbellum period, its status as a site of resistance depends solely upon its recovery. The confrontation with Southern white paternalism makes that recovery impossible for Tom Burwell. In an ironic contrast to the Du Boisian hero, Tom is powerful and passionate, "but the future he imagines is out of Booker T. Washington,"[18] which suggests for Tom a perspective based less in Washington and his philosophy of black enfranchisement through industrial education than it reflects a heroic stance that is counter to Du Bois. Intriguingly, "Blood-Burning Moon" ushers in *Cane*'s dreaming men of part two, replete with semicircle, the line drawn through notions of black labor and peonage in the South and their transitional phases in Washington and Chicago on the trek north. The second semicircle, which appears before "Kabnis," not only represents the completion of Toomer's spiritual journey but also is the signifier for his revision of double consciousness—an awareness of hesitation and irresoluteness, of gaps and fragments.

As the last story of the second part of *Cane,* "Bona and Paul" also provides an ironic contrast to the last story of the first part, "Blood-Burning Moon." As Tom Burwell's defiance of white hegemony in order to defend his affection for Louisa proves his undoing, that taboo of defiance is compared with the taboo of the mulatto student Paul Johnson's confused affection for the white coed Bona Hale. The several references to blood as metaphor in "Bona and Paul" provide interesting contrasts to "Blood-Burning Moon" with respect not only to the first story's title but also to some of the more harrowing details (including the haunting blues refrain) leading up to Tom Burwell's lynching. As William C. Fischer suggests, Paul's friend and roommate Art Carlstrom, who is not quite sure about Paul's identity, follows this line of liminal reasoning: "Dark blood: moony. . . . Dark blood; nigger?" (72), as if Paul's high sanguinity (evident from a dark hue) will deploy his racial aggression.[19] A return to Paul's musings about making love to Bona reveal his very different feelings: "Paul follows the sun to a pine-matted hillock in Georgia.

---

18. Scruggs and Vandemarr, *Terrors,* 156; Arnold Rampersad, *The Art and Imagination of W. E. B. Du Bois,* 67.

19. William C. Fischer, "The Aggregate Man in Jean Toomer's *Cane,*" 190–215.

He sees the slanting roofs of grey unpainted cabins tinted lavender. A Negress chants a lullaby beneath the mate-eyes of a southern planter. Her breasts are ample for the suckling of a song. She weans it, and sends it, curiously weaving, among lush melodies of cane and corn. Paul follows the sun into himself in Chicago" (71). Paul's remembrance takes place "in his room of two windows," in which one imaginatively frames himself and the other, Bona. A Chicago subway train traverses the space between the two windows, signifying the intervention of the machine in natural love, and Paul, as the hypertrophic "new American," appears helpless in his transition between the world he remembers and the one he struggles with in the present. It also strangely recovers an episode in Du Bois's "Of the Coming of John," wherein John's reverie in the New York music hall also transports him: "When at last a soft sorrow crept across the violins, there came to him the vision of a far-off home,—the great eyes of his sister, and the dark drawn face of his mother. And his heart sank below the waters, even as the sea-sand sinks by the shores of Altamaha, only to be lifted aloft again with that last ethereal wail of the swan that quivered and faded away into the sky" (*Souls,* 527). Here the "soft sorrow" of the music John culls for himself is a strain in the minor key, the wail of ironized, human pain that for Du Bois ranges across culture and can even be found in the compositions of Wagner. But Toomer's redaction in "Bona and Paul" of John's episode in *Souls* substitutes the technology of mass movement for high culture. In neither case is the song to be carried to fulfillment, for while the condition of high culture demands its hesitations and incompletions in Du Bois's men, Paul is similarly prey to the stasis of Chicago's "hurtling Loop-jammed L-trains" (71), where all movement grinds to a crushing uncertainty. In both cases the liminal return is itself a scene of frustration; as Du Bois suggests in "The Sorrow Songs" and Toomer in Paul's daydream, the absence or distortion of the father is engineered by imperatives of race and custom. It is just this paradigm of relationship that Tom Burwell wanted to destroy, not simply because of its interracial aspect, but because the historicized, racialized conditions under which these relationships are formed necessitate his erasure, thus ensuring the absence of a black male presence under a crushing hegemony and rendering his tragedy to song. The trek of the light that leads into Paul's heart began as a dawning on Tom's condition: it sets now over Paul, his confusion, and that of his contemporaries. Paul's reverie is also his legacy. It speaks to Tom's thwarted desire for Louisa and an evanescent peace for which he has nevertheless paid the ultimate price. There is additionally the constant reference in "Bona and Paul" to Crimson Gardens, wherein most of the drama is played out, and the night at the Gardens recalls the eerie red moon that foretells Tom's demise.

Paul is a representation of the song that heralds Toomer's new American, but while he possesses the wherewithal to undo the shameful legacy of slavery by acting decisively, he instead more consistently acts with confusion. In this instance, Paul becomes a Janus-figure rather than a Caliban or even an Ariel; to Bona, he is a scholarly rake, alternately seducing and repulsing her. But his schoolmates' behavior also dismays him because of the meaning of his being seen with a white woman. Paul's response of self-consciousness may appear simply to be a normal response to an abnormal situation, but it is crucial to an understanding of Paul, mightily divided as he is between sex and racial guilt. Paul feels this division as thoughts about Bona roll through him:

> From the South. What does that mean, precisely, except that you'll love or hate a nigger? Thats a lot. What does it mean except that in Chicago you'll have the courage to neither love or hate. A priori. . . . Well, never matter. You matter. I'd like to know you whom I look at. Know, not love. Not that knowing is a greater pleasure; but that I have just found the joy of it. . . . Even this afternoon I dreamed. To-night, along the Boulevard, you found me cold. Paul Johnson, cold! Thats a good one, eh, Art, you fine old stupid fellow, you! But I feel good! The color and the music and the song . . . A Negress chants a lullaby beneath the mate-eyes of a southern planter. O song! . . And those flushed faces. Eager brilliant eyes. Hard to imagine them as unawakened. Your own. Oh, they're awake all right. (76)

Paul is not unaware of a sense of his heritage, which offers him some measure of opportunity to break these particular slaver's bonds of racial guilt and enjoy Bona in a way that is at once nonracial and transindividual. But he never seeks to stand fast against guilt as it is imposed upon him; he never utters his approximation of Caliban's famous rejoinder on cursing in the acquired language. To Bona he displays instead a heady, erudite, and masculine veneer because he is conscious of "the convention in it"; it is a veneer that will itself eventually crumble before that final symbol of his guilt—the representation at the door of the Crimson Gardens of his own blackness.

As a further measure of Paul's voicelessness, his friendship with Art is one in which Paul's sense of his blackness is severely compromised. To Art, Paul is confused, "moony," practically nonverbal. Art, significantly because of his whiteness and partly through Paul's voicelessness, symbolizes the socioracial access to Bona that Paul does not have; he even assumes momentarily that Paul must not be black (for all their apparent closeness, Paul has never told him) because Bona, a white woman from the South, could not possibly want a black man. Whatever Art may think about Paul is sanctioned by Paul's voicelessness; Paul hands over to Art a measure of the construction of his identity. To this end, the story's homoerotic element should not be missed, for Paul's abjuration of his racial self is only one aspect of a cancellation of the masculine (read: heterosexual) self:

> Art has on his patent-leather pumps and fancy vest. A loose fall coat is swung across his arm. His face has been massaged, and over a close shave, powdered. It is a healthy pink the blue of evening tints a purple pallor. Art is happy and confident in the good looks that his mirror gave him. Bubbling over with a joy he must spend now if the night is to contain it all. His bubbles, too, are curiously tinted purple as Paul watches them. Paul, contrary to what he had thought he would be like, is cool like the dusk, and like the dusk, detached. His dark face is a floating shade in evening's shadow. He sees Art, curiously. Art is a purple fluid, carbon-charged, that effervesces beside him. He loves Art. But is it not queer, this pale purple facsimile of a red-blooded Norwegian friend of his? Perhaps for some reason, white skins are not supposed to live at night. Surely, enough nights would transform them fantastically, or kill them. And their red passion? Night paled that too, and made it moony. Moony. Thats what Art thought of him. Bona didnt, even in the daytime. Bona, would she be pale? Impossible. Not that red glow. But the conviction did not set his emotion flowing. (73)

Many colors surround and even define Art while Paul is but "a floating shade in evening's shadow." Color, while more regularly indicative of symbolic racial fidelity in the other stories, is also gender-typed (its importance to Dorris in "Theater" and Muriel in "Box Seat" is in large part more readily understandable on this ground), and these two functions of color as united in Art further illustrate Paul's gradual effacing of even the heterosexual element of his character.

The idea of the Calibanesque as devolving to the Arielesque in the manner of music and of voice-as-cultural-space develops its currency through the story as Art, while he and Paul wait for their dates in the dormitory parlor, is invited to sit at a piano and play jazz tunes. Again, while elsewhere regarded by Toomer as a music that spells the end of the romanticism of slavery, jazz is here seen as an important cultural signifier that is completely misread by Paul. Art, we are told, is simply tearing the house down with his playing, as "the picture of Our Poets hung perilously." The reference is of course to James Weldon Johnson's 1912 novel, *The Autobiography of an Ex-Coloured Man,* in which the protagonist, a deeply racially divided mulatto, himself misreads all of the signs of blackness. In his "Club," wherein a black elite (in many cases uncomfortable with the idea of a racial imaginary) entertains itself, a picture of Frederick Douglass hangs from the wall. The walls are otherwise covered with pictures of black prizefighters, jockeys, and entertainers, "every colored man in America who had ever 'done anything' " (*Autobiography,* 104).[20] The Ex-Coloured Man is also a pianist, who gains notoriety in the club by rendering Mendelssohn in ragtime. Paul, for his part, notes Art's playing and remarks to himself on Art's improvisational skills: "I've got to get the kid to play that stuff for me in the daytime. Might be different. More himself. More nigger. Different? There is. Curious, though" (73). But Paul's Manichean delusion crosses night and day and thus black and white, bestowing upon Art an aesthetic consciousness whose strange racialization is dependent principally upon the time of day it happens to be. Paul hears Caliban's "thousand twangling instruments," but never awakens from the dream. Similarly, Robert Stepto says of the Ex-Coloured Man that he must consistently "wrestle with questions of authorial control—especially as those questions persistently relate to a sense of self. Alienated from the deepest bonds of his race, he learns to play the music without reference to who is 'in the other room'—he becomes a musical technician bereft of an artistic soul."

20. For the historical background of the club, see David Levering Lewis, *When Harlem Was in Vogue,* 28.

Just as Art improvises jazz tunes under what to him would be the culturally significant gaze from "Our Poets," the Ex-Coloured Man bangs out melodies with a similarly blithe ignorance. But it is Paul who articulates both scenes for us, and as his sense of his blackness dissolves beneath the questioning gazes of the other patrons of the Crimson Gardens, his ability to read the cultural signs of blackness also diminishes: his lack of awareness progressively mirrors that of the Ex-Coloured Man. "Caught as he is in a kind of illiteracy that argues that technique can pass for art," Stepto writes, "it is also inevitable that the Ex-Coloured Man will unwittingly mistake the modulation and exploitation of race rituals along the color line for proper relations between artist and audience."[21] In this vein, Paul shows himself to be more than merely out of his cultural space, but to have relinquished the control of that space. Paul's limited awareness of his own "mixed blood," and of interracial sex, and the countervailing guilty awareness of the burning of the blood, as in Tom Burwell's crucifixion, represent a twisted double consciousness—or, perhaps more accurately, it is a double *un*consciousness, a tragic negation of both identity and heritage that Paul has, and shares as well with John in "Theater," Dan Moore, the Toomeresque narrator of "Avey," and the Ex-Coloured Man.

As Paul and Bona dance to the pitch of their passion, jazz acquires its full power in its sexualizing agency. But the deciding factor for their relationship comes in Paul's racialized guilt, which appears in the form of the black doorman. His face, "smiling sweetly like a child's," haunting Paul like a "dark spot" in the now perfect purple hue of the Crimson Gardens, is the mask that demands Paul's unmasking, and precipitates Bona's departure with shame perhaps, but certainly with her now true understanding of Paul's guilt. As Paul rushes back to justify his urge for Bona to this doorman, he acknowledges him as a uniformed authority—again, as in "Avey," a *policeman*—who exercises moral control over this sex act or even the consideration thereof. He is, however, only the representative of Paul's guilt and not the redemption of the Calibanesque voice. That voice was long ago lost by Paul, by Dan, and by John as it was lost by Caliban himself, who learned that the definitive utterance of a new free-

21. Robert Stepto, *From Behind the Veil: A Study of Afro-American Narrative,* 127–28.

dom is dependent upon infinitely more than the stuff that dreams are made of.

No Exit: The Sacrifice of Ralph Kabnis

"Kabnis" represents Toomer's return to rural Georgia from the urban centers of Washington and Chicago, thus completing for him the full yet fragmented circle of black experience that characterizes *Cane*. Kabnis, the mulatto teacher of heightened yet volatile double consciousness, exists tremulously in this setting, the Georgia of Tom Burwell in "Blood-Burning Moon." Set in the same theater of fear as was Tom, though unlike him, Kabnis displays all of the ambiguities of the men of part two. What makes Kabnis truly interesting, however, is that also unlike the male characters in part two—John, Dan Moore, Paul Johnson, and the Toomeresque narrator—Kabnis demonstrates the highest consciousness of his own failure to capture and utilize the voice of Caliban:

> Whoever you are, my warm glowing sweetheart, do not think that the face that rests beside you is the real Kabnis. Ralph Kabnis is a dream. And dreams are faces with large eyes and weak chins and broad brows that get smashed by the fists of square faces. The body of the world is bull-necked. A dream is a soft face that fits uncertainly upon it . . . God, if I could develop that in words. (81)

Kabnis here imagines the solace of a woman's presence beside him. In this moment, perhaps the one in which he is most honest with himself, he tells his imagined partner of his deepest fear—that of not fitting in, of utter rejection by society to the point of being destroyed by it, and his corresponding inability to characterize this vulnerability, to give it the verbal expression that might save him. The vast distance from woman, however, metaphorizing the same proximity he has to words of salvation, prefigures Kabnis's consignment to the racialized damned, excluding himself from all manner of redemption.

With Gorham Munson's formulation, this letter to Waldo Frank celebrating the coming-to-completion of *Cane* usually locates Kabnis as a mirror to Toomer the man as well as it suggests the fulfillment in *Cane* of Toomer as spectatorial artist.

Seventh Street is the song of a crude new life. Of a new people. Negro? Only in the *boldness* of the expression. In its healthy freedom. American. For the shows that please Seventh Street make their fortunes on Broadway. And both Theatre [*sic*] and Box-Seat, [*sic*] of course, spring from a complex civilization, and are directed to it. And Kabnis is *me*.[22]

Was the satisfaction of the Negro soul, by Toomer's lights, not to be found on Washington's Seventh Street? Was Kabnis looking for the "soul of himself" as planted there, only to discover a harvest elsewhere? Was Kabnis seeking to expunge, like Toomer, an indebtedness to masculinity that demanded a re-membering of the father? This extratextual instance only tantalizes; it does not make clear why Kabnis chooses to return to the South after having lived in the North. This additional feature of return, however, does further aid the consideration of Kabnis as the figure who absorbs the consciousness of all the men in *Cane*. As was the case in *Cane*'s previous portions, the author as spectatorial artist is offering himself for sacrifice; the heightened self-consciousness with which Toomer effects this sacrifice makes tangible for the reader the range of similar fragmentation as it exists among the other characters. But in Toomer's final expression of the psychic fragmentation of the African American male, Kabnis's racialized destruction gives broad dimension to the careers of the other men in this story and to those of the men in *Cane*'s other parts. Once hurled fantastically outside of the world of strife within liberty for the African American, Kabnis becomes the man at the opposite extreme of even the faceless men of "Karintha": as they are the fragmented souls between the post-slavery South and the alluring Jerusalem of the North, Kabnis has meekly returned, in body and spirit, to bondage.

Several commentators have noted that Kabnis's name is a pun on "cabins," the dilapidated, rat-infested dwellings that are home to the South's black poor, home to not only Kabnis but also the child Karintha and, in even more sinister fashion, Becky as well. But on the same ground of this paranomasiac function is *sinbak,* an anagram of Kabnis that is expressive of his mixed-race heritage as manifest in a misuse of sexual power,[23] and codified by Father John's

22. Toomer to Waldo Frank, ca. October 1922, reprinted in Kerman and Eldridge, *Lives of Toomer,* 98 (original emphasis).
23. Fischer, "The Aggregate Man"; Roberta Riley, "Search for Identity and Artistry," 480–85; Maria Isabel Caldeira, "Jean Toomer's *Cane:* The Anxiety of the

pronouncement that the great sin of whites was in their distorted interpretation of the Bible made in order to secure the ends of the slaver. Both Kabnis's fear and his intelligence give dimension to his distorted sense of place. Kabnis is a schoolteacher, an educated man who finds himself in deeply segregated environs with just enough naïveté to exist ineptly. It is just this naïveté which precludes his finding his voice, the stentorian Calibanesque utterance that will describe his experience as a felt reality for others.

William Goede remarks of Kabnis that Toomer has expressed in him the universal anxiety of modern man, the consuming effort to characterize lived experience with the word, to search for the inner matter of the descriptive text. The modern man as marked body, however, accelerates this anxiety. "It is precisely because he is Negro," Goede writes, "that his experiences formulate, rather than limit, distinctly and honestly, the tragedy of all life." Not only Kabnis's but also Toomer's entire career as first-person narrator and spectatorial artist throughout *Cane* becomes clearer in this consideration. *Being Negro* is precisely what Kabnis cannot do. Just as Toomer did at various points in his life (with the exception of the period during which he sought to market *Cane*), Kabnis summarily rejects any connection to his heritage. In following Goede's reasoning, then, to throw out one's Negroness is to discard the experience of tragedy, and also to test severely Munson's notion of the spectatorial artist. "What is experience and what is knowledge?" and "What is the world?" are questions that Kabnis fears and from which he runs. He is in many ways the modernist brother to many post-Reconstruction black male characters, who, because they were so thoroughly oriented to their class, chose to resist being affected by racial experience and who therefore moved indecisively, if at all. Kabnis's own ambivalence about class, heritage, and race are of course emblematic of Toomer's own struggles with a sense of place within and without the black elite, a milieu in which P. B. S. Pinchback was an intimate. This again points up the reading of *sinbak* as a possible anagrammatic meaning in Kabnis's name, because the movements of Pinchback and his circle were given significantly to an expiation of the perceived original sin of miscegenation through the invocation of class.[24]

Modern Artist," 544–50; Jack M. Christ, "Jean Toomer's 'Bona and Paul': The Innocence and Artifice of Words," 311.

24. William J. Goede, "Portrait of the Negro Artist as a Young Man," 73–85.

What we learn about this larger theater of fragmentation in the other characters, however, is seen through Kabnis as he acts as the prism of race and class consciousness. The others reveal themselves to us as they seize him by and contribute to his already well-nurtured fear and confusion. Kabnis thinks his principal failure to be his "soft face" as situated on the "bull-necked body" of the world. As this is his expression of the hated and insecure self, he searches naively and futilely for security in the self in other men. He appreciates what he feels to be the durability of Halsey, but in truth Kabnis entirely misreads this durability by ignoring Halsey's weakness. Though physically strong and wise in the ways of the South, Halsey is not above bowing and scraping before whites, and he uses Kabnis's own fears and weaknesses in order to fashion a broad paternalism toward him. Halsey is himself a lost figure whose miscegenated lineage is further compromised by its failure to meet the demands of its class. One of the portraits that hang in Halsey's parlor

> is that of an English gentleman who had retained much of his culture, in that money had enabled him to escape being drawn through a land-grubbing pioneer life. His nature and features, modified by marriage and circumstances, have been transmitted to his great-grandson, Fred. To the left of this picture, spaced on the wall, is a smaller portrait of the great-grandmother. That here there is a Negro strain, no one would doubt. But it is difficult to say in precisely what feature it lies. . . . To the right of the great-grandfather's portrait hangs a family group: the father, mother, two brothers, and one sister of Fred. It includes himself some thirty years ago when his face was an olive white, and his hair luxuriant and dark and wavy. The father is a rich brown. The mother, practically white. Of the children, the girl, quite young, is like Fred; the two brothers, darker. (85–86)

Halsey's is the lineage of an African American elite that did not sustain in all its generations the coveted characteristic of fair skin. It is not known whether the existence of his darker brothers made difficult a possible desire on his part to pass, but Fred Halsey has nevertheless determined to identify as a black man, and thus has made his uneasy peace with the American issue of race. Class, however, remains his nemesis, and it characterizes his every impulse. When confronted with whites and the possibility of having to endure racism, he is willing to defer his humanity so that he may later recoup the remaining aspects of the spirit of a superior class whose embrace has long since been attenuated.

Halsey's companion Layman moves under, beyond, and through Kabnis's every priestly or professorial pretension. He does this merely by telling the basic truth of the South, and it is a truth that paralyzes Kabnis with fear. Although Layman offers eminently practical advice, his judgments are so unadorned by thought that they contribute only the message of the everyday to black men. Layman's only message is to survive at all cost, which means survival with the exacerbated consciousness of dread. In Halsey's parlor, Layman has told Kabnis the story of Mame Lamkins, the pregnant woman who, along with her fetus as it was ripped from her body, was brutally murdered by the same lynch mob that sought her husband. This story worms to Kabnis's already well-established horror of the South just as a woman inside the nearby church shouts, exclaiming her connection with the Spirit—Toomer's emblem here for a Caliban-esque expressiveness, a voice that seeks in its way to answer Kabnis's newly refreshed anguish. The plaintive, high-pitched wail of the shout to glory had long been rejected by Kabnis as being in any way remedial to the hatred and the fear he shares with so many other African Americans. "We don't have that sort of thing up North," Kabnis tells Halsey. "We do, but, that is, someone should see to it that they are stopped or put out when they get so bad the preacher has to stop his sermon for them." Here Kabnis has relinquished access to the remedy of the voice of black pain. His ready-made connection to Northern attitudes of class, breeding, and behavior precludes any anticipation of hope. Halsey, who sees Kabnis's discomfiture, makes sport of it. "Yankees are right up t th minute in tellin folk how t turn a trick," he taunts. "They always were good at talkin" (89). But this is a hypocrisy that Halsey indulges in, with the phrase "turn a trick" being the key to understanding Halsey's bifurcated, compromised nature as well as his criticism of Kabnis's fearful equivocations. Again, this time in church, as the congregation reaches the height of its fervor, spiritually recalling its pain, the woman cries out dramatically; at this same moment, a rock with a threatening note tied around it sails through Halsey's window, and Kabnis is convinced that the message is for him. It reads, "You northern nig-

ger, its time fer y t leave. Git along now" (90). Later, as Halsey, Layman, and Kabnis are all drinking in Kabnis's room, Kabnis begins to
hear from far in the valley a third voice, again a woman's, whose
song is "a spark that travels swiftly to the near-by cabins. Like purple tallow flames, songs jet up. They spread a ruddy haze over the
heavens. The haze swings low. Now the whole countryside is a soft
chorus. Lord. O Lord" (96). Though Halsey's speculations about
Lewis interfere with Kabnis's recognition of the song, the failure on
Kabnis's part to recognize the song is tantamount to his fear and
class-based denial of the other two. This third woman's voice, a voice
that begins an ageless plaint and is soon joined by the community, is
again incompletely heard by Kabnis: it is the voice of feminine, and
now more crucially communitarian, distress that the spectatorial artist
does not answer.

> Th niggers, just like I told y. An after him. Aint surprisin
> though. He aint bowed t none of them. Nassur. T nairy a one of
> them nairy an inch nairy a time. An only mixed when he was
> good and ready—
> Kabnis: That song, Halsey, do you hear it?
> Halsey: Thats a man. Hear me, Kabnis, a man—
> Kabnis: Jesus, do you hear it?
> Halsey: Hear it? Hear what? Course I hear it. Listen t what
> I'm tellin y. A man, get me? They'll get him yet if he dont
> watch out.
> Kabnis: Get him? What do you mean? How? Not lynch him?
> Halsey: Na. Take a shotgun an shoot his eyes clear out. Well,
> anyway, it wasnt for you, just like I told y. (96–7)

Halsey correctly cites Lewis as the man for whom the note thrown
through the church window was intended, seeing Lewis as the perfect embodiment of masculine courage and class, both of which Halsey is aware are lacking in himself. Having already made his peace
with Southern racial codes through compromise with them, Halsey's
bedevilment by class allows him to subjugate the beleaguered Kabnis. For his part, Kabnis tries to hear this third voice in the valley and
its plaintive strain, but in being distracted by Halsey, he gives himself over not to faith, but to his fears. In seeking to maintain his fantasies of class, Halsey has always wanted Lewis to come to his shop
"to talk"; Kabnis, who already shares not only class affiliation but

also intellectual sophistication with Lewis, feels Lewis to be his alter ego. Lewis coolly dismisses the threatening note as a warning from blacks who think that his attitude of independence may have been stirring up hostilities among the town's whites. But Lewis's own fear of "the pain of the South," made evident in his flight from the party in The Hole, cannot address the racial hatred that is slowly consuming Kabnis.

In an incisive essay on *Cane,* however, Barbara Foley suggests that the Halsey-Kabnis-Lewis connection becomes plainer "if we read Lewis as an NAACP investigator . . . perhaps even a fictional recreation of NAACP Assistant Secretary Walter White." The story of Mame Lamkins that has so frightened Kabnis is an actual event in the bloody history of lynching in America—the murder and mutilation of Mary Turner, a pregnant black woman, that White investigated in 1919. Turner's lynching was but a part of a series of crimes committed by a white mob that hunted and slaughtered blacks in retaliation for the murder of a white landlord by a black sharefarmer. Turner suffered the fate that Toomer describes in "Kabnis," but as Turner's fetus spilled out, it was crushed under the heel of one of the mob. At this level, then, Halsey's desire to commune with Lewis may be more than ultimate class fantasy—Halsey may in fact be operating as Lewis's double agent, supplying him with information that may be useful in later prosecutions, perhaps, or even information serviceable to the end of petitioning Congress for the passage of the then-pending Dyer Anti-Lynching Bill (which was passed in the House but failed in the Senate in 1922). Toomer, who suggested to Frank his reluctance to project himself as a man of action in such dangerous circumstances, would perhaps more easily render a dimension of spectatorial artistry to the effort. As Foley writes, "for Toomer to portray Lewis as an investigator into the death of Mame Lamkins was to locate his own text in the specific historical context of this anti-lynching campaign."[25]

The foppish Hanby, headmaster of the school who summarily dismisses Kabnis for drinking in his room with Halsey and Layman, is partly modeled after Linton Ingraham, the principal for whom Toomer substituted at the Sparta Agricultural and Industrial College,

25. Barbara Foley, "In the Land of Cotton: Economics and Violence in Jean Toomer's *Cane,*" 181–98.

thus beginning for Toomer the theater of inspiration that matured into *Cane*. According to Foley, however, Ingraham was endlessly compromised politically by the white community, and Toomer must have found difficult the task of "the position of administering a school founded on Washingtonian principles of accommodation." Relative to his dissatisfaction in Ingraham, however, Toomer's ideal of manly struggle and participation is perhaps the place to which he himself cannot go. Though Hanby, upon employing Kabnis, may have lent inspiration to do the work of raising the next generation of blacks who might well be supplicants to potential white benefactors, Kabnis sees in Lewis a deep and enduring kinship and an intangible spiritual connection. For Lewis, Kabnis becomes "a promise of a soil-soaked beauty; uprooted, thinning out," a becoming though not a being, among the "new-world race" that Dan Moore imagines coming from beneath his feet in "Box Seat." Between Kabnis and Lewis "there is a swift intuitive interchange of consciousness. Kabnis has a sudden need to rush into the arms of this man. His eyes call, 'Brother,'" but in the very next moment, Kabnis has an urge that is just as overpowering to reject Lewis, heeding as he does the "savage, cynical twist about within him" (96). If we take Foley's suggestion in reading Lewis as a Walter White figure—and in accepting Toomer's declaration to Frank that Kabnis is a reflection of his author—Kabnis appears to be experiencing another dimension of the crisis of incommensurability that is the specific dilemma of the spectatorial artist. Toomer's desire to be a man of action could well have met with anxiety in the consideration of a figure like White, who like Toomer was a fair-complexioned African American, but who unlike Toomer willingly used his features to infiltrate white enclaves in the dangerous adventure of fighting racial injustice through investigating lynchings. White's realization of a black heritage, as he writes years later in his autobiography, would have laid bare to Toomer his own singular frustration at the intersections of race and masculinity:

> In that instant there opened up within me a great awareness; I knew then who I was. I was a Negro, a human being with an invisible pigmentation which marked me a person to be hunted, hanged, abused, discriminated against, kept in poverty and ignorance, in order that those whose skin was white would have

readily at hand a proof patent and inclusive. . . . No matter how low a white man fell, he could always hold fast to the smug conviction that he was superior to two-thirds of the world's population, for those two thirds were not white.[26]

Toomer's effort to historicize the text of *Cane* in the midst of White's investigations of racial terror makes Lewis not only a powerful symbol of justice but also the intellectualized fulfillment of the ideal of deracination that Toomer had, the best example of the distillation of all racialized sensibility into a homogeneous Americanism. On just this process of distillation, Toomer later writes in "The Blue Meridian" that "A million million men, or twelve men, / Must crash the barrier to the next higher form"; either sheer masculine strength or the strength of reason in assemblages such as juries will inaugurate the just nation of the American ideal.

But the "twelve men" of "The Blue Meridian" may also suggest an apostolic power, a power of faith, and this notion would seem consistent with Toomer's attraction to spirituality and particularly Gurdjieffianism, while it also would speak as well to his reverence for all forms of spiritual communion, at the time of the writing of *Cane* and beyond. While Foley and other commentators discuss Toomer's critique of Southern Christianity, this should not be confused with a rejection of the Christian ethic, whose reflections can be seen everywhere in *Cane*—from Barlo's disturbed and disturbing toss of the Bible onto Becky's death mound to Dan Moore's imagining of the "new-world Christ" to Tom Burwell's crucifixion. The one character in whom both a fragmented black masculine *and* feminine may find redemption is Father John, the blind and barely verbal old man who lives in The Hole, the cellar beneath Halsey's workshop. Ironically, it is Lewis—the Adamic figure who will soon flee his tainted Eden—who names the old man John, and even in this naming he is probably only preconscious of the many levels upon which this new appellation has import. Father John is not only John the Baptist, as Lewis has named him, but also Jack, John Henry, and High John de Conquer, rolled into one; his pathos recalls even Du Bois's tragic John in *Souls*. As a black Tiresias figure, he holds

26. Foley, "Jean Toomer's Sparta," 747–75; Walter White, *A Man Called White*, 11.

within him the aspirations of all African American men and women. He represents a return to "Box Seat," recalling the old sage of Dan Moore's delusion, the patriarch of the vast underground races whose incursion Dan senses: "Slave boy whom some Christian mistress taught to read the Bible. Black man who saw Jesus in the ricefields, and began preaching to his people. Moses- and Christ-words used for songs. Dead blind father of a muted folk who feel their way upward to a life that crushes or absorbs them. (Speak, Father!) Suppose your eyes could see, old man. (The years hold hands. O Sing!)" (105)

The overwhelming importance of Father John to the scene will ameliorate Lewis's sudden departure because Father John's tenure in the South, which is to say his tenacity in surviving it, authorizes him to bear its pain. Before Lewis leaves, however, he first recognizes Kabnis's own pain of fragmentation, constituted both of Kabnis's futile clinging to his own class affiliations and to the truth of his origins as represented by Father John:

> Lewis: The old man as symbol, flesh, and spirit of the past, what do you think he would say if he could see you? You look at him, Kabnis.
> Kabnis: Just like any done-up preacher is what he looks t me. Jam some false teeth in his mouth and crank him, and youd have God Almighty spit in torrents all around th floor. Oh, hell, an he reminds me of that black cockroach over yonder. An besides, he aint my past. My ancestors were Southern blue-bloods—
> Lewis: And black.
> Kabnis: Aint much difference between blue an black.
> Lewis: Enough to draw a denial from you. Cant hold them, can you? Master; slave. Soil; and the overarching heavens. Dusk; dawn. They fight and bastardize you. The sun tint of your cheeks, flame of the great season's multi-colored leaves, tarnished, burned. Split, shredded: easily burned. No use...
> (107)

As Hurston characterized him in *Mules and Men,* John (or "Jack") "is the great human culture hero in Negro folk-lore. He is like Daniel in Jewish folk-lore, the wish-fulfillment hero of the race. The one who, nevertheless, or in spite of laughter, usually defeats Ole

Massa, God and the Devil" (*Mules,* 253). Lewis has noted Kabnis's vulnerability to such power in that modernism's Manichean dualities, especially the overarching opposition white/black, are trapped within Kabnis and have begun rapidly to consume him. Both Lewis and Kabnis know that Father John's words are the words of salvation. Lewis's premature exit, however, exposes his own cowardice and thus ironically magnifies Kabnis, but does so by giving him only the veneer of courage. What Lewis avoids by leaving, however, is the deeper pathos that Kabnis displays through his desperate (and by now, unbeknownst to him, futile) attempts to retain a sense of self, to hold the shards and fragments of his manhood in place.

Paralleling Kabnis's rejection of Father John and further defining his fragmentation is a previous episode involving Kabnis, his robe, and the two women who join the men in The Hole, Cora and the darker-complexioned Stella. A cascade of antinomies continues to describe Kabnis's splintering, as the robe becomes his great garment of ambiguity; as Toomer describes The Hole and its contents, we are introduced to "a loose something that looks to be a gaudy ball costume dangl[ing] from a near-by hook" (104). It shortly becomes the robe of discursive authority as Kabnis, "with great mock solemnity," puts it on. That he becomes with this act "a curious spectacle, acting a part, yet very real" (105) suggests his pathetic desire to dissolve all ambiguity between the slow disintegration taking place inside him and the idealized self to which he clings. After having donned the robe, he seeks to make a distinction between the classical orator and the Sunday call-and-response preacher: "Preachers hell. I didnt say wind-busters. Y misapprehended me. Y understand what that means, dont y? All right then, y misapprehended me. I didnt say preachers. I said orators. O R A T O R S. Born one an I'll die one" (109). But classical oratory—the art of public persuasion—has always been decisive in the dissemination of religious doctrine. No one seemed to know this better than Toomer, through whom the malfeasant Barlo in "Becky" silently profanes both Becky's corpse and the Bible itself, but manages later to redeem himself in his grand communitarian gesture of the delivery of his vision in "Esther," which later becomes prophetic in "Blood-Burning Moon." Both oratory and preaching inhere in addresses from the antislavery pulpit, as well as in declamations like Frederick Douglass's, wherein selective readings of Christianity used to justify slavery were also criticized. John Callahan's remark that Kabnis's hostile pronouncement that Negroes are a "preacher-ridden race" echoes James Joyce's sentiment in *A Portrait of the Artist as a Young Man* that the Irish are a "priest-ridden race" is an apt pronouncement, but for Kabnis particularly, this is an empty statement.[27] His failed separation of oratory and preaching simply indicates another instance in which Kabnis cancels himself from language.

Rather than having dissolved ambiguity, Kabnis has instead tragically annulled himself by thus excluding himself from every manner of redemption. He has transgressed irrevocably against blackness by rejecting the spiritually charged voices of the women of the congregation—thus constructing an incommensurable chasm comparable to the unforgivable sin of uttering an oath against the Holy Spirit itself. This supreme violation both impacts and magnifies his torment, returning him irrevocably to another narrative: the story told by Layman about the horrific murder of Mame Lamkins. His only escape is to racial terror, to the contemplation of the hell which he feels remains for him, and its reification through the ritual of lynching:

> Th form thats burned int my soul is some twisted awful thing
> that crept in from a dream, a godam nightmare, an wont stay
> still unless I feed it. An it lives on words. Not beautiful words.
> God Almighty no. Misshapen, split-gut, tortured, twisted words
> . . . White folks feed it cause their looks are words. Niggers,
> black niggers feed it cause theyre evil an their looks are words.
> Yallar niggers feed it. This whole damn bloated purple country
> feeds it cause its goin down t hell in a holy avalanche of words.
> I want t feed th soul—I know what that is; th preachers dont—
> but I've got t feed it. I wish t God some lynchin white man ud
> stick his knife through it an pin it to a tree. (110)

The expanding discursive crisis of modernism is suddenly trapped within Kabnis, as the language of hatred propagates itself exponentially until it finally breaches the soul's ability to contain it. His realization of this, however, is ironic; he is only dimly aware of these implications in this curse against Father John: "Oh, I'm drunk an just as good as dead, but no eyes that have seen beauty ever lose their

27. John F. Callahan, *In the African-American Grain: Call-and-Response in Twentieth-Century Black Fiction*, 88.

sight. You aint got no sight. If you had, drunk as I am, I hope Christ will kill me if I couldnt see it" (113). But the blind man's vision of beautiful possibilities for redemption through the enactment of language—the call of pain and hopefully, the response of remorse—finally escapes Kabnis, who is on his way to indenture to Halsey, which is a certain social death. Father John's declaration that the sin of whites in making a mockery of the Word in support of slavery is itself a *fixed* sin (115) grants the opportunity for the redemption of whites but places the power to grant such redemption firmly in the hands of blacks as his statement points to this power as rendered by Christ in the Book of John: "Then he breathed on them, saying: 'Receive the Holy Spirit! If you forgive any man's sins, they stand forgiven; if you pronounce them unforgiven, unforgiven they remain.'" But Kabnis cannot participate in this redemption because he has secured his own spiritual and cultural damnation by insisting on his own fear and fragmentation. The overwhelming presence of words within him is instead a vast void, an inestimable and ever-expanding absence. With the trepidation of race and at the ground of class, he has not only returned to the crisis of incommensurability by rejecting the passion of the wailing women but he has also similarly denied the efficacy of Father John's simple healing, thus placing himself fantastically outside any redemptive possibility.[28]

If this is the final book of *Cane,* Toomer's saga of the black South, then "Kabnis" is also its "Revelation of John," in which all nature has condemned the world to its end. In this vein Toomer completes not only the cyclical pattern of the novel as suggested in the symbol of the semicircles dedicated to Waldo Frank on the page preceding "Kabnis," and not only as in the South-North-South movement of *Cane,* itself symbolizing first the slave narrative's movement toward freedom and then an imaginary of an ironic antithesis. He also leads us to a consideration of Kabnis's being lost in the Cocytus episode of Dante's *Inferno,* whose realm of fire and ice is reserved for those who have been treacherous to their masters—in Kabnis's case, his perfidy to both Father John and, by extension, to the spiritual significance of women's articulations of pain. This Dantesque theater is heightened

28. John 20:22, 23; Matthew 12:31; Mark 3:28–29; Luke 12:10. Kabnis's denials of the voices in church and in the valley thus recall the apostle Peter's three-time denial of Christ (Matthew 26:34; Mark 14:30–31; Luke 22:34; John 13:38).

but also momentarily relieved in the story by its own Beatrice, however, for after Kabnis's final vituperative salvo against Father John, Carrie Kate comes to rescue his emotions: "She turns him to her and takes his hot cheeks in her firm cool hands. Her palms draw the fever out. With its passing, Kabnis crumples. He sinks to his knees before her, ashamed, exhausted. His eyes squeeze tight. Carrie presses his face tenderly against her. The suffocation of her fresh starched dress feels good to him" (116). But this release is only ephemeral as Kabnis, who has repudiated the most salutary features of his culture, must suffer the fate of the unrepentant: as Father John joins in prayer with Carrie Kate, who herself has come full circle as the virginal reincarnation of Karintha, and as their spiritual energies unify to express the dawn of a new beginning—their "gold-glowing child"—Kabnis's subordination and indenture to Halsey, the judgment placed upon him for his yield to weakness, continues both immediately and ignominiously.

If Kabnis is consubstantial with Toomer as Toomer states in his letter to Waldo Frank, the consciousness that engages the sacrifice of the spectatorial artist is of significant note. "Much of the success of *Cane,*" writes Charles Scruggs, "arises from a tension between Toomer's real self—outcast—and his idealized self—the son who returned to the South to capture his racial heritage in song. Kabnis was the artist *manque,* the 'son' who returned to find that he had roots in neither black nor white world."[29] Kabnis's inability to resolve his crisis of incommensurability is Toomer's not very deeply sublimated explanation for his own self-exclusion. Toomer's drive to be "an American" was ultimately stimulated by a racialized guilt, a need to expiate the twinned sins of miscegenation and blackness. His assaults on the memory of his grandfather and his careful repudiation of his own African American past are probable testimony to this, and after the writing of *Cane* it may be certain that he retreated even further into the nether reaches of deracination, partly through his further involvement in Gurdjieffian spirituality. At the same time, however, Kabnis's tragedy problematizes this analysis of guilt in Toomer because Kabnis's ambivalences give shape to the bewilderment of the other men in *Cane.* What we learn of the men of *Cane*'s other parts and of Halsey and Lewis and Hanby and Layman is that they, as considera-

---

29. Scruggs, "Jean Toomer: Fugitive," 92–93.

tions of a fractured manly and political integrity, "balance, and pull against the weight of" Kabnis in a way similar to that in Louisa's mind as she thinks of definitions of the desirable in Tom Burwell and Bob Stone. Kabnis enters the theater of race and manhood to lend dimension to its pain, and he does so through his singular and terrible sacrifice. But as Toomer retreats into the world and its structures in an awareness that the absence of a politicized racial choice—his own species of fragmentation—disinvites him from participation in the redemptive acts of blackness, the spectatorial artist's willful exclusion from redemption makes Kabnis the most tragic of *Cane's* racially divided characters. Kabnis's fears already signal his surrender of his inheritance of the voice of Caliban, the bold voice of oppositional culture. But in disavowing the redemptive, healing powers of his community, of the voices of the women of Sempter's spirit of pain and of Father John, he unalterably sacrifices his *divinity*—in whose name his humanity, must be claimed.

4

HURSTON'S MASCULINIST CRITIQUE
OF THE SOUTH

> It was early night in the village. Joe Clarke's store porch
> was full of chewing men. Some chewed tobacco, some
> chewed cane, some chewed straws, for the villager is a
> ruminant in his leisure. They sat thus every evening os-
> tensibly waiting for the mail from Number 38, the south-
> bound express. . . . They all talked a great deal, and every
> man jack of them talked about himself. Heroes all, they
> were, of one thing or another.
>
> —Zora Neale Hurston, "The Eatonville Anthology"

It is by now an article of faith in the canon of African American literary criticism that Zora Neale Hurston is the progenitor of the black
female voice in the twentieth century. Her female characters, whether
in her novels, her stories, or her folklore, shape readings of Southern
black life through a continuous expression of that voice. That expression is itself a call to consciousness for women everywhere:
Pheoby, the hungering listener to Janie's tale in *Their Eyes Were
Watching God,* hears that there are two things that people must do
in order to approximate the complete life: "they got to go tuh God,
and they got tuh find out about livin' fuh theyselves" (*Their Eyes,*
183). But Janie's quest is more a spiritual than a geographic one—
that is to say, she grows this already burgeoning subjectivity not by
moving from the largely agrarian South to the swiftly industrializing
North as part of that Great Migration that could no longer endure

the South's various dangers, but only by engaging in a spiritual self-confrontation and in risk-taking. Nothing Janie says to Pheoby has anything to do with boarding a train, or hitching a ride, or going to sea. In fact, in an early short story of Hurston's, "John Redding Goes to Sea" (1921), the protagonist pays ultimately for taking Janie entirely too literally. In "John Redding," home is an objectification that shelters, even if it stultifies. Significantly, the notion of black romantic heroism that Janie fashions for Pheoby in *Their Eyes* has everything to do with remaining in and nourishing Southern black culture: the totality of meaningful experience for the questing black character is circumscribed by the South, a culture Hurston understood, as did Jean Toomer, to be on the verge of extinction because of the absence of its existence in the broader American cultural imaginary. Hurston's geography of the Jook as exporter of black performative culture in "Characteristics of Negro Expression," an article that appeared in Nancy Cunard's 1934 anthology *Negro,* extends (starting from Key West, Florida) no farther north than North Carolina, and no farther west than Nashville, Tennessee. These are the rough borders of what may be called Hurston's "hermetically sealed" South, a South she held inviolate and thoroughly removed from the cultural critique of Northern urbanity. Her sense that "the Negro farthest down" would be corrupted in body and spirit by the Northern cityscape was even more keenly felt than Toomer's, who risked an intimate textual subjectivity in "Kabnis" to prove the point.

Even in her 1942 autobiography *Dust Tracks on a Road,* Hurston is mostly silent about her experiences in the North, nearly as if she intended to wall off forever the racism she experienced at Barnard College in New York, or even the recognition she enjoyed from such academic luminaries as Franz Boas, Ruth Benedict, or Melville Herskovits. As regards the subject of black masculinity, she may have been in her personal relationships so frequently disappointed by the worst aspects of black men's urban sophistication that the purer natures she understood while growing up in the South and then re-encountered while collecting folklore years later resounded in her with striking familiarity. The successful black men in her novels, however, are men who would probably not fare well in the North because they are already spiritually corrupted in what was perhaps to her the least corrupting place on earth. At the least, the wholeness of the black South she portrays depends significantly on these men, as she appears to wish them developmental rather than devolutional. It is in just this instance we regard them as important to black women, as part of the message women like Pheoby must hear. At the end of Janie's tale, Pheoby exclaims: "Ah means to make Sam take me fishin' wid him after this" (*Their Eyes,* 183), which suggests that the strongest hearing that Pheoby—and Janie's larger female audience—have given is also the one that must happen across genders. But while there may yet be hope for Sam, black men are otherwise roundly critiqued in Hurston's novels, and they in turn are used to critique the imperatives that have corrupted them—namely those of economics, politics, and power. The racism that is the legacy of the antebellum period has been the continual miasma of the South, one that has defined it ultimately as a region unto itself. Hurston sets the task for herself of examining the black South, and as she suggests in numerous places, explaining it to us. For the purposes of focusing on elements of black manhood as they are treated in Hurston's novels, I would like to look first at her last novel, where examinations of black life and particular critiques of black manhood are perhaps least apparent.

Seraph on the Suwanee, appearing in 1948, is Hurston's effort to depart from the traditional formula for the African American novel, that in which black characters control the movement of the text through their shaping of themselves as subjects. Herschel Brickell in *The Saturday Review of Literature* called *Seraph* "a moving novel of life among the Florida Crackers,"[1] which characterizes the novel as something of a departure from the by then well-established career of Hurston's writing, one in which blacks figured significantly at the center. Unlike Hurston's second novel, *Their Eyes,* or *Jonah's Gourd Vine,* her first, wherein white presences figure only infrequently, *Seraph* depicts white life as innocent and powerful by turns as it follows formulas designed and sanctioned by the American pathology of racism and its liminal conduit, American popular culture. Thus in the descriptions of the lives of the white Jim and Arvay Meserve, not only do black voices both male and female occupy a lower register but also their senses of subject-orientation and purpose are similarly diminished.

---

1. Herschel Brickell, "A Woman Saved," 19.

Seraph is the story of Arvay Henson, a deeply introverted young woman who meets the handsome and manly Jim Meserve in Sawley, a small town whose largest employer is its turpentine mill. Though Jim's character seems "typically American"—which is to say, indicative of vision, purpose, and the ability to seize opportunity in a forceful, masculine way—it is exacerbated in this relationship, for he demands that the woman's role as being entirely inferior to man's reflects the natural order of things. One of the possible readings of Jim's surname is "Me-serve," which suggests his intention that Arvay be subordinate to him. But Jim's typicality is given some dimension by the fact that he loves Arvay so much that he feels his role, however hierarchical, is to conquer the world for her and give her the spoils. Another possible reading of Jim's name, then, suggests that *he* will serve Arvay as much as he will expect her to serve in return. The heart of the conflict in the novel is Arvay's refusal to understand Jim's love for her, though it must be said that Jim, in fantastic displays of insecurity, seeks affirmations of love from Arvay that often can only be considered cruel or stupid. Many readers have been dissatisfied with the novel's ending, wherein Arvay finally realizes that her marriage—despite its peremptory and abusive nature—is the only thing that anchors her and gives her life purpose and dimension. The novel has been considered an unusual departure for Hurston, whose canonical status as a black woman writer of considerable impact has otherwise held significance for women and feminists everywhere. *Seraph* thus remains a problem text, making new departures for feminism, and making what appear to be very different, un-Hurstonlike claims for black agency as well. Though Arvay Henson may ultimately want and seek love just as much as does Janie Crawford, Arvay appears to represent womanhood as it should *not* be, a condition traditionally and completely dependent on a masculine control of economics and environment. Such control as represented by her husband, Jim, while ostensibly accruing to Arvay's good, expresses masculine abuse and a phallic insistence on power. But Ann duCille reads Arvay as having emerged victoriously from this apparently hopeless situation. At the end of the novel, the reconciliation she achieves with the unregenerate Jim is termed an "active submission"; she "reinvents herself as an actor in a marriage she wants to maintain." Rather than supinely surrendering to the prison-house of the feminine, her reconciliation with Jim is seen as being "heroically comic";

she is regarded as having effected "a claiming, rather than a surrendering, of self" (*Coupling,* 151). While this indicates the tone of contemporary feminist criticism on *Seraph,* however, little has been written on the fact that Hurston appears also to have allowed through Jim's centrality in the novel a range of irrecoverably disabling behaviors in its black men. There is a mapping in *Seraph* of Southern black maleness that speaks to the fragmentation of black masculine entelechy, and makes its own limited pronouncements upon black possibility. It reveals, at the least, the theater of stasis and limited participation for black men that is a quite ordinary part of modern capitalist progress. In charting this field of the masculine, its implications for African American men and its career in Hurston's novels, we may first consider this passage from *Seraph* in which the relationship between Jim Meserve and his close friend Joe Kelsey, a black man, is described:

> Every Southern white man has his pet Negro. His Negro is always fine, honest, faithful to him unto death, and most remarkable. Indeed, no other Negro on earth is fitten to hold him a light, and few white people. He never lies, and in fact can do no wrong. If he happens to do what other people might consider wrong, it is never his Negro's fault. He was pushed and shoved into it by some unworthy varmint. If he kills somebody else, the dead varmint took and run into the pet's knife or bullet and practically committed suicide just to put the pet in wrong, the low-life-ted scoundrel-beast! If the white patron has his way, the pet will never serve a day in jail for it. The utmost of his influence will be invoked to balk the law. Turn go *his* Negro from that jail! (*Seraph,* 61)

What Joe Kelsey embraces in this moment, and indeed in every contingent moment as a black man in the South, is his subordination to a white masculine ideal of racialized comradeship in which Jim Meserve is his ultimate protector. This is not unlike Jim's ordinary paternalism toward Arvay, who, like Janie in Jody's estimation of her intellectual faculties in *Their Eyes,* "can see ten things and not even understand one." Interestingly, Hurston's remarks about the "real" South, whose tone is derivative from a much earlier essay in *American Mercury,* reify Nanny's lament in *Their Eyes* that "de white man throw down de load and tell de nigger man tuh pick it up" by compromising black male possibility and independence. That essay,

"The 'Pet Negro' System," is a clever parody of this curious Southern relationship, as it mixes folk humor with the language of biblical text. Nanny's complaint, however, has at least the force of folk law ("Honey, de white man is de ruler of everything . . . so fur as Ah can see") in that it checks the humor of the essay while giving ironic dimension to what we understand in *Their Eyes* to be Nanny's limited view of the world and the place of developing young women like her granddaughter Janie in it. David Goldfield charts this deleterious relationship in the history of Southern race relations. Blacks who assumed any voice with respect to their own affairs at all "faced loss of property, legal harassment, eviction, denial of credit at the store, and violence. Black lives and livelihood literally depended upon whites, so many blacks, especially in rural areas, ingratiated themselves with powerful whites. . . . This lingering paternalism sealed black dependence."[2] In this light, it will be *Janie's* blindness to the fact that black masculinity suffers overdeterminations of various kinds. Hurston charts with particularity the racial dissonance between men over several years and works, suggesting a shaping of black sexual politics by an overarching whiteness whose presence, except in the case of *Seraph,* is rarely invoked.

Joe's general attitude toward women seems to be the crucial factor determining the advice he gives Jim on how to win Arvay's devotion: "Most women folks will love you plenty if you take and see to it that they do," Joe says. "Make 'em knuckle under. From the very first jump, get the bridle in they mouth and ride 'em hard and stop 'em short. They's all alike, Boss. Take 'em and break 'em" (*Seraph,* 46). This is one of the most problematic episodes in this "problem" text, for Hurston appears to ask here that Joe, as a black man for whom the stereotype endures, be accepted as the spirit of Jim's sexual violence against Arvay. Several commentators have remarked about Jim's rape of Arvay, but there is little commentary on its racialized nexus, Joe Kelsey.[3] This particular aspect of the rape episode in *Seraph* can be (and perhaps tacitly has been) dismissed as

---

2. Hurston, "The 'Pet Negro' System," 593–600; David R. Goldfield, *Black, White and Southern: Race Relations and Southern Culture, 1940 to the Present,* 30.

3. See, for example, Lillie P. Howard, "Marriage: Zora Neale Hurston's System of Values," 256–68; Laura Dubek, "The Social Geography of Race in Hurston's *Seraph on the Suwanee,*" 341–65; Ann duCille, *The Coupling Convention: Sex, Text, and Tradition in Black Women's Fiction;* Claudia Tate, *Psychoanalysis and Black Novels: Desire and the Protocols of Race.*

one of the novel's unevennesses. But the question persists: How indeed, pet Negro or no, could a black man presume to give such information to his white counterpart? Though this may be bold license on Hurston's part, its implications are monumental. Despite the fact that Joe does not quite use the word "rape" in counseling Jim, this is precisely what Jim performs. But Joe discusses the subjugation of women as if he were discussing the domestication of livestock. Given the long history of the lynching of black men on false charges of rape, it is certainly a word that Joe *cannot* use. Jim not only uses the word, but does so imperiously in addressing Arvay: "Sure you was raped, and that ain't all. You're going to keep on getting raped" (*Seraph,* 57). Only in Jim's mind does the moment of rape signify his marriage to Arvay, but if there is any doubt, only a white, male juridical power can sanitize this crime:

> But, but, you just got through saying that you meant to keep on raping me. That . . .
> You got that right, and I mean to tell you, rape in the first degree. We're headed for the courthouse now, just as fast as we can wheel and roll. And the minute we get there, we're going to take out some papers on it. (57)

In her study of *Seraph,* Claudia Tate owes the strange racialization of its characters to the idea of masking, the carnivalesque, and the joke.[4] Black folk humor, especially that of Hurston's stamp, is a well-settled fact, but the nether side of this jest is Joe's subordination to Jim in every sense—even that of Jim's sexual education and masculine prowess. Some aspect of the joke may reside in Jim's demonstrated desire to legally marry Arvay after the rape, wherein a legal cleansing not only mitigates Jim's violence but absolves Joe as well. The Southern legal system is one to which only whites have recourse, however; the pain of ridicule and unlawful arrest from whites that John and other blacks evince at his divorce trial in *Jonah's Gourd Vine* and the similar trepidation expressed at Janie's murder trial in *Their Eyes* indicate that this is a system that blacks would do well to avoid. The same system that would sanction the white man's rape will doubly enforce the absence of the word "rape" in the mouth of the black man: it must never be uttered, and here the suggestion of sexual-

---

4. Tate, *Psychoanalysis and Black Novels,* 164–70.

ity, for the sake of Joe's own self-preservation, becomes of necessity a genuine, reified bestiality. The issue of Jim's marriage to Arvay, then, does far less to absolve Joe than to diminish him. In an effort to destabilize any valuation of Jim's masculinity, Hurston further—and necessarily—engineers Joe's diminution.

While it may appear that Hurston has not only sacrificed black male agency but also specifically employed white masculinity to do it, a closer look at her efforts reveals a deft critique of masculinity as coupled with racial terror. Though it was undoubtedly present throughout the history of the black in the West, Thomas Gossett writes that by 1900 the concern for the black male's sexual longing for white women became exacerbated by many Southern office-seeking politicians of the time. To men such as J. K. Vardaman of Mississippi, "Pitchfork" Ben Tillman of North Carolina, and Georgia's Tom Watson, the Negro was thoroughly unredeemable from his lusts, and incapable of any action but rape.[5] That could not be the simple case with Joe Kelsey, however, for *without the word in his mouth,* he is thoroughly implicated in Jim Meserve's effort to reassert his masculinity via the sexual violation and control of Arvay Henson—an instance of facilitation that far less renews the Southern white male call for the preservation of white womanhood than it reveals the white male desire to express his sexuality in ways his society deems taboo. Hurston's investment in Joe's bestiality thus pays dividends in Jim's fear of sexual guilt, which is ordinarily manifest as a paradigm of desire and aversion for adventures in black sexuality felt even by Southern racist politicians. As Winthrop Jordan suggests, the pure animalism of Joe's description of the control of women reaches Jim in a way that intimates Jim's prescience. "Ever since the days of confrontation in Africa," Jordan writes, ". . . the Negro-ape connection served as a sufficiently indirect means by which the white man could express the dim awareness of the sexual animal within himself." This phenomenon is located and given flesh by Gossett in the racially divided South: "One still hears," he writes, "the idea expressed by white men in the Deep South that they wish they could be Negroes, at least on Saturday nights."[6] In the good-natured banter that courses through *Seraph,* Joe succinctly tells Jim about what

5. Thomas F. Gossett, *Race: The History of an Idea in America,* 271.
6. Winthrop Jordan, *White over Black: American Attitudes toward the Negro, 1550–1812,* 491; Gossett, *Race,* 273.

must be to Jim the dubious but tantalizing virtues of black pleasure: "If you ever was to be a Negro just *one* Saturday night," he says, "you'd never want to be white no more" (*Seraph,* 44).

Early in the novel, a sketch of Jim Meserve reveals that he "was obviously Black Irish in his ancestry somewhere," an impression owing to his "thick head of curly black hair" and "long black lashes, so that they were what the Irish called 'set in with a sooty finger'" (*Seraph,* 7). Jim differed also from the other residents of Sawley in that his ancestors "had held plantations upon the Alabama River before the War," which makes ironic Jim's present state as being similarly situated with the men of Colored Town in comparison with the white feudal power that was his heritage. Jim's dark features, represented in his ancestry only vaguely, and the grandeur of his ancestry itself as it was concentrated in wealth, social prestige, and political power, configure a curious crossing of whiteness with blackness analogizing both past and present, poverty and wealth. Though they held an unquestioned economic and social power that epitomized the masculinity of the South, the Cavalier planters from whom Jim is descended were unable or unwilling to marshal their true resources in the face of crisis. This tradition of Southern aristocracy both flourished and faced its demise during the antebellum period; the French interpreter of American mores and manners, Alexis de Tocqueville, wrote of the Cavalier in 1835 that he loves "greatness, luxury, renown, excitement, enjoyment, and above all, idleness. . . . [He] has the tastes, prejudices, weaknesses and grandeur of every aristocracy" (*Democracy,* 375-76). William Taylor charts the career of the Cavalier through his literary representations in nineteenth-century Southern literature. "[The Cavalier's] characteristic improvidence," writes Taylor, "his almost childish impetuosity and irresponsibility, his lack of enterprise and his failure to move with the times—in sum, his inflexibility and inadaptability—spell his doom."[7] What Vardaman, Tillman, and Watson also revealed at the turn of the century when they determined the Negro's bestiality was both the immediate loss of white masculine power as they knew it in the Cavalier, and the continuing threat of black migration that increased toward the end of the century. Both events had their effect on white South-

7. William R. Taylor, *Cavalier and Yankee: The Old South and American National Character,* 148, 154.

ern manhood, for they made increasingly difficult the ability to realize power ever again through the control of black labor.

As the Meserves, particularly Arvay, engage in typical deroga-
tions of blacks and Europeans alike (*Seraph,* 116–21), Joe's subordination to Jim, despite the absence of the ravages of slavery, becomes
all the more commonplace. The mention of the plural in the description of Jim's background—*plantations*—further centers Jim in the
Cavalier mold, placing his descent from one of the greatest estates of
the South, with acreages so large that they were subdivided, with
several managers working hundreds of slaves, as was the J. A. S.
Acklen estate in Louisiana,[8] or Wye House of Edward Lloyd in
Maryland, given its notoriety by Frederick Douglass as the "Great
House Farm" in Douglass's 1845 *Narrative.* The glorious past of the
Meserves was forged in the expansion of slavery, made possible by
the first wave of the Industrial Revolution, the invention of the cotton gin, and the gradual expansion of the Calhoun South. But at the
ground of class Hurston is careful to make social capital out of the
fact that the fortunes of war had not been with Jim's family: "Not
that Jim Meserve had come among the people of Sawley with anything," Hurston writes, though we are led to understand that he definitely "had a flavor about him. He was not meat any longer, but he
smelled of what he had once been associated with" (*Seraph,* 7). Thus
begins the odd democratization of the turn-of-the-century South in
Seraph. For a considerable portion of the novel, Jim's fortune is made
by running a still that Joe runs at a profit, and it is an enterprise that
is lucrative to both men. But also interesting is the fact that the mechanized source of income in which both share is a still instead of a
cotton gin. Later, that land is cleared by "gangs of husky black
roustabouts rumbling past in truck loads, singing, chanting, laugh-
ing as they went to the swamp . . . swinging shining axes to rhythm,
felling the giant trees" (*Seraph,* 195) for Hatton Howland, the new
husband of Jim's daughter Angeline, rendering a reconstitution of
the old hierarchy. But at least at the outset, despite the fact that Joe
runs the still for Jim, the fact of its illegality makes both men vulnerable (though Joe would pay a greater price if caught), and
through a new valuation of class difference, curious allegiances are

8. Kenneth M. Stampp, *The Peculiar Institution: Slavery in the Ante-Bellum
South,* 42–43.

formed. Jim Meserve, then, for all his boisterousness, swagger, and virility, is a descendent of the old order that itself had attenuated its power through its own insouciance. Much of Tocqueville's description can be found in Jim's character, and while he cannot return absolutely to the racial hierarchies of the old South, he can seek to regain his ancestral glory by preserving some of the economic ones. The nineteenth-century Cavalier becomes the modern twentieth-century American opportunist, and what gives Jim his wide appeal is his ability to step from the failed feudalism of his forebears into a thriving arena of capitalism he creates. As he seeks security for his new wife, he ventures, jobless and somewhat desperate, to Sawley's "Colored Town" to find crews that will work with him in the orange groves. A new masculinity (though a familiar capitalism) is both rendered and preserved through the text as we are told that Arvay is unaware that Jim "had finally decided that since the colored men did all of the manual work, they were the ones who actually knew how things were done" (*Seraph,* 74).

Jim's dependence on Joe to erase his earlier lack of knowledge about how to gain advantage over Arvay's resistance is crucial, for in the present as in the past, he can in his milieu easily be seen to lack masculine wherewithal and sexual savvy. Indeed, his later transformation into a provider and a keen observer of the workings of capital is seen, in his relationship to Arvay, to be bound up with his ability to control and own sexually. "The worker is conventionally discussed," writes Carole Pateman, "by defenders of socialism and capitalism alike, as if the fact of his masculinity and that he is a husband is quite irrelevant to his working-class consciousness." It is this sexual—and economic—wherewithal that is presumed in Jim's conversation with Brock Henson, Arvay's father, as Jim asks her hand in marriage. Brock shares with Jim the mock formula for determining a young woman's fitness for marriage: she is put in a barrel, and if her head sticks out, she is eligible; if not, the top of the barrel is sawed off to make the adjustment. In this presumably jesting moment Arvay is trapped by what Pateman calls the "law of male sex-right," the patriarchal decree of civil society that the bodies of women become the property of men. But what is also important here is Hurston's preservation of Jim's innocence in that he has been given the right to Arvay's body via the civil machinery, and lacks the sexual wherewithal to secure it. Even more insidious is that this lack of sexual "know-how" is reciprocally illustrative of Jim's overall innocence, even to the point of Joe's thoroughgoing shielding of his masculinity. The art of the sex crime Jim soon commits is bestowed upon him by the putative original possessor of a dangerous black sexuality, which thus exculpates Jim from his rape of Arvay. In one sense, Joe could do nothing else, since his social and legal protections depend entirely on his ability to satisfy Jim. As Philip Brian Harper suggests, nothing more definitively foregrounds the validity of one's masculinity than the realization of a threat against it, and while Jim's lack of knowledge about how to claim his wife is the very horizon of such a threat, the additional fear that an inferior blackness was responsible for eradicating it can be summarily dismissed—indeed, it already has been—by the fact of the existing racial hierarchy.[9] What Joe is unable to escape is that Jim's conception of manhood curiously overmatches his, being doubly grounded as it is in an ethos of conquest and ownership.

On the other hand, while Jim's double-edged paternalism preserves the white masculine imperative, his solicitation of sexual "help" from an inferior still compromises a *consciousness* of control. When Joe tells Jim how the thing is done and punctuates his tutelage with the appellation "Boss," he has redeemed Jim's whiteness, as if the idea to rape could not have come from Jim. Though in other ways he helps build the Meserve fortune, Joe is in this most outstanding instance fundamentally implicated in another of Jim's hegemonic imperatives: after his taking of Arvay, Jim tells her not only that she had been raped but also that "the job was done up brown" (*Seraph,* 42), a punning reference to Joe's dark but thorough pedagogy. This blend of innocence and aggression paves the way for Jim's later unchallenged status as both owner of Arvay's body and as local preeminent capitalist, but it also places black Joe Kelsey in the ironic position of vicar of Arvay's defloration. This is one joke after which though the listener laughs, laughter comes uneasily.

There may be a litmus test for the effect of this episode upon the entire novel, but it unfortunately may never be taken. Its visual aspect and thus its translatability to film would have offered its own

9. Carole Pateman, *The Sexual Contract,* 1, 140, chap. 5; Phillip Brian Harper, *Are We Not Men?: Masculine Anxiety and the Problem of African-American Identity,* 25.

critique of American racial policy, particularly as that policy is ordinarily generated through popular culture. Six years before the publication of *Seraph,* Hurston wrote to Carl Van Vechten that the "tiny wedge" she had gained as a screenwriting consultant at Paramount Studios in Hollywood in 1941 and 1942 had given to her "hopes of breaking that silly old rule about Negroes not writing about white people." She was, she told Van Vechten, "working on a story now." Claudia Tate writes that *Seraph* was intended to be not only a bestseller but also eventually a screenplay, thus the reason for this black novelist's shifting the white presence to the center of the novel. If so, then the purpose of Hurston's critique of Southern life on behalf of black self-conscious personhood would seem to fall both to the demand of the marketplace and to Hurston's desire to enter it. Another Hurston essay that appeared in *American Mercury* in October of 1943, "High John de Conquer," rendered fragments of the series of African American folktales about the mythical slave who was usually able to deceive his masters, thereby gaining a measure of ease and comfort for himself and his fellows in bondage. His transcendence is a part of collective black memory, where such tales of derring-do inform and distribute the spirit of black possibility. But after emancipation, John ceased to have the same spiritual appeal as in antebellum times. John's minions, at the end of the war, "had their freedom, their laugh and their song. They have traded it to the other Americans for things they could use like education and property, and acceptance . . . White America, take a laugh out of our black mouths and win!" (*Complete Stories,* 139).[10] It may be reasonable to speculate that this essay, along with the "Pet Negro" essay in the same journal in May, both having come soon after the letter to Van Vechten late in 1942, may have begun the politically perfidious path along which Hurston had devised *Seraph.*

What might Hurston have been thinking? She had never been wealthy, had been nearly always in debt, and certainly by 1943 had ached to produce another novel and make the enterprise a truly lucrative one. Could she have been prepared to sell the black visage and voice in doing so? Though the evidence points to such a possibility, the potential visual impact of the episode would seek to deny

10. Hurston to Carl Van Vechten, November 2, 1942, quoted in Hemenway, *Hurston,* 308; Tate, *Psychoanalysis and Black Novels,* 163.

it. In writing against the heritage of racist one-dimensionality that has characterized American film, James Snead observes that "throughout the history of Hollywood cinema . . . blacks' character is sealed off from the history into which whites have trapped them" (*Representing,* 20, 26). The racial binarism, the narratological veil between black and white as described in Snead's remark, is itself a signifier of black misrepresentation; he correctly suggests here that what is knowable about black character is dependent not on its tradition of narrative ideology as transmitted through American film, but upon the persistence of the black character to challenge the ideology by revealing itself. Hurston was almost certainly familiar with Margaret Mitchell's novel *Gone With the Wind* (1936), wherein Rhett Butler took Scarlett O'Hara in a rape scene whose visual representation in the 1939 film version acquired all of the sweep and splendor one might imagine for a Depression-era audience thirsting for the hardness and virility of a man's man who takes both his enterprise and his woman with force. Though Hurston appears to construct *Seraph* along the basic lines that Snead suggests, Jim Meserve, who for his whiteness would be in the popular imagination similarly heroic, would never find audiences fully appreciative of his manly vigor, bound as it is to Joe's tutelage. Had the film been made, it in this instance would likely have belied its textual foundation. Otherwise, history might have had to wait for the discovery of a director's cut that revealed the crucial colloquy between Joe and Jim that had been deleted from the final release. It would be just so, for no strain of a supremacist ideology of white American masculinity could support such an episode's articulation of its deepest secret, and with its inclusion, as is the case with the novel, comes every skepticism of Jim's fitness to lead. Hurston, then—at least with her book—appears to have planned, with the deft use of the beast in the jungle, to distribute wholesale her own brand of snake oil.

But Hurston does not end her critique of the South simply by garnering either a textual heroism for Joe Kelsey, or even absolution for him because of his necessary dependence on the "pet Negro" system. While it is obvious that Joe lives in a position racially subordinate to Jim, it is Joe who, finally, renders advice to Jim on how to win a woman—not with compassion and empathy, but with sexual violence. Because a white male patriarchy had for so long commanded such overwhelming power over black men, the stance of the powerful was the only stance left for the powerless to embrace, and it is Joe's wisdom, passed on to Jim, that stands as a metaphor for this dynamic. Joe Kelsey is doomed to embrace only the worst aspects of a stereotypical masculinity. Jim bestows upon his pet Joe his idea of blackness: Joe is someone who "had plenty experience with women, certainly" (*Seraph*, 45). For his pains, Jim receives a dark night of the soul—or at least a gray one—in which he then ponders the efficacy of the borrowed power that will breach Arvay's resistance. bell hooks, in discussing her upbringing, recalls some of the men she grew up with as "black men who chose alternative lifestyles, who questioned the status quo, who shunned a ready-made patriarchal identity and *invented themselves.*"[11] Joe Kelsey is an exemplar of the sort different from what hooks describes, as he has drifted far from this island of independence. Ann duCille aptly remarks that "black Joe's notion of gender relations is no different from that of white Jim" (*Coupling*, 125), which figures a patriarchal conspiracy against Arvay that is not limited by racial difference. But as mentioned previously, Joe's historicized animalism describes him in terms of a different variety of sexuality. Joe's wife, Dessie, herself demeaned by Jim's expectation that she will tend to Arvay's needs during her pregnancy, is also ensnared by the popular construction of masculinity. As she says to Arvay, "I declare! That husband you done married is all parts of a man. . . . Youse knocked up" (*Seraph*, 62). Manhood, to Dessie, ostensibly means having the wherewithal to "take" a woman and impregnate her; perhaps the particular force with which he does this affirms that he is also solely responsible for her changed biological state. It may be significant that Dessie accepts this state of affairs for women with far more aplomb than Arvay, who is confused and frightened after her encounter with Jim; there may be, after all, something chilling in this acceptance, because Dessie was also visited by the lust of the beast, and had performed upon her body an act for which there was no name.

While *Seraph* is a novel ostensibly about the interconnections among marriage, power, and whiteness, it also forges subtle and incisive critiques of black and white masculinities. Before we pronounce Joe saved by subterfuge, Hurston forces us to her critique of the black masculine, for Joe is deeply implicated in Jim Meserve's

---

11. bell hooks, *Black Looks: Race and Representation*, 88 (emphasis added).

career in the novel. Joe represents to Jim the "return of the re-pressed," the exotic, psychic mentor, the madman in the attic. He is not in *Seraph* the isolated object of the American cinematic gaze; through one dramatic instance, he definitively *participates* in the life of his white counterpart, motivating his most base and tyrannical act. But the crucible of this participation is Jim's own configuration of the American dream, fashioned as it is by the worst aspects of male-ness: the abuses of capital, power, and sex. Joe's implication in white, male, capitalist desire is indeed found by Hurston to be a destructive influence to African American maleness; Hurston's own correctives are more sanguinary representations of manhood, found in other more comprehensive aspects of pan-African culture.

NATIONHOOD, GENDER, AND "THE STRIFE OF FREEDOM"

A very different construction of black maleness appears at the focus of Hurston's 1939 novel, *Moses, Man of the Mountain.* In the same year, Sigmund Freud published his famous essay "Moses and Mono-theism," which also argues that the name Moses has Egyptian, rather than Judaic, origins; Hurston's biographer, Robert Hemenway, al-lows for Hurston's possibly having seen the article, but suggests also that she may have come upon this idea independently. In the novel the biblical Moses emerges as a pan-African folk hero, by Hurston's having imaginatively relocated his heritage in Egypt rather than in Judea and by presuming Moses to have given the gift of monotheism to the Hebrews. This relocation becomes a transcendent reconfigura-tion of biblical myth as it Africanizes the theme of leadership as en-gaged by the great individual mind, and that mind's struggles with methodological doubt. Hemenway writes of Hurston's Moses that "once he was demystified . . . the analogy between biblical history and the black American past became real and immediate, an allegory relevant to the oppressive circumstances that black people encounter in any age."[12] Zora Hurston the anthropologist and cultural historian had known even before *Tell My Horse* the importance of the biblical Moses to the pan-African world. In this volume she begins to rumi-nate about the far-reaching cultural implications of the myth: "It is

12. Hemenway, *Hurston,* 260.

more probable that there is a tradition of Moses as the great father of magic scattered over Africa and Asia," she writes. "Perhaps some of his feats recorded in the Pentateuch are the folk beliefs of such a character grouped about a man for it is well established that if a memory is great enough, other memories will cluster about it, and those in turn will bring their suites of memories to gather about this focal point, because perhaps, they are all scattered parts of the one thing like Plato's concept of the perfect thing" (*TMH,* 117–18).

Hurston's effort to locate Moses' origins on the African continent may have had much to do with preserving the ideas of harmony and the possession of the "strife of freedom"—the responsibility there-for—that so motivates the novel. Hurston was already using as copy one of the most important books of the Bible, and the tension be-tween the austerity of the biblical text and her effort at freer play have been discussed. But she understood the importance of the story of Moses in the Book of Exodus to Africans everywhere, as well as the importance of preserving the elements of leadership, patriotism, and nationalism in the biblical text for the aggrandizement of the African Moses. Hurston's device for projecting this view of Moses is the same as that which rendered the tension between his blackness as conceived by Hurston and the historicity of the biblical text— Moses' use of African American folk speech. "Hurston's most effec-tive device for bringing Moses down to earth is the manipulation of his speech," writes Hemenway, who here discusses Hurston's tem-pering of Moses' austerity as he ascends to greatness. But the location of African American folk speech in *Moses* and among the Israelites has another importance—the final location of African America in a milieu that existed before capitalism. Hurston's Moses is cast, then, in the African American grain, as African American folk expression gives life to his career in the novel. As Moses descends from the mountain with the Commandments, he discovers that his brother Aaron has been indulgent in sinfulness just as have the other Israel-ites. After Aaron gives his feeble account, Moses answers: "Aaron, you haven't said a thing yet and that is because you haven't thought a thing yet, nor felt anything except your own importance. Your whole body is nothing but a big bag to toe your littleness in" (*Moses,* 238). Hemenway, while recognizing the richness that such expres-sion lends to the narrative by reforegrounding the biblical story in African American cultural terms, notes also that the narrative thus reforegrounded also lends to a textual tension between the idea of the traditional, biblical Moses as emissary of God and the idea of Moses in mystical and kabbalistic lore, Moses as the original conjure-man. But such tension can act as well as a metacommentary upon different levels of the narrative: the theme of authority versus resistance is evident at various points in the text as the Israelites doubt Moses even after major successes; the theme natural versus divine, as regards the entities "magic" or "conjure" in pan-African syncretism; and the special qualities of grace, as in traditional Judeo-Christian thought. The problem here can also be doubly manifold: there may be genuine difficulty, finally, in determining what characteristics of all that is should be assigned to the natural and what to the divine. There is thus exposed the existential consciousness which of necessity must exist between each of these master oppositions, and there is also exposed the methodologically doubting consciousness now thrust into a role of leadership, a consciousness at once both individual and communitarian. "Even in a primitive collective, as in every human community," writes the Christian philosopher Paul Tillich, "there are outstanding members, the bearers of the traditions and leaders of the future. They must have sufficient distance in order to judge and to change. They must take responsibility and ask questions. This unavoidably produces individual doubt and personal guilt. Nevertheless, the predominant pattern is the courage to be as a part."[13] Hurston seeks to approximate in her reconfiguration of Moses a very different construction of maleness from the type sometimes found in her South, for example by Joe Kelsey in *Seraph*. The representation of capable black masculinity located in Hurston's Moses is rooted in other, secularized black folk representations of male strength, such as High John de Conquer, Stackolee, and Shine. Here, however, Moses is first among equals, as Hurston sketches his introductory:

> Africa has her mouth on Moses. All across the continent there are the legends of the greatness of Moses, but not because of his beard nor because he brought the laws down from Sinai. No, he is revered because he had the power to go up the mountain and to bring them down. Many men could climb mountains. Anyone could bring down laws that had been handed to them. But who can talk to God face to face? Who had the power

13. Ibid., 259–62; Paul Tillich, *The Courage to Be,* 92–93.

to command God to go to a peak of a mountain and there demand of Him laws with which to govern a nation? What other
man has ever seen with his eyes even the back part of God's
glory? Who else has ever commanded the wind and the hail?
The light and darkness? That calls for power, and that is what
Africa sees in Moses to worship. (*Moses,* xxiii–xxiv)

The novel opens as a bildungsroman as, on Hurston's new scaf-
folding of an African origin, Moses learns the intricacies of life and
power from the slave Mentu, continuing the oral transmission of
wisdom from old sage to young seeker. In this relationship, even the
loss of virility, inevitable to every man, can be conveyed with wonderful humor: "When one is too old for love," Mentu says to the young
Moses, "one finds great comfort in good dinners" (*Moses,* 42). Despite Jethro's hatred of seeing a maturing Moses "wasted on a woman"
because of the latter's obvious leadership capabilities, Moses' great
love is Zipporah, Jethro's daughter. Moses yields to her in spite of
what Hurston casts as being her childishness and her class consciousness, both of which are manifest in her desire to lord before
the other women of her class her marriage to an Egyptian noble. It
may at first appear, however, that with respect to Moses' personal relationship to Zipporah, or more broadly, his ordinary relationship to
women, that Mentu gave the growing Moses quite the wrong advice—that is, as a contemporary mind would have it, advice laden
with sexism. Mentu counsels the young prince Moses that

> male man was made with five strong senses to gather the truth
> of things and his mind is a threshing floor to clean his truth in.
> This is often an unhappy thing, for man sees himself as he
> really is. Thus he is made very miserable. But he does not de-
> stroy himself because the female man was made with squint
> eyes so that she sees only those things which please her. And
> her threshing floor is cramped and cluttered. She cannot sepa-
> rate the wheat from the chaff. But she achieves a harvest that
> makes her happy. When she sees man fleeing from his bowl in
> horror of himself, she feeds him from her own dish and he is
> blindly and divinely happy. Ah, yes, the female companion of
> man has the gift of the soothing-balm of lies. (*Moses,* 39)

But this lesson from Mentu is in one sense not qualitatively different
from the authorial narrative opening of *Their Eyes,* in which men's

and women's values are structured according to their respective re-
flective perceptions, that is, their genderized world views:

> Ships at a distance have every man's wish on board. For some
> they come in with the tide. For others they sail forever on the
> horizon, never out of sight, never landing until the Watcher
> turns his eyes away in resignation, his dreams mocked to death
> by Time. That is the life of men.
>
> Now, women forget all those things they don't want to remem-
> ber, and remember everything they don't want to forget. The
> dream is the truth. Then they act and do things accordingly.
> (*Their Eyes*, 1)

These paragraphs—representing what I would call Hurston's "folk
phenomenology," remarkable for its pith, its truth-telling value in its
examination of our rituals in the actual world—are more remarkable
still not only for their being suited to the novels and situations in
which they appear but also for their innate consistency, which lends
much to their interchangeability and thus the retention of that descriptive value for the characters and situations in either novel. In
each case men are described as capable (and sometimes even lucky
enough to beat the odds despite an extreme probability of failure),
yet flawed.

In the *Moses* passage quoted previously, man is often made
"very miserable" by his too-clear reflection in the mirror of his discovered truths. The element of hope in the passage quoted from
Their Eyes, which would be the chief motivator in either case, is
usually "mocked to death," corroded utterly by time. Women appear to have a greater facility with reflexive truths. In both the quo-
tations, they are unlike men in confronting these truths in that they
can achieve sensibility and turn it into praxis. In the narration
opening *Their Eyes,* the dream becomes truth, and upon this occurrence, women "act and do things accordingly." Similarly, the
woman in Mentu's description in *Moses* "achieves a harvest that
makes her happy" despite her inability to winnow through conflicts that only make men miserable anyway. Her ability to feed her
fragmented, disillusioned mate from her bowl, however—to fortify
him against his most vulnerable moment—makes him ecstatically
happy, "blindly and divinely" so. It seems likely that Mentu's description could well describe the men of *Their Eyes,* Logan, Jody, and Tea
Cake, with the possible exception of the aspect of introspection,

which only Tea Cake seems to possess, and here only minutely. The description of men in *Their Eyes* could describe Moses in his ascendancy, as his entire career is marked by episodes of doubt of one sort or another, usually methodological. Janie in her relationship to Tea Cake (and perhaps in her first years with Jody) could be a woman of Mentu's description; the narrative opening from *Their Eyes* may describe any of the women in *Moses,* but Miriam most often comes to mind in this vein because she is the only woman in this novel who consistently expresses her desires through her own agency.

Even though social roles for women, as well as perceptions of them, were limited centuries ago, there is nevertheless rendered in *Moses* a sense of the natural and national imperative toward the realization of goals as shared between genders. Again, this idea is expressed in concentrated form in Mentu's speech to Moses. It might be said, again, that Mentu's last remark to Moses—that woman "has the gift of the soothing-balm of lies"—is itself sexist, as if woman, as the saying goes, "speak with forked tongue." But lies are here not simply untruths. They are rather precisely what Mentu says they are, a "soothing-balm," a salve against the pain of ordinary existence. Mentu is speaking from his position as a slave, knowing this pain as the *only* form of existence. It is the idea of "lying" in African American folklore that applies here, rendering not only the doubleness of the word "lie" in this context, but also fixing the terms of interpersonal and thus national harmony, as Barbara Johnson describes it. "If, as Hurston often implies," Johnson writes, "the essence of telling 'lies' is the art of conforming a narrative to existing structures of address while gaining the upper hand, then Hurston's very ability to fool us into thinking we have been fooled—is itself the only effective way of conveying the rhetoric of the 'lie.'" Though Johnson here speaks principally of the use of black signifying among Hurston's characters, the description of this strategy as regards Mentu's use of speech is doubly applicable as what appears to be at issue in Mentu's remark is actually Hurston's own effort at the "lie." The ambiguity in Mentu's remark is seized and redoubled by Hurston, who as author and as woman is herself appropriating and reforegrounding the elements of sexism in the remark, claiming for herself and for the woman in Mentu's example a rhetorical power that for blackness on the one hand, and for the feminine on the other, is expressed as the relational, or oppositional, voice.[14] Mentu's "complicity" in Hurston's strategy allows woman's recognition of man's vulnerability rather than its sacrifice, and by also allowing subterfuge, claims the harmony between the sexes important to nation-building. Even Mentu's neo-biblical appellations "male man" and "female man" dissolve into a rhetorical ambiguity that itself qualifies as equality; if man can be both male and female, then "man" loses its primacy over "woman."

As previously suggested, this reading may suggest several things. First, it may mean that Hurston, in writing *Their Eyes* in 1937, found working models for descriptions of gender and race that may have guided her through much of the writing of the novel. For example, Henry Louis Gates remarks that Hurston, through a process of tropological play which induces formal revision, is connecting rhetorically with Frederick Douglass's 1845 *Narrative,* as the opening paragraph of her novel reflects Douglass's famous apostrophe to the ships moving across the wide expanse of the Chesapeake Bay: "You are loosed from your moorings and are free! I am fast in my chains, and am a slave! You move merrily before the gentle gale, and I sadly before the bloody whip! You are freedom's swift-winged angels, that fly round the world; I am confined in bands of iron! O that I were free!" (*Narrative,* chap. 10). At least as evident, however, are what appear to be Hurston's rhetorical comparisons with the tale of bondage and escape often considered the "female companion" to Douglass's, Harriet Jacobs' 1861 narrative, *Incidents in the Life of a Slave Girl.* This narrative, though it opens interestingly with the narrator's remembrances of a strong-willed, largely free family, has at its very beginning an interesting warp with respect to identity: "I was born a slave; but I never knew it until six years of happy childhood had passed away" (*Incidents,* 1). Compare this with Janie's earliest self-realization in *Their Eyes,* wherein she recognizes herself in a photograph: "Ah was wid dem white chillun so much till Ah didn't know Ah wuzn't white till Ah was round six years old. . . . Ah looked at de picture a long time and seen it was mah dress and mah hair so Ah said: 'Aw, aw! Ah'm colored!'. . . . But before Ah seen de picture Ah thought Ah wuz just like de rest" (*Their Eyes,* 8–9). Janie's folk expression revises the dilemma she shares with Jacobs, thus establishing

14. Barbara Johnson, "Thresholds of Difference: Structures of Address in Zora Neale Hurston," 317–28; Fredric Jameson, *The Political Unconscious,* 84.

for both of them a sisterhood without the trappings of sentiment; each woman's objectification through race as constructed by the men in their lives becomes virtually indistinguishable, as the reasons for the depredations upon Jacobs by Flint and Sands are mirrored in those upon Janie by Jody and Tea Cake. The placement of these tropes near the very beginning of the narrative, as well as Hemenway's observation that the experience of ethnographic work in Haiti for the creation of *Tell My Horse* "released a flood of language and emotion" which was itself connected to a passionate but failed love affair of Hurston's, suggests that these metaphorized descriptions of gender may have been not only an important focus in *Their Eyes* but also its chief organizing principle. Second, the efficacy of these models in *Their Eyes* suggests that Hurston may have found them serviceable once again in *Moses,* the novel she produced five years later. Karla Holloway calls the voice in the four opening paragraphs of *Their Eyes* a voice that "philosophized like a distant and wise observer. . . . The narrative voice that works like this one establishes a relationship within the characters rather than outside of them."[15] Mentu is the wise observer in the early chapters of *Moses,* and his very similar pronouncement upon men and women sets the stage for their movement through the novel without objectifying them. His is not, finally, a sexist utterance, but rather a fulfillment of a more wholesome theme, which is also a central theme of the novel—the achievement and then the securing of the harmony of the entire nation. As Moses brings Israel to Jordan, Hurston summarizes his triumphs:

> He had given Israel back the notes to songs. The words would be according to their own dreams, but they would sing. They had songs and singers.
> They might not be absolutely free inside, but anyway he had taken from them the sorrow of serving without will, and had given them the strife of freedom. He had called to their memories the forgotten words of love and family. They had the blessing of being responsible for their own. (*Moses,* 283–84)

The thematic support here emanates from the story of Moses and Zipporah, which, though a story of a union sealed by devotion, is not without its difficulties.

15. Gates, *Signifying Monkey,* 170–72; Hemenway, *Hurston,* 230–31; Karla F. C. Holloway, *The Character of the Word: The Texts of Zora Neale Hurston,* 53.

It is also intriguing that despite the ultimate similarity of the *Moses* and *Their Eyes* passages, there is a rhetorical sense that nevertheless imposes a crucial qualitative difference. In the *Moses* passage, man and woman come together in an effective, mutually satisfying way. In the passage from *Their Eyes,* the separate descriptions of men's and women's minds remain separate; there is no rhetorically intended harmony. Due to the thematic importance of each passage to its respective larger text, the *Moses* passage acquires its structure through the nature of that novel's master theme—the nation's health through strong leadership—and the rhetorical bifurcation of the sexes in the passage from *Their Eyes* is fulfilled through Janie as protagonist, the development of whose black female voice depends largely on an acknowledgment of separateness that exists at the behest of an androcentric, capitalist imperative. The idea of black men being forced to accept the demands of white patriarchal structures is given expression by Hurston in *Their Eyes,* as Nanny, locked into her exceedingly narrow view of not only black womanhood but all life as well, nevertheless accurately depicts the degradation that black women experience: "Honey, de white man is de ruler of everything as fur as Ah been able to find out. Maybe it's some place way off in de ocean where de black man is in power, but we don't know nothin' but what we see. So de white man throw down de load and tell de nigger man tuh pick it up. He pick it up because he have to, but he don't tote it. He hand it to his womenfolks. De nigger woman is de mule uh de world so fur as Ah can see" (*Their Eyes,* 14). Nanny admits that this point of view is limited ("so fur as Ah can see"), and her entire life demonstrates this condition. She lives it even by being called Nanny, never having had the opportunity to choose her own appellation, or to have her own granddaughter, Janie, choose one of her own. (Janie's nickname is "Alphabet" because so many people had given her "different names.") As "Nanny"—caretaker of the children of the white Washburn family—she is defined in the postbellum world by gender and class as well as race, aspects of the new configuration of an economy that is at once capitalist and American. That black men adopt the role of tyrant is a condition that she endures, and as expressed to Janie, it is also the fear that mirrors the advice given by Joe Kelsey to Jim Meserve in *Seraph*. Nanny interestingly describes "the white man" and "the black man" separately at the beginning of the passage, but as soon as a relationship between them is established—which relationship can only be unequal, one disadvanta-

geous to black men—the black man becomes deeply rhetorically
subordinated, immediately becoming "the nigger man." Nanny's en-
trenched biases, restrictive though they may be to Janie's development, describe acutely the psychosocial and psychosexual dilemmas
of black men. They do so because they are from a woman's perspective, finally; Nanny's well-nurtured cynicism itself becomes the
ironic clarion call for alternative appraisals of masculinity.

Nanny's musing that black men may have true power in some
other locale indicates the peculiar American character of the race
and gender problems she understands. Such a statement brings into
sharper focus the notion that *Moses,* as a much later work and because of its grounding in a very different time and place, is somehow
closer to a visualization of alternative possibilities, and it also suggests that Hurston herself felt that these possibilities were on some
plane realizable. But if African American men remained unregenerate, it remained for Hurston to find some means by which the dishar-
mony and disunity their actions promoted would be sanctioned. If
Hurston had determined that the errant behavior of African American men was Western in origin—because capitalism's economic
and social injustices could only be seen as having been an always-
already—then such a retributive agent would have to have its provenance in a place (and a time) that is beyond the structures of
capitalism and beyond any earthly pattern of organization. It would
have to be based in an ethic of humanity that would also transcend
every category of race.

5

ZORA NEALE HURSTON AND THE ROMANCE OF THE SUPERNATURE

Black men in Hurston's novels and stories, when guilty of abuses against black women—which is to say as well that they are also guilty of abuses against nature—are met with powerful and consuming responses to their transgressions.[1] Toomer's African American men are similarly violative of a Southern sense of nature that is closely identified with its women, but their flaws are merely exposed. They presumably live on long after their stories have ended; a broadly redemptive closure is not a feature of the tales in *Cane*. Toomer's men perhaps continue to be swept along by forces they do not fully understand, if at all. But the forces of nature take rein in Hurston's narratives as if they suddenly become aware of things radically gone awry, and work toward a restoration of order from the disorder created by these errant men by destroying them.

This cosmic temperament in Hurston's novels manifests itself as being the sum of the forces of nature, and for this it is neither purely Judeo-Christian nor purely pan-African. It is primarily pan-African, however, for our understanding of its agency is based upon its being driven largely by pan-African symbolism. For its ability to assume for itself not only all of the forces of nature but also the principal human religious systems that categorize their control, I am given to calling it a Supernature, in that capitalization seems to lend to an

1. SallyAnn Ferguson, "Folkloric Men and Female Growth in *Their Eyes Were Watching God*," 185–97; Missy Dehn Kubitchek, "'Tuh de Horizon and Back': The Female Quest in *Their Eyes Were Watching God*," 19–33.

117

appreciation of its infinite power. The sense of *romance* in its agency is derived partly from the program for the poetry of the English Romantics, which involved the synthesis of the human mind with the whole of creation, the result being a more harmonious, a more sensible world; in fact, the result of such a union is a world that is far more attractive than even the most wonderfully imagined version of this one. Representing itself as a serene, intoxicating, and therefore welcome habit of the mind, the union is fulfilled "by consummating a holy marriage with the external universe, to create out of the world of all of us, in a quotidian and recurrent miracle, a new world which is the equivalent of paradise." In the thinking of major writers in England and Germany during this period, this union was central to a constellation of similar ideas regarding "the history and destiny of man and the role of the visionary poet as both herald and inaugurator of a new and supremely better world."[2]

The significance of this union for Hurston is in its strong resemblance to nature's motivating intelligence in her novels and stories; it parallels the description of the Romantic tendency to synthesize the work of the human mind with the limitlessness of the mind of God. In a similar vein, the ethnographic work with which Hurston began her career, the discipline which preceded her mature writing, was itself, in part, the deep mythic basis on which she built her fiction, a basis that includes pan-African, Judeo-Christian, and Greco-Roman elements.[3] Unlike either the supernal celestial force of the Romantics or the deistic plenipotentiaries of comparative mythology, however, Hurston's Supernature does all of its work on *foreign* soil—that is to say, that unlike Jehovah or Zeus, the power of the Supernature is exercised in a domain that is unlike that of the origin of its subjects. It has made its own one-way, nonstop flight from Canaan (and Dahomey) to the remote pavilions of succeeding generations. As regards Joe Kelsey in *Seraph,* the relative absence of the Supernature is a point to which I will return, but the absence of Supernatural retribution in *Moses* is immediately significant, for if Moses is the Supernature's interlocutor, his status as "the original conjure-man" makes him Nanny's black man who "somewhere over the ocean . . . is in power."

2. M. H. Abrams, *Natural Supernaturalism: Tradition and Revolution in Romantic Literature,* 28, 31.
3. Cyrena N. Pondrom, "The Role of Myth in Hurston's *Their Eyes Were Watching God,"* 181–202.

For Hurston, the great sin of African American men is the very source of their fragmentation—their apparently preconscious eagerness to embrace the worst aspects of a system inherently inimical to their interests. Though Hurston herself might have characterized her opposition to the influence of social and economic hegemony on African Americans in quite this way, she might not have, for instance, thought of the evils of capitalism in logical opposition to alternatives proposed by communism, given her lifelong distrust of Marxism and its structures. She did feel that as a matter of course, solutions to the difficulties of African Americans lay significantly in their own broadest appreciations of their cultural valuations. But the failure of the African American men in Hurston's novels to embrace these cultural valuations indicates their seduction by some aspect of the imperative of capital. As Hemenway describes, though without necessary attention to gender: "Instead of transforming her observations about the distinct culture of black people into the idea of a distinct black political movement or a collective alternative to capitalism, Zora reacted to criticism by retreating from the brink to which her theories had led her. She found a personal litmus test for racial politics that tested for only two things—a pathological stereotype and an individual pride. . . . If someone did not support her effort to celebrate the folkways of black people, he was assumed to have an insufficient pride in his own culture."[4] But the seductions of capitalism are at once racialized and gendered, as Nanny acutely observes: white men rule, and black men, alienated from atavistic principles of communality and partnership, and in America having no legitimate role to assume, give the burdens bestowed upon them to black women. This is a grave offense by black men against black women as seen by a woman passionately driven to interrogate racism and sexism in America through the development of the black female voice. Hurston believes that black men should participate in this process as well, however—developing their own voices alongside those of black women— and that they so often appear to choose against this communitarian effort gives expression to the value of atonement (at-one-ment) that Hurston's Supernature embodies.

In the novels, then, Hurston's cosmic system enters the lives of men and women to restore order, but that restoration depends on the

4. Hurston, "Crazy for This Democracy," 45–48; Hemenway, *Hurston,* 334.

destruction of the black male body, an instance that seems at best uncharitable since black men are but the instruments of the structures and ideologies that control them. As is the case with Toomer, Hurston's black men are governed by an aspect of unendurable bifurcation—which is only in one sense the specter of Du Boisian double consciousness. Dan Moore, Paul Johnson, and, most notably, Ralph Kabnis all experience the attenuation of the "dogged strength" necessary to keep the "two warring ideals in one dark body" from ripping that body apart, though that attenuation is also perhaps revelatory of just who these men really are. As Du Bois wrote in *The Souls of Black Folk,* the African American, in wishing to merge his African and American selves "into a better and truer self," realizes that "America has too much to teach the world and Africa" (*Souls,* 365). But the lesson is likely a costly one, since both slavery and its aftermath of black peonage, as Du Bois well knew, were inextricable from capitalism. Hurston records her well-known distrust of Du Boisian and other forms of "race consciousness" in *Dust Tracks,* wherein the validity of the blues or Spirituals or other forms of black expression were denied by "people [who] made whole careers of being 'Race' men and women" (*DTR,* 218). This general antipathy is perhaps another motivation toward Hurston's construction of an insular black South, where black folk culture speaks of itself, and *in* itself, beyond what she understood as a black class awareness grounded in an Americanism that sought to exclude as much as it professed to defend.

Hurston would have those ideals sundered on behalf of "Negroness" and counter to Du Bois, for she is actually maintaining a philosophical consistency in making a radical rhetorical return to the psychosocial, psychocultural, and psycholinguistic wholeness of the black body. Her effort makes the counterstatement to what Hortense Spillers, in her analysis of Atlantic slavery, calls "a *theft of the body*— a willful and violent . . . severing of the captive body, from its motive will, its active desire." Spillers further contests that "the sociopolitical order of the New World . . . *represents* for its African and indigenous peoples a scene of *actual* mutilation, dismemberment, and exile." Gender difference disappears at the ground of this trauma, for the black body, male or female, was desired for both its labor and its degradation. Blacks in captivity—or blacks in community, similarly situated through the legacy of slavery, establish "a private and particular space, at which point of convergence biological, sexual, social, cultural, linguistic, ritualistic, and psychological fortunes join" ("Mama's," 67; original emphasis). As black men engage in those structures and embrace those ideologies that disrupt this cohesion—as they participate in these for gain that is at best illusory to them—they risk the obliteration of that space, undoing the work of transindividualism. To call Hurston's Supernature a manifestation of sexism, then, would not be accurate. It is far more a restoration of this psychic space, a calling to account, an atonement for risking communitarian healing. It is also a call that is heeded by contemporary black women writers: what is found by these writers to be necessary in the reconstitution of the black male image is just this call to restoration in the name of a rejection of existing hegemony.

It is not surprising that Hurston's cosmology would include a force that was prepared to challenge "the New World order," or that she chose a force that hailed from the African pantheon. Though she was long aware of its existence in African religion (perhaps its most dramatic representation occurs in her 1926 short story "Sweat"), it is the Haiti portion of Hurston's record of Caribbean folklore, *Tell My Horse,* that describes the pan-African mythic elements of the Supernature. The chief god (or *loa*) of Voudou is Damballah, a god of beneficence to whom believers pray for good works. Damballah's symbol in pan-African religion is the snake, which exists beyond the ordinary associations of deception, disgust, and death made with snakes through Christian iconography. The caduceus, the ancient symbol of health and well-being associated today with the medical profession, can be traced back approximately twenty-six centuries before Christ to ancient Mesopotamians who considered the intertwining serpents to be symbolic of the god who conquers all illness. In ancient India, the caduceus was also found engraved on stone tablets that were placed at the entrances of temples as votive offerings.[5] In African culture, health and well-being include the support and healing of family and salutary relations between the sexes—the space of habitation of the transindividual. The very strangeness to the West of the snake's Asian and pan-African mythic function also informs its efficacy. It is perhaps not surprising that the snake as

5. For a critical discussion of the retention of this symbolism in contemporary African literature, see Robert Serumaga, "A Mirror of Integration," 71–80.

signifier would be chosen as a chief trope in Hurston's symbology; its antithetical status in the symbology of the West determines its irremediable othering.

It may also not be surprising that Hurston begins her project for the restoration of order in her semiautobiographical first novel, *Jonah's Gourd Vine,* for to be certain, charity begins at home. *Jonah* foregrounds the black male voice with a supporting yet unappreciated black female impetus behind it, which in some ways mirrors the lives of Hurston's own parents, John and Lucy Hurston. In the novel, Lucy Potts Pearson gently though consistently prods John Buddy Pearson to make the most of his gift, the powerful and persuasive style of oratory that characterizes his preaching. John, however, despite Lucy's tremendous love and support, is unable to repay Lucy with, at the least, marital fidelity. He is a man possessive of not only unusual physical strength but fair skin as well, and the fascination he thus holds for women proves fatal. His arrival as a young boy from a place forgotten by both time and Reconstruction reveals the tragic unself-consciousness that was so much a part of growing up on one side of the Songahatchee Creek. This location is an intriguing one, which may include Hurston's verbal play for "Songhay hatched you," which is more than simple verbal play: it tends to explain John's Africaneity despite his lack of awareness, and it also aids in defining the very different worlds of the two banks on either side of the creek, as well as it explains John's stepfather Ned Crittenden's character and the importance of his inability to cross over to the other side. The very newness and excitement of women, machines, and rudimentary education on the other side eventually exploit his vulnerability and corrupt his nature. As he stands before the approaching train on the creek's bustling, industrious side, he becomes Hurston's perfect and shining example of the fragmentation of the black male in the theater of the modern.

If we are to garner any sympathy for John, it might be remembered that he is as he is partly because of Ned, his malevolent stepfather who wants only to control John by prolonging his captivity on his side of the creek, and thus prolong John's ignorance; Alf Pearson, the town's leading white citizen, and John's biological father (though John does not know this), at least initially chuckles and winks knowingly at John when he discovers John's liaisons, and later helps John avoid arguably deserved jail time. To remember all of this is to understand on one level John's vulnerability and the fact that he has never learned responsibility. But John, who becomes a man of the cloth, and is thus invested with the grave duty of teaching responsibility to his congregation and community, is deeply remiss as a spiritual leader; he is at variance with his own sense of responsibility, which conveys the deeper meaning of the sentence with which he swaggers at the pulpit, "Ah takes mah text, and Ah takes mah time." His sense of right and wrong and his ability to exercise restraint should be considerably greater than that which he possesses. Additionally, Lucy, though she acts for the greater good of John and their seven children, could be said to be adhering too closely to the demands of her class when she tells him: "Jus' you handle yo' members right and youse goin' to be uh sho 'nuff big nigger" (*Jonah,* 112).

Big Nigger was an early working title of *Jonah,* revealing not only John's stature in the community but also ironically the possibility of enticements of various sorts to which powerful men may fall. It is also otherwise a term awash in irony, as its oxymoronic effect suggests its impossibility at the level of its utterance, and thus a fragmentation, a frustration in realization to its bearer. Though the principal theme of the novel is John's inability to reconcile his abilities as a man of God with his libidinous appetites, nothing beyond the Judeo-Christian fear of retribution common to such behaviors lends an awareness to the retributive function of the Supernature as constructed. In a foreshadowing of the final efficacy of the trope, Hurston reveals the eventual disintegration of the relationship between John and Lucy. The innocent courtship between John, then sixteen years old, and Lucy, then eleven, carries with it a sense of foreboding as John, in chivalric play with Lucy, kills the water moccasin that had been a perceived threat to Lucy for as long as she was able to remember. There is also an instance later in their lives, in which Lucy's metaphor, meant to warn John against the possible treachery of both the congregation and the inner circle of deacons, unwittingly demeans the ancient symbolic value of the snake, which is one of benevolence: "Friend wid few. Everybody grin in yo' face don't love yuh. Anybody kin look and see and tell uh snake trail when dey come cross it but nobody kin tell which way he was goin' lessen he seen de snake. You keep outa sight, an' in dat way, you won't give nobody uh stick tuh crack yo' head wid" (*Jonah,* 112).

These instances, like others in Hurston's novels, reveal aspects of structural ambiguity in her texts. John, for his lusts and the neglect of his gift, and Lucy, who far more innocently has succumbed to American fantasies of class, embrace a Western psychosymbology as directed by Western religion; they see snakes as either dangerous beasts or agents of evil. Yet they relate strongly to other aspects of pan-African folk tradition, such as the dancing and drum-playing at the big hoe-down at the beginning of *Jonah* and the "lying and loud-talking" that are so much a part of *Their Eyes*. In the episode in *Jonah*, drums and the dance are the order and spirit of the night's festivities, as the folk engage in communal festivity that is at the heart of their African origins. The end of the feast means the end of the visitation of the spirits: "The fire died. The moon died. The shores of Africa receded. They went to sleep and woke up next day and looked out on dead and dying cotton stalks and ripening possum persimmons" (*Jonah*, 32). John, who later excludes himself from all good, is here at one (at/one) with communitarian spirit. In a dramatic contrast, the concluding scene of desolation describes their collective plight, the separation from Africa and African sources of communion.

The train holds a double valence for John that is more powerful than it appears is rendered in the text. At John's first encounter with a train, references to the engine's sides, which "seemed to expand and contract like a fiery-lunged monster," its subsequent rattling off down the track, and John's effort to "keep sight of the tail of the train" (*Jonah*, 16) all render the train's metaphorized snakiness, thus prefiguring the divine retribution awaiting him. But John mistakes the train station for a cotton gin, a landmark he is given by a passer-by in his effort to locate Alf Pearson and find work. The cotton gin that John imagines he sees, while representing the mechanization and thus the expansion of slavery, can mean John no good as he seeks a way "across the creek," but neither does the actuality of the train that pulls into the station. The train represents both freedom from Southern white exploitation, tropologically common to African American literature and song, and a metaphoric agency of evil as rendered in John's dramatic "damnation train" sermon, borrowed by Hurston from the Reverend C. C. Lovelace in an effort to display John's great gift. In his incisive study of *Jonah*, Eric Sundquist remarks that "the elaborate trope of the 'damnation train,' whose cow-catcher pierces Jesus' side and releases his sacrificial blood in the Lovelace sermon, is reduced to a burlesque figure in the train that smashes into John's Cadillac after his last act of infidelity." He continues in this vein by saying that Hurston's investment in the train as symbol of renewal and hope, "its rich association with movement and migration in modern black history, its embodiment in work songs and the blues of the endless toil of black America . . . are diminished in the comic instrument of reprisal" (*Hammers,* 76). In doing so, Hurston unleashes something of her own moral sanction against her own father, whom John Buddy so closely resembles.

Issues of reprisal within a comic vein may well be at work here, but it also appears that Hurston, while investing the symbol of the train with aspects of movement and migration, blues and labor, is also simultaneously involved in a significant *di*vestiture of these associations, in order to destabilize, as would later be the case in *Seraph,* the fixity of certain valuations. I want to reiterate the doubleness that so often manifests itself in the text, and suggest again that Hurston invests some of these time-honored symbols with an ambiguity which itself provides this destabilization. After the conflicting but conflated Western and pan-African representations of the snake as both evil and salubrious, there is yet another conflation of these with the train itself along the same lines. Though Hurston does reconstruct the lore of the train with both movement and blues, and with these, salvation, she compromises them all in the Lovelace sermon in the very fact of the train as a vehicle of damnation. It is "de damnation train/Dat pulled out from Garden of Eden loaded wid cargo goin' to hell," and it could only have been stopped by Jesus, who "stood out on her track like a rough-backed mountain/And she threw her cow-catcher in His side and His blood ditched de train/He died for our sins" (*Jonah,* 181). In the consideration once again of Hurston's insulated South, this duality of the train might suggest a conveyance that goes nowhere. The entire later section of *Jonah* dealing with the northern migration of African Americans for jobs, which includes mock debates over the ultimate efficacy of the theories of Du Bois and Washington and the trustworthiness of Woodrow Wilson relative to that of Theodore Roosevelt, ends with a veiled derision for the Migration. It is also important to note that the entire section, as regards the entire novel's context, goes nowhere as well: it appears to have been added adventitiously by Hurston, in an effort to inveigh once more against the "promised land" of the North. If we return to the novel's beginning and John's first encounter with a train, we recall that he is met there by another Negro who, when asked where the train is going, answers laconically "with the intent to convey the impression to John that he knew so much about trains, their habits and destinations that it would be too tiresome to try to tell it all" (*Jonah,* 16). It is quite possible that John's interlocutor knew only as much as he, and certainly we as much as they, since no one is told where the train is from, or even where it is going.

If anything regarding *Jonah*'s train symbolism is comic, or ironic, as these elements tend sometimes to overlap, it is this scene, but again, as in *Seraph* and the notion of the joke as indicative of the movements through the text of the Meserves or the Kelseys, it is just this quality of doubleness, of dubiousness, that governs these tropological principles. Ideas of movement, and particularly of migration, are compromised again and again in *Jonah*. In John's second encounter with the train something of a warning is given against the indulgence of his wanderlust, thus reinforcing Hurston's felt uniqueness of her South: "Soon in the distance he heard the whistle . . . and around the bend came first the smoke stack, belching smoke and flames of fire. The drivers turning over chanting 'Opelika-black-and-dirty! Opelika-black-and-dirty.' Then as she pulled into the station, the powerful whisper of steam. 'Wolf coming! Wolf coming! Wolf coming! Opelika-black-and-dirty, Opelika-black-and-dirty! Auh—wah-hoooon'—into the great away that gave John's feet such a yearning for distance" (*Jonah,* 41). The train remains dragonlike, but here it also recalls the machinery of the cotton gin that John thought he saw when coming to Notasulga for the first time. Opelika, Alabama, seat of Lee County, is east and north of Notasulga, and at the eastern end of what was known as the Black Belt, called this not for its African American population, but for the wide expanse of rich, dark soil that girded the state, thus ensuring a perfect cotton crop. Its growing importance to the textile industry at the time of the writing of *Jonah* interestingly casts the town as one in transition, perhaps characterizing also the unease with which Hurston viewed Northern urban culture. The "wolf" is this urbanity in sinister blend with vestiges of slavery, giving the train an eerie ambiguity similar to that of Tom Burwell's fiery tomb, the old factory building of "Blood-Burning Moon." There as here, the body's dismemberment is effected between two industrial revolutions—or rather, as a result of both of them.

The train that kills John hits while John is driving his Cadillac, which is both a class-bound, mechanistic symbol of John's reestablishment in the community and a signifier of his wanderlust and sexual prowess (it is given to him by his third wife and is used for his final assignation). John's doubleness is itself the novel's cartography; like Jean Toomer's men, he is everywhere represented as a figure of duality that is indicative less of the socially remote double consciousness of Du Bois than it is of a more generalized, more fundamental doubleness that is powerfully indicative of pan-African tradition and represents itself also in flirtations with Manichean modernism. As a representative of Moses, whom Hurston would later characterize as "the original conjure-man," John was of the brotherhood of the "two-headed doctors" of Vodun, leading and controlling his congregation spiritually with the great gift of his voice. He was Kata-Kumba, "the drum with the man-skin" (*Jonah,* 29), the timbre of pan-African spirit and nation. As local spiritual leader of an African American congregation in the South, John occupies what had been since Reconstruction the only source of social and political power at all reasonably available to black men. Eric Foner describes the postbellum black church as having been "the first social institution fully controlled by black men in America"; it was from the pulpit that such matters as the adjudication of family disputes and sanctions against adultery had issued.[6] As powerful as his preaching is, however, he cannot overcome his unfitness in this area. A deep and infectious doubleness seizes John here: on one hand, there is his responsibility to the community, framed by the beauty of his great gift; on the other, his powerful and self-destructive sexual appetite. Rather than being Du Bois's scion of double consciousness, he is instead Hurston's "na'chel man." Lucy, after John's many betrayals, captures this doubleness in an opposition of language and action, the maintenance of which opposition marks his slow descent toward destruction. "Big talk ain't changin' whut you doin'," she says. "You can't lick yo'self wid yo' tongue lak uh cat" (*Jonah,* 128–29).

John has endured, though unconsciously, various kinds of doubleness. On the other side of the Songahatchee, he is in logical opposition to his stepfather Ned Crittenden, who has doomed himself to a fatal subservience and a love of whiteness for its own sake and also

6. Eric Foner, *Reconstruction: America's Unfinished Revolution: 1863–1877,* 92–93.

harbors a hatred of John because of his obvious mixed-race ancestry. This ancestry is of course the element of doubled beauty that gets John into trouble with women as well. With respect to the side of the creek where Lucy lives and where there is relative prosperity and opportunities for self-expansion, John is at first an outsider trying to fit in, and in this regard is as close as Hurston will allow to urbanization. John, upon having crossed the creek, "could see houses here and there among the fields—not miles apart like where he had come from" (*Jonah,* 13). But as preacher and as pillar of the community, John has for his wife transgressed utterly against the best of what he is, the spirit of Damballah, in that he has compromised for Lucy the sanctity of the home. For Carole Boyce Davies, "the mystified notions of home and family are removed from their romantic, idealized moorings, to speak of pain, difficulty, movement, learning and love in complex ways," suggesting of course that such demystification— such nefarious doubling—is ultimately engineered by men.[7] Immediately after Hurston renders a narrative taste of the best aspect of John's doubleness, his preaching—"he rolled his African drum up to the altar and called his Congo gods by Christian names. . . . so effectively that three converts came through religion under the sound of his voice" (*Jonah,* 89)—she unveils the scene in which Lucy, nursing their youngest child, and with little food to feed the others, tries to fend off her oldest brother Bud, who demands and eventually gets Lucy's and John's marriage bed as collateral for the three dollars he is owed. John's career at this point is a dark one indeed, for his lusts have taken precedence over the protection of his family. His bad conscience, even under better conditions, would have had him react with anger had he heard Walter Mosely's slur of John as "a wife-made man," because this element of doubleness—this crossing of his great gift with a woman's support—would have been seen by his masculine vanity as weakness and not as the ground at which gender difference metamorphoses into spiritual confluence. The power of the train to rectify John's duality through its own structural ambiguity, its own irony, is the power of Damballah to restore order by wresting the sanctity of voice from its corruption. Though John's death is in fact a classic deus ex machina ending in which God and

7. Carole Boyce Davies, *Black Women, Writing, and Identity: Migrations of the Spirit,* 21.

machine are conflated, it is difficult to read the train, as does Hemenway, merely as "a symbol of the white man's mechanized world,"
thus pointing to a portion of the narrative that does not seem to fit
neatly into the whole. But in consideration of the supernal conflict
between what John tragically unsays in his life as opposed to the
transformative and life-affirming power of what he says in the pulpit, we are aware that his death occurs not "by chance": a more trenchant reading of *Jonah* is captured in Hemenway's remark on John's
fateful, final meeting with the train: John is ultimately "doomed to
cultural collision rather than to self-understanding."[8]

This kind of duality appears not to reach into the heart of *Seraph
on the Suwanee,* since Joe Kelsey's transgression is not a transgression per se: he rather acts in situation with the stereotypical, and at
least part of this activity is a subversive feature of the text, as the
centrality of Jim Meserve's masculinity is arranged principally to be
interrogated. But for that part of Joe's tenure as Jim's pet Negro that
may have had its deleterious effects on Dessie, Joe must recompense
through, among other things, a sense of his own cultural uncon-
sciousness. It is Joe who teaches Jim's son Kenny not only how to
play the guitar but also how to render through it the cultural sensibilities of black musicianship. The blitheness of the appropriation by
whites of the blues is reflected in Jim's sense of the theft as being an
economic inevitability, a *telos:* "White bands up North and in different places like New Orleans are taking over darky music and making
more money at it than the darkies used to," he says. "Kenny claims
that it is just a matter of time when white artists will take it all over.
Getting so it's not considered just darky music and dancing now-
adays. It's American, and belongs to everybody. . . . He aims to be
the first one to make it something for the public, and he might be
right for all we know" (*Seraph,* 202). African American blues is
here recast from its formerly private and necessarily secret forms
and origins in slavery into a public, homogenized, American medium, which means the appropriation of specific ethnic forms of
expression (and they were this because they were engendered in
isolation) by a demand that is at once white and capitalist. Kenny's
appropriation is far less indicative of a hybridization of artistic forms
in an interdependent, multicultural milieu than it is an affirmation

8. Hemenway, *Hurston,* 200 (emphasis added).

that the potential success of the received form will accrue only to him. Intriguing too is Kenny as double here, for his trek to New York, a dubious northern "migration," is a cultural warp captured by Hurston as a theft, this time of the balm of pan-African cultural material; the urgency with which he phones his parents to tell them his decision to leave only moments before his train leaves is rendered ironically with the suddenness and the mystery of the escaping slave.

Pan-African religious and folkloric symbolism also suffers an appropriation by whiteness in the episode in which Jim seeks to prove to the phlegmatic Arvay his love for her. He chooses to wrestle a large water moccasin, the spectacle of which Jim wants Arvay to witness. Jim's struggle and eventual draw with the rattlesnake is doubly intended: Jim's response to Arvay's failure to help him with the snake becomes the catalyst for Arvay's journey toward self-realization; on the other hand, Jim's unbridled, arrogant sexism is recompensed by the snake's tearing away at the flesh on Jim's torso as it coils around his body. But Jim, after having escaped certain death, decides against killing the snake. "He's a gentleman who never picks a fight," Jim says of the snake, "and never is known to run from one that anybody picks with him. And till the day he dies, he is one general that never loses a battle. I like that kind of a heart. I tried him fair, and he was the best" (*Seraph,* 258). This is a decision that enjoins another irony: Jim's interlocutor is Jeff Kelsey—Joe Kelsey's son—who insists that because the snake came so close to killing Jim, "he's got to go way from this world" (*Seraph,* 257). But Jim is not merely romanticizing his battle with the snake. He acknowledges the superior power of Damballah and states as well that Hurston's snakes, for this reason, are not predatory. Jeff misses the importance of letting the snake live, however, and in doing so allows this time an oblique appropriation of pan-African religious sensibility by the white Jim Meserve. Jeff is possibly thus destined to follow the fates of the transgressors of the values of Damballah as he follows at least in sensibility the killer of the snake in *Jonah.* As a gesture of gratitude for having saved Jim's life, Jeff becomes Pet Negro Junior: in an ironic twist, Jim tells Jeff to take the rest of the day off, to "gwan home and get in the bed and make things tough for your wife" (*Seraph,* 257). This directive is startlingly similar to the advice given much earlier to Jim by Joe Kelsey on how to subdue Arvay. The failure for men to convey gentleness in giving physical love to women

(for this is not, after all, the language of real men) is now perpetu-
ated in *Seraph* with this irony, an irony that includes transvaluations
of race and culture: while appreciating and appropriating pan-African
values, Jim manages to return to a younger generation of African
American men precisely those corrosive ideals about love as taught
to him by a black man of his own generation. This is a fully realized
cultural fragmentation for African American men, cast into relief by
Hurston; the racialized and sexualized dead end previously fashioned for Joe Kelsey is now reconstituted for his son.

Hurston's fullest use of the retributive factor of pan-African religious symbolism is found in *Their Eyes*. The greatest irony in this
comes from the fact that many readers remain dismayed by the idea
that Hurston tacitly sanctions violence against women in this novel,
though it seems well settled, however, that Hurston has indeed not
allowed Tea Cake to escape accountability for having struck Janie. It
also appears discrepant that even though Jody dies, he is not seen to
have paid definitively for having beaten Janie, or for his ordinary
mistreatment of her for most of their marriage. Even Nanny, Janie's
beleaguered grandmother, dies shortly after striking Janie for the latter's refusal to marry Logan Killicks. It is not the case, however, that
Nanny answers to the Supernature as do Hurston's male characters.
In fact, she parallels in many ways Hurston's own maternal grandmother, who leaned so hard on young Zora for being the daughter of
the deeply disliked, light-complexioned John. This moment from Hurston's autobiography is configured in much the same way as Nanny's
discovery of Janie's kissing Johnny Taylor at the gate in *Their Eyes:*

> My grandmother worried about my forward ways a great deal.
> She had known slavery and to her my brazenness was unthink-
> able.
>
> "Git down offa dat gate-post! You li'l sow, you! Git down!
> Setting up dere looking dem white folks right in de face! They's
> goine to lynch you, yet. And don't stand in dat doorway gazing
> out at 'em neither. Youse too brazen to live long."
>
> Nevertheless, I kept right on gazing at them, and "going a
> piece of the way" whenever I could make it. The village seemed
> dull to me most of the time. If the village was singing a chorus,
> I must have missed the tune. (*DTR*, 46)

In the novel Janie is protected by Nanny, who because the other
black children tease Janie for her advantages, builds a house in the

backyard of the white Washburn family for whom she works. Though this may easily be seen as a poor woman's tender sacrifice, the larger remembrance of Hurston's grandmother in the character of Nanny is given to us as a belated complexity, as Janie relates to Pheoby in one of the returns to the novel's outer frame: "Ah done lived Grandma's way, now I means tuh live mine" (*Their Eyes,* 108). The episode in the novel is set in the larger theme of the shared pain of black women across the generations, as Nanny has performed the difficult task of raising two young black women, though not without her poignant intervention. Though Nanny dies a month after the altercation with Janie, this death nevertheless sets the stage for Hurston's own feelings about violence, for no one who strikes Janie leaves this novel alive.

Logan Killicks actually fares better than most anyone else who knew Janie intimately: though he at one point threatens even to kill her, she manages to leave him before he does express violence (if indeed he ever would), and thus exits the novel intact. But Logan's own death is spiritual, not physical, and for this variance, a physical demise might have been preferred. Logan, according to Nanny, is the possessor of "the onliest organ in town, amongst colored folks," in "a house bought and paid for and sixty acres uh land right on de big road . . ." (*Their Eyes,* 22). Logan is the expression of dead and deadening property; interestingly, no music is ever heard from the organ he owns, a silence that has its own bearing on the marriage bed. Moreover, he does not exemplify the leisure that would presumably emanate from such holdings, as after a hard day's work, he is unprepared to wash his feet even when Janie has set water for the purpose. Unsurprisingly, Nanny recommends Logan as a mate for Janie, since he represents a sense of security as wrapped in stasis. For most of a life marked by slavery, Nanny has never known black maleness as stability in nurturance. Love is frivolous and unreliable, and the only respectable black masculinity could be a masculinity-in-modernity, its counterpart in slavery never having been palpable. It is captured in feminine terms by Janie as she later remembers her grandmother, a woman for whom "sittin' on porches lak de white madam looked lak a mighty fine thing to her" (*Their Eyes,* 108). Sometime after the wedding, Nanny assures Janie that she need not be embarrassed if she is pregnant, because she is legally married "same as Mis' Washburn or anybody else" (*Their Eyes,* 21), which

determines the social function of marriage not through the imaginary of its fruitfulness, or even through its bare legality, but through
whiteness. Racism and bondage have of course severely limited the
vistas of human possibility for Nanny, but they have also done this
through the distorted lens of the black masculine, as even her emergence into freedom is as desolate as the retreat into property is to
Logan, whose home "was a lonesome place like a stump in the middle of the woods where nobody had ever been" (*Their Eyes,* 20).

Janie's utter dissatisfaction with her life with Logan leads her to
seek love and adventure with the thrilling Jody Starks. Jody is "a
cityfied, stylish dressed man with his hat set at an angle that didn't
belong in these parts. His coat was over his arm, but he didn't need
it to represent his clothes. The shirt with the silk sleeveholders was
dazzling enough for the world" (*Their Eyes,* 26). Jody thus features
many attractions to women, but emanating from him is the very first
sign of danger: "He was a seal-brown color but he acted like Mr.
Washburn or somebody like that to Janie. Where would such a man
be coming from and where would he be going?" In other words,
Jody's demeanor is strangely reminiscent of that of the white head of
the home in which she was raised if only because it is unusual that
black men can also display that demeanor. It is altogether unusual at
this period in history that black, dark men like Jody, in all his finery,
can simply be walking, particularly by themselves, down a Southern
road. Curiously absent from this scene as constructed by Hurston are
the local white sheriffs and their nominally deputized cohorts, who
would seize men in far less sartorial splendor than Jody on charges
of vagabondage for cheap labor on neighboring estates, or in some
cases even those far removed from the town or district of the arrest,
and the states of Alabama and Florida gained particular notoriety in
the late nineteenth century and during the first third of the twentieth
for abuses in the system that quite often meant the death of the ac-
cused.[9] Nevertheless, Jody, especially as compared to Logan, is a
pleasant apparition. Perhaps it is his dress, producing the corresponding silence in the text about what his fate could have been long before advancing toward Janie's gate, that indicates this. His ambition

9. Milfred C. Fierce, *Slavery Revisited: Blacks and the Southern Convict Lease
System, 1865–1933,* 82–88; Noel Gordon Carper, "The Convict-Lease System in
Florida, 1866–1923," 58–59; George Washington Cable, *The Silent South,* 84–96,
174–75.

and energy, qualities commendable in the notion of nation-building, are even seductive here: "He was glad he had his money all saved up. . . . He meant to buy in big. It had always been his wish and desire to be a big voice and he had to live nearly thirty years to find a chance" (*Their Eyes,* 27). This sense of masculine drive as carefully cultivated by Jody pervades his character and works to the same result as Logan's presence in the text. It expresses itself less in his aggressiveness in building Eatonville than in his use of his ascendancy to control others and to isolate himself, and Janie, from them. Jody's rise to power in Eatonville takes with it the suggestion that the acquisition of that power was inexorably the result of his having assumed a capitalist patriarchal role that is normally thought occupied only by white men. Even the black men of the town accept this model, as they grow skeptical of Jody's drive; meanwhile, Jody develops and projects an anticommunitarian spirit, a class consciousness that amplifies the imbricated discomfitures of race and gender:

> He bought a little lady-size spitting pot for Janie to spit in. . . . It sort of made the rest of them feel that they had been taken advantage of. Like things had been kept from them. Maybe more things in the world besides spitting pots had been hid from them when they wasn't told no better than to spit in tomato cans. It was bad enough for white people, but when one of your own color could be so different it put you on a wonder. It was like seeing your sister turn into a 'gator. A familiar strangeness. You keep seeing your sister in the 'gator and the 'gator in your sister, and you'd rather not. (*Their Eyes,* 45)

This description of Jody's developing consciousness of class is contrasted to our earlier introduction to him. Jody's risk then was heroic; his desire for a "big voice" is very like the actuality of John's in *Jonah.* Both have their potential for serving their communities in terms of rendering a beneficent stewardship. Jody's doubleness, however, is manifest with widening poles of alienation and familiarity, of "outsidedness" and "insidedness" as regards the rest of the town. His "familiar strangeness" is interestingly coded by whiteness, thus securing with race the veil of exclusivity whose design began with patterns of class. Jody's own annoyingly consistent epithet, "I god," speaks for itself in depicting his awareness of his power; while it is expressed as a note of exasperation toward the frustrating slowness of his fellow townspeople, it is also *in this same effect* his discursive formation of his sense of masculine control. It is by contrast tempting to think of Hurston's dismantling of Jody's despotism in the use of the simile of the sister and the alligator: Jody has become the principal beast in his own "class menagerie," but the use of the envelope *sister* first powerfully undercuts Jody's sham masculinity in this instance.

Janie's emergence from this difficulty is effected through the forces of nature. Though the marriage bed of Janie and Jody has been violated by neither party, Jody's ego has been assaulted by Janie's ever-expanding voice. His beatings of Janie find their cumulative effect in the slap he gives her after her final retort: "Humph! Talkin' 'bout *me* lookin' old! When you pull down yo' britches, you look lak de change uh life" (75). From this point, Jody's slow deterioration is immediate: "A little sack hung from the corners of his eyes and rested on his cheek-bones; a loose-filled bag of feathers hung from his ears and rested on his neck beneath his chin. A sack of flabby something hung from his loins and rested on his thighs when he sat down. But even these things were running down like candle grease as time moved on" (77). The ensuing kidney disease Jody contracts is also the metaphor for his impotence. By "winning" at the dozens in quite the way she has, Janie has effectively shouted Jody's penis into quiescence: as if the shadow of Damballah had descended, she has, in no uncertain terms, "killed the snake." This death enjoins a revelation, as the descent of Jody's phallus is followed by Janie's uncovering and unwrapping the bountiful head of hair she had tied up at his behest, a metaphor for the female voice long checked and held in abeyance by a fractured yet uncompromising male hegemony.

Tea Cake, however, does become Janie's spiritual savior as he shares his life with her in the Florida Everglades. He is even reminiscent of a more pleasurable part of Janie's past: the tall, thin man who walks into the shop recalls Johnny Taylor, the young man whose kiss over the gate sends Janie into a reverie identifying love with all nature, and Nanny into her repressive tirade that leads to Janie's unwanted union with Logan Killicks. Tea Cake represents inclusion and recognition as well as he does heightened adolescent sexuality: "Somebody wanted her to play. Somebody thought it natural for her to play. That was even nice" (*Their Eyes,* 91–92). This begins Janie's return to the Garden of Eden, now fulfilled in the freer, more communal

life of the Everglades; Tea Cake's easy, generous manner inspires
Janie's return to herself and makes possible her discovery of a world
that accepts her. Even Tea Cake's style of wooing is different and
exciting: he tells Janie that she is beautiful, but instead of merely
objectifying her beauty for himself, he instead challenges her to ap-
praise it through the lens of her own ego, the mirror. Tea Cake thus
engages a Lacanian construct that proves empowering for Janie:

> Umph! umph! umph! Ah betcha you don't never go tuh de
> lookin' glass and enjoy yo' eyes yo'self. You lets other folks git
> all de enjoyment out of 'em thout takin' in any of it yo'self.
>   Naw, Ah never gazes at 'em in de lookin' glass. If anybody
> else gits any pleasure out of 'em Ah ain't been told about it.
>   See dat? You'se got de world in uh jug and make out you
> don't know it. But Ah'm glad tuh be de one tuh tell yuh. (*Their
> Eyes,* 99)

But Tea Cake proves himself to be imperfect in a number of ways.
When he stays out all night and cavalierly spends Janie's money, his
sense of his own poverty has become greater than that of his integrity. Here, cash represents his sense of worth: "When he found
out how much it was, he was excited and felt like letting folks know
who he was" (*Their Eyes,* 117). The party he orchestrates with the
money is one to which he would not invite Janie; he tells her that he
is afraid that he will lose her if he risks taking her among "railroad
hands and dey womenfolks." "Tain't my notion tuh drag *you* down
wid me," he says. The legitimacy of his reasoning is tainted, first by
the fact that he has "lowered" himself with *her* money, and second,
by his assumption of a higher station accorded her because her skin
is fair. It is paradoxically his sense of her worth that lifts him up,
making him, in his mind, more man than the man he is. Even after
Janie reassures him that she claims no station for herself and wants
only to share the life that shames him, he demonstrates instead that
he can be merely a possessor of property, namely Janie herself ("From
now on you'se mah wife and mah woman and everything else in the
world Ah needs" [*Their Eyes,* 119]), and that he can risk his life
through gambling (a manly adventure existing on the periphery of
every class stratum) to maintain his possession: "Ah no need no assistance tuh help me feed mah woman. From now on, you gointuh
eat whutever mah money can buy yuh and wear de same. When Ah

ain't got nothin' you don't git nothin'" (*Their Eyes,* 122). That Janie acquiesces to all of this may in fact reveal *her* fragmentation, for after her tenure as the wife of Mayor Joe Starks, she is unable to realize that Tea Cake's descent to the thrill of life at the lower depths is as dangerous and as debilitating as was her apotheosis.

The material basis for Hurston's determinations against violence between the sexes is probably her tempestuous relationship with her ultimately nameless Caribbean lover, which precipitated the writing of *Their Eyes:*

> He was a *man!* No woman on earth could either lend him or give him a cent. If a man could not do for a woman, what good was he on earth? His great desire was to do for me. *Please* let him be a *man!*
> For a minute I was hurt and then I saw his point. . . . [H]e wanted to do all the doing, and keep me on the receiving end. He soared in my respect from that moment on.

> One night (I didn't decide this) something primitive inside me tore past the barriers and before I realized it I had slapped his face. That was a mistake. He was still smoldering from an incident a week old. A fellow had met us on Seventh Avenue and kissed me on my cheek. . . . So I had unknowingly given him an opening he had been praying for. He paid me off then and there with interest. No broken bones, you understand, and no black eyes. I realized afterwards that my hot head could tell me to beat him, but it would cost me something. I would have to bring head to get head. I couldn't get his and leave mine locked up in the dresser-drawer.
> Then I knew I was too deeply in love to be my old self. For always a blow to my body had infuriated me beyond measure. Even with my parents, that was true. But somehow, I didn't hate him at all. (*DTR,* 253, 257; original emphasis)

Zora's impatience with being struck, even by her parents, carries with it curiously racialized and gendered stigmata in that Zora's father, the doctrinaire John Hurston, had a fair complexion; there was as well the influence of Zora's maternal grandmother mentioned above, who hated John for his fair features and who herself took delight in punishing Zora, especially when Lucy would not.[10] A curious play

---

10. Hemenway, *Hurston,* 72.

among the elements of maleness, femaleness, power, and physicality seems to emerge here. Zora Hurston as we know her—writer, intellectual, feminist—would not only refuse to back down from a fight but also would hardly return, it would seem, to a relationship in which she had experienced violence. But this single experience, as in the excerpted portion above, appears somehow denuded of every sense of an imbalance of power, as in ordinary descriptions of gendered abuse; both combatants, wounded both psychically and elsewhere, like survivors in life's common contests, are probably evenly matched. This is the only way in which the Hurston we know remains palpable. The respect she gives to him after acceding to his impulse to give as she receives really comes after a granting of a request; it is a benevolence *she* bestows, as she allows him to maintain a masculine veneer, the only protection he knows. It would thus seem that violence, as a medium of human exchange, is a carefully maintained issue in Hurston's writing. The entirety of chapter 15 of *Their Eyes* is devoted to Janie's jealousy over Nunkie, a younger woman who ostensibly devises ruses to be close to Tea Cake. Janie's anger is directed toward Tea Cake (possibly conveniently, since Nunkie has run away), and it is an anger not manifest in the ineffectual flailings of wronged, hysterical women one might remember in Hollywood B-movies. As discussed in the previous chapter, Hurston would later seek to undermine fixed race and gender ideologies in even this medium in writing *Seraph*. Janie clearly intends to do damage, however, for they "fought from one room to another . . . and Tea Cake kept holding her wrists and wherever he could to keep her from going too far" (*Their Eyes,* 131). But because Janie's violence is generated from love, she is not bound to the laws of retribution.

In both *Jonah* and *Their Eyes,* violence occurs to form turning points in the novels when both John Pearson and Jody Starks have reached the zeniths of their success. Hurston's men thus follow a continuum of benevolence and abuse, which, while familiar behavior, serves as a paradigm for the erosion of values suffered by Toomer's men on their trek north. If even an incremental Northernness is a metaphor for spiritual corruption, then it should be remembered that Jody's trek to Eatonville began in Georgia; John, corrupted by women and power in *Jonah,* hails from Notasulga, which is north and west of the Eatonville that he helps to develop. Tea Cake, on the other hand, the best of Janie's three husbands, is from Orlando—well south of Janie's Eatonville home. Janie's first meeting with Tea Cake, however, is the result of misdirection, as the ball game attended by everyone in town that day is in Winter Park, which is just southeast of Eatonville. Tea Cake is thus only "north of south," and technically lost. For all of his goodwill, then, he was perhaps better situated with crowds and raucous fun in Winter Park than in the rarefied space he shared with Janie, who was quickly gaining wisdom.[11]

The fair-skinned Turner family, a radical reflection of the Washburns with whom Janie lived as a child, seeks to have Janie "class off" from the others living on the swamp. Tea Cake, in retaliation born of wounded racial and masculine pride against the Turners, beats Janie to mark his dominion. It is this beating that falls under sanction, for it is generated by anger that itself is derived of Tea Cake's persistent class consciousness. This beating and the reasons for it of course set into motion a chain of events that lead to Tea Cake's killing by Janie in self-defense, but the fact of the beating has created a silence about its existence in the text among many feminist critics, though some have focused upon Janie's apparent balancing of the scales through the shooting. For example, Alice Walker finds that "an astute reader would realize that this is the real reason" Hurston has allowed Janie to kill Tea Cake: because Janie has been humiliated by the whipping her husband gives her, and seeks to vindicate herself through his death.[12] Hurston writes that Tea Cake hits Janie "not because her behavior justified his jealousy, but it relieved that awful fear inside him. Being able to whip her reassured him in possession. No brutal beating at all. He just slapped her around a bit to show he was boss. Everybody talked about it next day in the fields. It aroused a sort of envy in both men and women. The way he petted and pampered her as if those two or three face slaps had nearly killed her made the women see visions and the helpless way she hung on him made men dream dreams" (*Their Eyes,* 140).

Though there is much to consider in Walker's reading of the episode, there is no indication in the text that Janie had any such perspective on the assault. Walker's "astute reader" must indeed take great pains to make any assessment other than that which suggests

11. See *DTR,* 22–23, where the women in Hurston's family seem fully capable of holding their own.
12. Alice Walker, *In Search of Our Mothers' Gardens,* 305–6.

that Janie responds to the beating in much the way the community does, and that their "visions" and "dreams" are significantly representative of community acceptance of generalized violence against women (which includes even the *victim's* acceptance of it).[13] This is a reading that seems to lend more to Walker's point about battering, for it also speaks to the fragmentation of the values of an entire community—and Hurston had already set the matter of misogynist violence within the context of the unaware or even uncaring community in the early short story "Sweat." With as much as has been written about Hurston's steadfast allegiance to community, some mention might again be made of Hurston's not-infrequent positioning of community *away* from the immediate concerns of the developing voice/ the voice in peril. Despite abundant evidence of her insistence upon the sanctity of the community, even unto the erection of ideational borders on its behalf in "Characteristics of Negro Expression," Hurston sometimes deploys a politics of distance for the black female presence. Perhaps one notable episode of this kind in *Their Eyes* involves Mrs. Carter's flirtation with Jody for the sake of extra meat, on the basis that her husband doesn't feed her. This has become a quite ordinary joke in town that depends on elements of power and helplessness, but it fuels Janie's ire against anyone who would speak on behalf of these sexist elements and perpetuate them as part of the lore of the community. This unstable narrative relationship that Hurston seems to have with her community may stem from the refusal, against the young Zora's insistence, of neighbors and relatives to honor her mother Lucy's wish not to engage aspects of traditional folk ritual at the moment of her death. "I was to agonize over that moment for years to come," she writes of the incident. "In the midst of play, in wakeful moments after midnight, on the way home from parties, and even in the classroom during lectures. My thoughts would escape occasionally from their confines and stare me down" (*DTR,* 88). Nothing in these passages is conclusive in Lucy's death having fashioned a deeper inner consciousness to be reconciled with an outer, but in several episodes throughout Hurston's fiction women who hear the voice of fear within are elsewhere discussed and ultimately ignored by neighbors. Additionally, some of the more nettlesome episodes in her ethnographic work—for example, the class disparities with the residents of the sawmill camp she has to mediate

13. Barbara Christian, *Black Women Novelists,* 60.

in *Mules and Men,* and the disdain she displays for Haitians that dissolves into pettiness in some instances, a virulent nativism in others in *Tell My Horse*—reveal a discomfiture, an unreconciled striving against other communities that creates its own problems regarding principles of objectivity in anthropological study. Though Hurston makes many happy and fruitful connections in community settings, there are also frequent, definitive, and recognizable disjunctures in these relationships. If the passages from *Dust Tracks* quoted previously are a useful measure, they resemble the incommensurability of distance in Toomer's identifications with women toward symbolic wholeness that appeared to begin with the imperiled health of his mother, Nina. The remaining parent in each case is the opaque or absent father, who seems from this perspective to drive the considerations of gender that work in the authors' texts.

The relationship of the community to the individual continues to oscillate with perilous consequences, particularly for Tea Cake. Between the elements of class to which he succumbs and the feverish bestiality to which he descends lies the irony of Tea Cake's wisdom, a device he ordinarily uses for thwarting the sting of Mrs. Turner's idiocy. There is an inherent morality and even a kind of folk gentility that crystallizes around the remark he makes to her: "Aw, don't make God look so foolish—findin' fault with everything He made" (*Their Eyes,* 139), and it is in moments like these that Tea Cake is able to transcend dangerous categories of class consciousness. But Hurston's informing us that the season has begun to change, signaling the onrushing return of the community—that "the sun was cooler and the crowds came pouring onto the muck again"—reveals once again Tea Cake's desire to possess, to "show people who he is." In whipping Janie, he makes this show to his fellows, but he has also made himself tragically and unheroically vulnerable to whiteness, thus ironically contrasting Jody's heroic vulnerability to it at his entrance in the novel.

In these last fateful chapters Hurston focuses upon the forces of nature and the ways in which they effect their power against one who himself, at least initially, was in the novel the man most in harmony with nature and thus the man best suited for the woman who closely personified that nature. Truly it is no accident that Hurston calls Tea Cake's idea to whip Janie a "brainstorm" (*Their Eyes,* 140); such a term provides its own ironic turn toward not only the feverish storm that later whips into his mind, forcing Janie to choose between her

life and his, but also the hurricane itself, the manifestation of the
Supernature whose power is interpreted through the extratextual life
given it by the further descriptions of the Voudou pantheon in *Tell
My Horse.* Damballah's malevolent counterpart in other Voudou cults
derives from a long list of spirits who have the same names as the
Rada gods, but they also have a second name—*ge-rouge,* meaning
"red-eyed." Damballah Ge-rouge, then, is potentially good, but he is
also potentially evil or dangerous. One of the sacrificial animals of
one Voudou sect, the powerful Petro Quita Moudong, is the dog
(*TMH,* 164–67); these elements take their places in the last portion
of *Their Eyes,* emerging from entropy with shadows of Judeo-Christian
myth. As the hurricane whips to greater fury, Tea Cake, beyond being
Janie's savior, emerges for one last time as a Moses-figure. He manages to save a man who is caught between a swinging sheet of tin
roofing and a rattlesnake that has lengthened its body against the
wind. The snake, of course, is as stiff as the staff of Moses; by telling
the man that the snake will not bite because it is afraid of being
blown away, Tea Cake reenters the text as a deliverer, and in a small
yet crucial way, as a conjure man. It is the unregenerate part of Tea
Cake's nature that makes him act *against* nature, and forces the hand
of countervailing powers. The rabid dog riding on the back of the
cow is an ironic, sinister inversion of Christ's ride into Jerusalem.
The dog is thus also, provocatively and parodically, the "cow-
catcher," the extension of the locomotive that destroys John in *Jonah*
as well as it pierces Christ's side in the Lovelace sermon there, thus
perhaps emphasizing the best of what both John and Tea Cake *could*
have been; as for Christ as well as for these, it emphasizes the co-
nundrum of being both human and divine.

At the moment the dog bites Tea Cake high on the face, a different
tropological play is effected. It was Tea Cake who struck Janie's face,
thus the precision of the retribution—but more than this is what
Hurston is doing in appropriating the idea of the pan-African mask.
She visits the mask as a sign of the changing same, that movable
quality of the self that is foregrounded and backgrounded as situations warrant. Houston Baker, who earlier described the mask as a
"repository" of the black spirit, here extends his discussion of the
trope of the mask. The mask of the white minstrel as a weapon against
black subjectivity—that is, the fact of burnt cork itself as painted on
the face—is also for Baker "the space of habitation . . . for the deep-
seated denial of the humanity of inhabitants of and descendants

from the continent of Africa."[14] Tea Cake engaged in this denial of humanity when he struck Janie, perversely courting whiteness to reaffirm an illegitimately masculine blackness, when he "just slapped her around a bit to show he was boss"—when he felt he needed to court the footlights, and play the role. As this mode of violence reasserts difference that is gender- as well as class- and even race-oriented, it also reenacts the trauma of slavery in the theft and inhumane possession of the black body. In Tea Cake, who held such bright promise for Janie at our introduction to him, Hurston renders also in this trickster-as-bluesman her warning against the insidiousness of hegemony. Despite his attractiveness, Tea Cake is nevertheless determined by those other seductions that have plagued the African in his whole time in the West. In this connection, Tea Cake's "mask" is disfigured in retribution, just as Sykes's facial disfiguration in "Sweat" is effected by the snake meant to kill Delia for the misvaluation of self that underwrites injustice. It is therefore arguable that the scene in which Janie shoots Tea Cake, except for its acute dramatic pitch, is superfluous, for Tea Cake, at the moment of the bite, is really already dead. Both Janie and Tea Cake are only dimly aware of the expressed power of the Supernature, as reference is made, if not specifically to the *ge-rouge,* then to some other quality in its eyes. As Janie says to Tea Cake after the storm: "You was twice noble to save me from dat dawg. Tea Cake, Ah don't speck you seen his eyes lak Ah did. He didn't aim tuh jus' bite me, Tea Cake. He aimed tuh kill me stone dead. Ah'm never tuh fuhgit them eyes. He wuzn't nothin' all over but pure hate. Wonder where he come from?" "Yeah, Ah did see 'im too," Tea Cake replies. "It wuz frightenin'. Ah didn't mean tuh take his hate neither. He had tuh die uh me one" (*Their Eyes,* 158). At this point, the feral eyes of the dog are opposed to Janie's eyes, in whose beauty Tea Cake once reveled and which he once revealed to her. He misses the irony in once having the pleasure of eyes that gave pleasure; here, in the face of retribution, the eyes represent the hate that Tea Cake refuses, the hate that was also implicit in his errant effort to reassert himself, and the hate that he is soon completely to become. Similarly, the locomotive that John Pearson meets for the first time in *Jonah* possesses proleptically a "great eye beneath the cloud-breathing smoke-stack" that "glared and threatened" (*Jonah,* 16).

14. See chap. 3, note 12.

Janie's perspective of her murder trial has little to do with what the juridical can do in deciding her fate, for despite Tea Cake's ultimately fallen nature, her bond to him renders something of the communitarian spirit that holds a crucial lesson for all those present, black or white, who would judge her. "She was in the courthouse fighting something and it wasn't death," Hurston writes. "It was worse than that. It was lying thoughts. She had to go way back to let them know how she and Tea Cake had been with one another so they could see she could never shoot Tea Cake out of malice" (*Their Eyes,* 178). But an array of ironies surround Janie's acquittal: even though her freedom is the only just course, it is an overdetermination of Southern justice that juries are white, and given the ordinary valuation of black men's lives by them, it seems not at all unusual that an all-white, all-male jury would find a black woman innocent in the death of a black man. Another silence in the text is manifest in that her freedom, her widowhood, and her relative wealth add to her attractiveness and suggest sexual possibilities, however obliquely, for the members of her jury. The phalanx of white women appears to know this; they crowd around Janie after the verdict and are sympathetic and protective of her, as the black community, "with heads hung down, shuffled out and away" (178). But the black community was the one from which nurturance was somehow expected. It was this community that should have come to both Janie's and Tea Cake's deliverance by not condoning Janie's whipping. Forever suspended is the community's understanding of the flaws in Tea Cake's earnest expression of black manhood, and thus any possibility for its mediating them. The irony doubles upon itself, however, when we consider that given these common determinations about maleness, the local black community, in large measure, could not avoid coming to many of the same conclusions about black life as did Tea Cake; it could not avoid being shaped by their forces as was he. It was probably impossible, then, for the community ever to help Tea Cake— and itself—in this dilemma of a shared fragmentation, and probably impossible for it ever to understand the tragic and supernal irony he uttered to Janie at the instant of the dog's bite, at the moment the Supernature had completed its task: "You don't have tuh say, if it wuzn't fuh me, baby, cause Ah'm *heah,* and then I want yuh tuh know it's uh man heah" (*Their Eyes,* 159).

6

PROMISED LANDS

The New Jerusalem's Inner City and
John Edgar Wideman's Philadelphia Story

All black men have a Philadelphia. Even if you escape it,
you leave something behind. Part of you. A brother
trapped there forever.

—John Edgar Wideman, *Reuben*

In his biography of Hurston, Robert Hemenway examines one of the
chief conundra in her autobiography, *Dust Tracks on a Road*. Calling attention to Hurston's early New York years, when she studied
anthropology at Barnard College under Ruth Benedict and Franz
Boas and gained her first successes as a writer, Hemenway notes
her silence in *Dust Tracks* on this period: "She is searching for an
appropriate voice for the post-Eatonville Zora Neale Hurston."
That Hurston does not discuss the post-Eatonville years fully—the
racism she must have suffered at Barnard and in other venues of
this new urban existence—is testamentary not only to her individual complexity but also, among other things, to a politics of pride,
a total refusal to enroll in "the sobbing school of Negrohood."
Francoise Lionnet-McCumber comes to Hurston's defense by calling *Dust Tracks* an "autoethnography," that is, "the process of defining one's subjective ethnicity as mediated through language,
history and ethnographical analysis," whose "an-archic" style "is
not anchored in any original and originating story of racial and

sexual difference."[1] These positions represent the wide poles of opinion on Hurston's view of her post-Eatonville success in the North. There seems ample room for all similarly competing claims, for while they of course contribute broadly to Hurston's own complexity as a narrator of human experience, they also share a perspective on what she herself must have encountered in this new milieu. Advantages of social access to which she was attracted were deceptively woven with the coruscating racism that she was challenged to defy. While this may yet appear to be an oversimplification of both Hurston and black urban life, it is still not without its own reflection on her relative silence about that life in her autobiography, or its virtual omission in her novels. While enjoying the exploration of New York in the 1920s, this feisty, intellectually curious black woman experienced to the fullest the hostility of environs that welcomed none of these characteristics. She saw in the city's shining Northernness a dangerous duplicity, and reflected her uneasy triumph over it in such representations as the $12.74 Macy's dress and new Chevrolet she strove to transcend to gain acceptance in the Florida sawmill camp whose folk she returned to in *Mules and Men.* In few other places do we see the urban Hurston, however, as she contributes with her silence to the mixed history of the city in African American writing.

To Paul Laurence Dunbar and Nella Larsen, the city was a venue of loathing and despair, and the locus of truly dangerous effects. The family of Berry Hamilton, the loyal black servant in Dunbar's 1902 novel *The Sport of the Gods,* was first seared by Southern racism and then exquisitely devoured by the great maw of New York. Helga Crane in Larsen's *Quicksand* (1928) could never anchor herself safely in any city in either the United States or Europe. The grayness of Chicago or New York or Copenhagen is replicated in Anne Grey's and Robert Anderson's eyes, and the eyes of all of the other malevolent or misguided mixed-race personae who surround her. In Wallace Thurman's *The Blacker the Berry* (1929), Emma Lou Harris runs from Los Angeles to Harlem to prove that dark skin is not a curse, only to have her fear made real once again. And as is again the case in *Quicksand,* psychoracial confusion is the subject within the context of the city in the entire second section of *Cane.* Small wonder, then,

---

1. Hemenway, *Hurston,* 283; Francoise Lionnet-McCumber, "Autoethnography: The An-Archic Style of *Dust Tracks on a Road,*" 242–43.

that Hurston's characters never leave the South. While Toomer's characters—particularly his male characters—do leave, they take with them their psychic disconnection from the feminine whose healing even then could possibly have allowed new political and social possibilities. These two large elements—regional and/or social insularity and psychosexual disaffiliation—play a significant part in the literature of African American manhood even through the watershed "school" of Richard Wright, but new strategies for the reduction of these appear well after the last wave of the Migration. They arrive in a new venue, the arena of the postmodern city, where the black text, the written record of opposition, supplements and expands Paul Johnson's effete plaint, Tea Cake Woods's seductive blues refrains, and Tom Burwell's final, flame-enveloped scream.

As Charles Scruggs makes clear, in among several of Du Bois's works, but most prominently in *The Philadelphia Negro* (1899), it was the civilized and civilizing activity formed by the black elite that would provide the "centre" around which urban black life would successfully coalesce. For Du Bois, the lifeblood of this center of black urban success—its chief organizing principle—is the university, the source of ideas and the articulation of challenges for the forging of human leadership. It is therefore the exclusive training ground of the talented elite, but much more is at stake in Du Boisian thinking here than class consciousness and class exclusion. The hope of the city and its seat of learning is to eradicate racism and create civilization. Not only the Northern city but also the Southern city should be so equipped: as his dialectic with Washingtonianism continues in *The Souls of Black Folk,* the future of American civilization remains uncertain while the Southern Negro's access to education remains thwarted. For James Weldon Johnson, the acquisition of culture had meant a relative yet crucial freedom in the context of his own life; he felt the most fortunate circumstance of his entire life to have been "reared free from undue fear or esteem for white people as a race; otherwise, the deeper implications of American race prejudice might have become a part of my subconscious as well as of my conscious self" (*Along,* 78). Though often conveyed with a sense of "divine right," there is more than a smarmy elitism being produced by these black men of privilege. What is revealed beneath this is a variation of perspective, a peek from behind the Du Boisian veil, a way of knowing fashioned by cultural oppression. Within this ethos is grounded as well a culturally designed sense of manhood, constructed not because it is vacated by the ethos of the white masculine but because it inexorably accompanies the feeling that imagining progress without it is unthinkable. Johnson's assumption of learning at Atlanta University was one that imbued him with a value of manhood in the Victorian sense, rendering to him the fount of world culture.[2] For Du Bois at Harvard, the citadel of citadels, psychosocial opposition on the grounds of an embattled manhood seemed never to end. His tireless, finely intellectualized sense of outrage, as David Levering Lewis ascertains, "must have been regarded by him as the only face worthy of being presented to a white society whose philanthropy was at best incidental and capricious, and at worst serving increasingly to segregate and emasculate his race" (*Biography*, 98).

The men of the black elite thus appeared to feel their oppression with a heightened awareness of their own masculinity, a feeling that such consciousness necessarily insulated them from racial epiphenomena, though Anna Julia Cooper had earlier regarded their conservatism as having been manipulated by white male hegemony and thus unsupportive of progressive black feminism. In what seems an about-face and a keen awareness of Cooper's critique, Kautilya, the Princess of Bwodpur in Du Bois's *Dark Princess* (1928) appears to be a self-directed, intelligent and intrepid young woman, fully prepared for social engagement and political change with her lover Matthew, but she is in fact surrounded by a retinue of male protectors who know what is better for her, and she exists for most of the rest of the novel as a vessel for his seed, which becomes the hope of a multiracial, intersubjective humankind. Johnson's introspective Ex-Coloured Man finds no safe niche in New York, the modernist City of Exiles; he is prey to ambiguities and tergiversations of many kinds, including the homoeroticism of his relationship with his millionaire patron, as suggested in the text. The Ex-Coloured Man inexplicably avoids the university, which, presumably, would have "set him straight"; in his relationship with the patron, the stylized, urbanized sexual tableau that is inserted into the breach of sensibility he has developed metaphorizes the bondage and feminization of the black

2. Charles Scruggs, *Sweet Home: Invisible Cities in the Afro-American Novel*, 21; Eugene Levy, *James Weldon Johnson: Black Leader, Black Voice*, 28–29.

male as it reinvokes the theme of subordination. After Toomer's and Hurston's excursions into the realm of the black masculine, there would be few portrayals of black maleness that emphasized inter-subjective possibilities for them by allowing critiques of the sexual and societal pressures upon them without the usual props of other exclusionary behaviors. Naturalism, as the dominant form of liter-ary expression in American writing after about 1940, left little room for male characters, black or white, to combat systematic racial and class oppression through alterity and, as an element of that alterity, principled associations with women. If the metropolis as symbol of capitalism had failed man the agent of nature, then particularly in defense of his generations to follow, he was impelled to meet this foe with an unwavering, masculine force, while the recipe for such force usually included women's subordination. Anxieties about the fear of the success of the Depression's direct attack against masculinity were not only in literature but also everywhere in popular culture, and be-came one of the most enduring features of modernity.[3]

As Brian McHale notes, the postmodern novel's ontological struc-ture seeks to intend a world rather than to disclose it, and nearly any world that could be imagined was preferable to the one available. Postmodernity as a feature of the novel was at least capable of re-lieving the literary realism of the androcentric Black Consciousness movement from the feminist backlash of the late 1960s as it de-manded of black male writers new perspectives in which to frame masculinity; by atomizing the valuations and binaries of modernity, masculinity was thus able to embrace an alterity and a critique of the masculine self that made manhood as an ethos far more semiperme-able, far more inferential than referential. The examples of two of John Edgar Wideman's later works, *Reuben* (1987) and *Philadelphia Fire* (1990), make such deft critiques of the sexual divide and seek to invert the relation of the black masculine to the *topos* of the city on the hill. Though most of his novels and stories are set in Pitts-burgh, the city of his young adulthood, these novels have their psychic center in Philadelphia, where Wideman studied, taught, and coached athletics, a city whose black population since the publication of *The Philadelphia Negro* has been chronically unable to organize itself

3. Anna Julia Cooper, *A Voice from the South,* 134–40; Michael Kimmel, *Man-hood in America: A Cultural History,* chaps. 6–7.

politically.[4] The combined effect of the twin critiques of gendered disconnections and the New Jerusalem is the effort of postmodernity in these works, a project allowing the reclamation of people and politics. While his earlier works, particularly the Homewood trilogy— *Damballah* (1981), *Hiding Place* (1981), and *Sent For You Yesterday* (1983)—discuss the means to appreciating black male differences at various points, both *Reuben* and *Philadelphia Fire* appear to have their most sustained critiques not only of the city versus the black masculine but also of the black masculine itself.

Reuben purports to be a lawyer, trained at the University of Pennsylvania, who has returned to Wideman's mythical Homewood neighborhood to ply his trade. His training, however, has mostly been at the keyhole of the dorm rooms of white law school fraternity boys, the same boys who later humiliate him and kill his lover, the prostitute Flora. His client base is not that of the talented elite, but rather Homewood's poor, black population, Philadelphia's most easily victimized segment; they are, as he later tells his friend Wally, "a better class of people . . . our people . . . the best" (*Reuben,* 197). He is something of a savior to this community, as its members take their cases to him and have them solved; he has acquired a magical, oracular significance to the neighborhood, for it appears that he has always been there, in an old trailer that sits in a vacant lot. His ability to get results for community members in difficulty with the law is legendary, and he charges next to nothing for his services. Though he is fit to represent the vocational ideal of the talented Negro of the beginning of the century, he lacks what would have been his ideal physical characteristics. Except for the Vandyke beard he wears (which suggests a Du Boisian bearing), Reuben, small and hunchbacked, recalls the early-twentieth-century essayist and reformist Randolph Bourne, who is perhaps best known for his writing first for Herbert Croly's and Walter Lippmann's then-fledgling *New Republic,* and then for the short-lived journal the *Seven Arts,* inveighing throughout against America's role in World War I risking mentors, associates, and friends; he was also an early member of "Young America," that cadre of writers and intellectuals of which Jean Toomer

4. Brian McHale, *Postmodernist Fiction,* 9–11; Miriam Ershkowitz and Joseph Zikmund, eds., *Black Politics in Philadelphia,* 84–144.

was a part. In an article published in the *Atlantic Monthly* in 1911, Bourne dramatically outlines his particular phase of difference, writing of his inescapable sensitivity toward "the inevitable way that people . . . have of discounting in advance what one does or says. The deformed man is always conscious that the world does not expect very much from him."[5] The application of Bourne's remark to blackness or to any other marginalized difference is of moment here, particularly for Reuben, as both his blackness and deformity make their separate claims upon his place in the world. But there is a savvy, a feisty resilience that both men share; as was the case in the presence of the misshapen but redoubtable Bourne, one was careful in speaking to Reuben; there were always "certain words you didn't want to say, certain lines you didn't want to cross" (*Reuben,* 1).

At the time of his death, Bourne had left unfinished his searing indictment of government and war, *The State.* Government, to Bourne, is "the idea of the State put into practical operation in the hands of definite, concrete, fallible men. It is the visible sign of the invisible grace . . . the word made flesh. And it has necessarily the limitations inherent in all practicality. Government is the only form in which we can envision the State, but it is by no means identical with it." The "state" in *Reuben* is the web of the Pennsylvania legal bureaucracy and its laws that ensnare Homewood's black folk; the instant case involves Kwansa, a single mother whose drug addiction and former lover have conspired to take her baby boy Cudjoe (whose name is the same as that of the adult protagonist in *Philadelphia Fire).*[6] Refusing his social heritage as a member of the talented elite, Reuben nevertheless retains some of its trappings; to retain a professional demeanor, he wears a jacket and tie in a blistering summer heat made all the more intense in his small, stifling trailer. The lore of the community paints Reuben as surreptitiously wealthy, and thus either unwilling or too crazy or too wily to spend his money; in short, they have consigned him to a world of his own. But in that world Reuben is engaged in a form of intellectual resistance, an activity that seeks to complete his already deep inversion of the notion of the talented elite and its locus of possibility as the city on the hill.

5. Randolph Bourne, "The Handicapped—By One of Them," 321.
6. Bourne, *The State,* 1; Bonnie TuSmith, ed., *Conversations with John Edgar Wideman,* 166–67.

Chief among Reuben's passions are a series of photographs by nineteenth-century British photographer Eadweard Muybridge, taken under the auspices of the University of Pennsylvania. The series, entitled *Animal Motion* (1887), featured subjects both clothed and naked, depicting graphic studies of human movement for the uses of artists and scientists. Reuben's fascination is with the photographs' ability to show a grace and beauty he contrasts with his own broken body, and through them he reasons his own exclusion from a bodily humanity: "All pictures in the book are black-and-white, since they predate the technology of color photography. Reuben wonders what shade of gray his brown body would have registered, what he'd look like without clothes climbing stairs with a Greek water jar balanced on the hump of his right shoulder. What caption would fit him. Would he exemplify a disease? Would Muybridge have recruited him? Would he have answered Muybridge's knock?" (*Reuben,* 16). But in delaying the answers to these questions, he preserves the sanctity of the body and his own body's usefulness; in the very next moment he also sacrifices ideations of the body to speculations on intellectual talent and the motion of the law:

> All motion a series of stills succeeding one another fast enough to create the illusion of motion. The law was a series of steps. Each step depends on the one before it, as he'd assured the young woman in his office. The law created its particular fiction of motion, its metaphysical passage from disorder to equilibrium, unfair to fair, chaos to order, by establishing a series of steps—a due process. If those steps are followed, so the fiction goes, there is motion, progress, results can be reached, the world made a better place for litigants, for all of us. (*Reuben,* 16)

It is through this lens of Muybridge that Reuben is seen to be perhaps most like Bourne, for it is also Bourne's incisive introspection that drives him to reinvent the world:

> Human affairs seem to be running on a wholly irrational plan, and success to be founded on chance as much as on anything. But if [the handicapped man] can stand the first shock of disillusionment, he may find himself enormously interested in discovering how they actually do run, and he will want to burrow into the motives of men, and find the reasons for the crass in-

equalities and injustices of the world he sees around him. He has practically to construct anew a world of his own, and explain a great many things to himself that the ordinary person never dreams of finding unintelligible at all. (*Radical,* 79)

Reuben's mission is to unencumber his clients from the law, to effect change by producing the fiction of progress, just as Muybridge's stills, taken individually, produce the fiction of motion. "Law was detail work," he mused. "Freezing things into unnatural frames. Forestalling an inevitable conclusion by the logic of another conclusion, just as inevitable if the dice are given a slightly different spin" (*Reuben,* 17). In this the very idea of the body, and particularly the black body, is implicated. The least movement of the black body, the body desired in slavery, was determined incrementally by law; each new law, in ensuring the domination of the body, enhances the power of the last one to control. Reuben's "freezing" is a reversal of this control, an arrest of the discursive minutiae of law to permit its deconstruction and restore a spirit of freedom. Similarly, at the end of a later Wideman novel, *Two Cities* (1998), the aging Martin Mallory leaves behind at his death his innumerable candid photographs of members of the community that Kassima and Bob distribute to the neighborhood by giving them to the attendees at Mallory's funeral; their effort in doing this is to remind their neighbors of their own virtues and dissuade them from lethal, internecine warfare. As Kassima and Bob have temporarily separated because of Kassima's fear that an instance of Bob's bravado on the basketball court could have cost him his life, a loss that would only refresh for Kassima the pain of already having lost her husband and son, the photographs that they spread in this communitarian gesture also heal their relationship. Unlike Muybridge's photographs, however, which depict movement gradually, in continuous frames, Mallory's are discontinuous, but with the fluidity of everyday life in each frame. In a return to ideas from English Romantic poetry, such as those that appear to suggest the workings of the supernatural in Hurston's novels, Mallory's photos taken individually, as might the sum of any of Muybridge's sequences of human effort, suggest those deep, recurrent illuminations, the incandescent Wordsworthian "spots of time" in *The Prelude* that become translated into the "epiphanies," or sudden, cataclysmic insights of later literature, from Joyce to Faulkner to Kerouac. In a second letter he writes to the Swiss sculptor Alberto

Giacometti, known for abstract works that so closely resembled the human body in movement, Mallory is indeed happy that the first letter had not been answered, for the prospect of Giacometti's being perhaps "beyond the reach of words" has placed his second writing in a realm as rarefied as that in which he believes his pictures to reside. This second letter to the sculptor is projected "outside ordinary day-to-day time, into a space where your figures live, fixed and dancing, metal and flesh, entering and leaving time through the needle's eye of each beholder" (*Two Cities,* 90–91).

This distillation of Mallory's individuation into his art—a revaluation of the spectatorial artist—is in *Reuben* translated into Reuben's envy of Muybridge's "egomania transferring to monomania" (*Reuben,* 15), as he regards Muybridge's name and its metamorphosis into painstaking efforts to register human movement: born Edward James Muggeridge in 1837, Muybridge changed the spelling of his name— "complicating" it because he guessed that early Anglo-Saxons must have spelled Edward in this way. As well, "Reuben" is an anagram for "Bourne," which, though Reuben is unaware of this fact, encourages the drive and alterity that he seeks. The name, properly bestowed, is inextricably bound with the body. Egomania and monomania as shared between the photographer and the lawyer, between both manipulators of the static in free play, become kinship; while staring at the photographs, Reuben understands his relationship to Muybridge as "two men unawares, moving toward the same corner in the same city. One says a name he's never said before, and in an instant he's staring into a face that couldn't have shocked him more if it had been his own. And maybe it is" (*Reuben,* 20). As Reuben understands the complication of names as legal things, that complication returns in the persons of Kwansa and her lost little boy, Cudjoe. Kwansa's given name, Lily, is replaced by the name of the African American holiday constructed to recapture lost values of the African past; similarly, she names her son Cudjoe because she does not want him to bear a slave name. As Reuben points out, however, Cudjoe was a name commonly given to slaves by their masters; as such, the child not only remains bound by the stigma but is also thus inexorably part of a broader network of misnaming that informs his status, sensibility, and even praxis as a person of color.[7] The renaming

7. Boyce Davies, *Black Women, Writing and Identity,* 9.

of the misnamed must thus be consistent with what will invest, potentially, with power. Similarly, the complication of legality with access occurs in Hurston's *Their Eyes,* as Janie, in her childhood known as "Alphabet," sheds throughout her development the names that become useless as she advances toward a realization of her worth.

In continuing his imaginary conversation with Muybridge, Reuben learns that there are endless cycles of existence that replace the old by inaugurating the new. The photographer explains that as the old order expires, it rather implodes to reveal a final energy, "a final, life-sustaining flash of spirit" (*Reuben,* 61). This lesson has personal value for Reuben as he carries with him his brother as represented by a talisman. The talisman mirrors the shape of Reuben's own body; it is bullet-shaped, though not a bullet, "but a man, severely stylized, African style, all torso and brow and arching crown" (*Reuben,* 65). Through this brother, a twin, Reuben seeks to reclaim his own body, while always having had the task of reclaiming the bodies of others. Long before the present case of Cudjoe's disappearance there was that of Reuben's twin brother, perhaps even less healthy than he, separated from him at birth; preceding the disappearance of Reuben's twin is the conviction of murder of Wideman's own brother Robert, who, imprisoned for life in Pennsylvania, is the subject of Wideman's personal reminiscence in his *Brothers and Keepers* (1984). While Reuben's earliest memories of his brother take the form of mystic visions—recollections of being separated from him practically in the womb—they are intertwined with vague remembrances of his mother from this same time, a presence he can only approximate: "He can't be remembering that woman born in another century who lay down and spilled him out upon the damp earth. Like a doe in the forest. Not only him. Two of them all spotty like fawns. A dark one and a light one. Twins on a bed of soft earth and leaves and grass. He cannot be remembering because it happened too long ago. Was he ever that young once?" (*Reuben,* 64) The autobiographical Wideman recalls how the conditions that led to his brother's imprisonment also fashioned the gradual estrangement that his mother felt from both her sons:

> Even though the strands of the net—racial discrimination, economic exploitation, white hate and fear—had existed time out of mind, what people didn't notice or chose not to notice was

> that the net was being drawn tighter, that ruthless people out-
> side the community had the power to choke the life out of
> Homewood, and as soon as it served their interests would do
> just that. During the final stages, as the net closed like a fist
> around Homewood, my mother couldn't pretend it wasn't there.
> But instead of setting her free, the truth trapped her in a cage as
> tangible as the iron bars of Robby's cell. (*Keepers*, 74–75)

Brian McHale's declaration that the "dead author" of postmodern
criticism is "free once again . . . to break in upon the fictional world"
(*Postmodern,* 199) describes Wideman's freedom to do this in *Reuben.* In this Wideman most resembles Toomer as spectatorial artist,
the artist who performs many of *Cane's* critical and political deictic
functions while also inviting readerships to share the task of critique. But in *Cane* the spectatorial artist sacrifices the self to inaccessibility, to momentary or permanent incommensurability in order
to shape this critique. In Wideman's novel, Reuben honors his brother
by adopting the fetish, by "keeping the body of his brother always
with him," realizing through one of his visions that his dead brother
was in "a vast, gray prison in a cell too small for a dog, from which
he'd never be released" (*Reuben,* 66). Though for a time Reuben has
been remiss about observing the rite, the remissness itself has ensured a double inaccessibility, recalling also Reuben's distance from
his mother. He later has the "manshape" identified for him in a
dream, spoken by "a voice Reuben could only describe as 'on high'"
(*Reuben,* 66); from this moment on, the voice that identifies Reuben's nameless brother is never again heard, only echoed in this
identification by Reuben's own voice. Reuben here begins a ceaseless quest for a meaningful masculinity, whose recovery is a more
decisive way of embracing the work of the world. In a reversal of
Psalm 121 ("I will lift up mine eyes unto the hills, / from whence
cometh my help"), the "voice from the hill" that Reuben hears, that
of a deity, remote and demanding observance, is singular and final:
"'On high' didn't repeat itself. Once was enough. [. . .] A steel door
slammed behind him. Iron clattered against iron, bolts rammed
home, keys twisted in locks, tumblers fell. Reuben would need all
the days of his life to examine the black cell, become acquainted
with the brother sealed there" (*Reuben,* 66).

This twinning by which Reuben finds himself so inextricably engaged has its roots in the *marasa* (or *marassa*) principle of Haitian religion, and it is a duality that afflicts Ralph Kabnis as well. The *marasa* is the Haitian Voudoun sign for the Divine Twins, and the Haitian version of the androgynous Yoruba god Mawu-Lisa, who populated the world through the figure of Legba, god of language and literacy. Maya Deren locates the *marasa* concept partly through the Dahomean *tohwiyo,* the ancestor of a clan from whom all its members claim unilateral descent; these ancestors "are considered to be the offspring of one human and one supernatural parent," which recalls Kabnis in that he absorbs, or reflects, all of the male characters in *Cane.* In VèVè Clark's discussion of literacy and social change in the African diaspora, *marasa* is "a mythical theory of textual relationships" based on the sign of the twins. This blend of androgyny and literacy is important to discussing the black oppositional text, but perhaps the most important feature of this aspect of *marasa* is that of displacement. *Marasa,* which Clark suggests as being "movement beyond the binary nightmare," remarks that a good deal of the writing characterized by its elements involves, for example, environmental upheaval—such as the hurricane that hits the Everglades in *Their Eyes.* The simple male-female binarism that characterizes much of Hurston's novel is ruptured and broadened by the hurricane, and made far more complex in its aftermath than before it. This rupturing by *marasa* presence is again reflected in both Kabnis and Reuben with respect to aspects of "double consciousness due to color, class and educational differences experienced by one individual." The contemporary association of the *marasa* with Christmas—as Christ had parentage both human and divine—doubly reflects Kabnis's struggle, both in terms of Christian sacrifice and at the ground of race. In Reuben's hazy memory he recalls his and his brother's coming to being as the birth of "a dark one and a light one," so herein lies a difference in color—but broadening this difference is the multilayered subtextual comment upon these as values, thus compounding the delicate intricacy between Reuben's (and Wideman's) this-worldliness and his brother's other-worldliness.[8]

Since the time of Reuben's dream, he has slept with his talisman around his neck, and has invoked the name in prayer of the god who

8. Maya Deren, *The Voodoo Gods,* 44–45; VèVè Clark, "Developing Diaspora Literacy and *Marasa* Consciousness," 40–61.

watches over his brother whenever he has needed aid. But though in the Haitian and West African pantheons this god would ordinarily be Legba, Reuben calls upon Thoth, the Egyptian god of learning and, more specifically, of writing. This difference is probably akin to the adult Cudjoe's location of masculine identity in the Greek isles rather than in his native Philadelphia at the beginning of *Philadelphia Fire;* while this Cudjoe spans an ocean to find healing aid, Reuben's effort to achieve the same spans a continent. These different dramatizations point up the differences between the two men: as Reuben struggles toward fulfillment through senses of history, writing, and community, *Fire*'s Cudjoe, whose Atlantic trek is less a diasporic fertilization than the simple mapping of a vast void, is consistently unable to find solace in these. But Reuben's perversion of Thoth's iconographic pose generates an upheaval of representation regarding this deity's sacred animals, the ibis and the baboon. Reuben curiously omits the ibis, recalling the baboon as the only referent: "Oh Thoth, patron of scribes. Full moon springing from the head of Seth, god of darkness. Thoth the "reckoner of days" in his moonship. Reuben couldn't recall how or why the baboon became Thoth's totem animal. Yet a baboon, brow furrowed in deep thought, middle finger searching his asshole, was a perfect emblem of the writer. Thoth and sloth. A baboon marooned in the moon" (*Reuben,* 67). This ironic representation of writing through what is a blasphemous rendering to a deity also recalls racist representations of the black as simian, and is bound up in Reuben's doubt that he can in fact render any good in the present case of the lost child, or in any case where his special services may be needed. Not only does Reuben feel himself incapable of making new law to locate Cudjoe, but it is the very foreignness of his invocation—an act of *mis*placement of which he is unaware—that further compounds his difficulty, as it does for the other Cudjoe, the adult protagonist of *Philadelphia Fire.* That Thoth's original Egyptian name, Djhowtey, is elided in the West, giving readier access to the Greek form, renders what Carole Boyce Davies suggests as being a crucial difficulty in the construction of ethnic identity. As they exist through the fact of colonization, taxonomies such as Negro, black, or African American fashion a map of misnaming whose inconsistencies and inaccuracies, much like those in Hurston's *Moses,* complicate the making of subjectivity.[9]

9. See note 7.

Hurston's use of pan-African myth to reference the black masculine is reflected in Wideman's novel; for the health of Reuben's masculine self-worth such as he has configured it, it is probably the invocation of this deity with its Egyptian name that will yield the greater effect. In the myth of Osiris, Djhowtey was the guardian of the pregnant Isis; after the birth of her son Horus, Djhowtey healed the injuries inflicted on him by Seth, Osiris' nemesis. The myth is woven through the novel, as it is Reuben's chosen task to help the mother of a lost child. But throughout it all, Reuben lacks the personal confidence to see through his several tasks of recovery, a condition that is exacerbated by his subsequent arrest and the revelation in the local papers of his many sleights-of-hand on behalf of Homewood's most needy—performances that may have, for their daring, done at least as much harm as good. Despite the controversy, however, it is the effort of his humanity that matters most.

Reuben's confidence in that humanity is shaken at least as much by his failure to save his girlfriend Flora as it is to free his brother. Just as his brother's body remains in a sort of prison, so does that of Flora, the sex worker who is eventually murdered by the white fraternity boys Reuben worked for while a student. Flora's body is so much a source of her pain that she is left only with reciprocating that pain as a means of survival. "What I know best is how to use people," she says. "This body's loaned to me and I rent it out. I'm sick of it. I don't live in it anymore" (*Reuben,* 83). Though their only encounter is a brief one, Reuben and Flora share and cancel out their tortured selves; through Reuben, Flora is ransomed from her body's ordinary use, desiring only his human sensitivity to relieve her indenture to it. Through Flora, pleasure and sexual self-confidence are revealed to Reuben; similarly, he is liberated from his broken corporeal shell. But Flora's death cuts short this liberation, punctuating the tension of sex and death that existed between them. Reuben's engagement in both the rendering and receiving of education is an ironic one, as it metaphorically inverts the notion of the New Jerusalem; Flora's house sits atop a high hill, and the old trolley Reuben takes to get there clatters as it goes, "inching up the steep grade where the tracks parallel the black iron fence of a cemetery" (*Reuben,* 72). This foreboding image doubly critiques the notion of the shining African American mecca as it also recalls Toomer's Washington, whose "ballooned, zooming Cadillacs / Whizzing, whizzing down the street-car tracks" in "Seventh Street" bespeak a dangerous modernity, and whose "white and whitewashed fence" will be washed again by the forceful, northward-moving black blood of Migration as it seeks to survive the effort to build cross-racial citizenship.

Another reclamation project appears in the person of Reuben's friend and former classmate Wally, an athletic recruiter for the university, who comes to Reuben to solve his legal dilemma of misused university expenses. Reuben's exterior life represents aspects of the deep isolation Wally felt while a student. Reuben, for Wally, is not only the medium through which he crystallizes his despair but also the release from that despair—a release into fragmentation and confusion. As a college freshman, Wally's confusion and isolation began with his presentation of self among his white teammates: "The whole bunch of them must have talked it over. You know. My teammates. What should we do about Wally and that silly nigger hoodlum way he wears his ties? One guy volunteered to do the dirty work. The others lined up behind him. Shaking their heads, smiling. Nothing personal, Wall. Nobody in this life had ever called me *Wall* till those white boys got hold to my name" (*Reuben,* 111–12). The necktie and the attention Wally gives to it together function as the rope around his neck at the lynching he has constructed in his mind, while his self-negation is secured by his classmates' truncation of his name. As a black recruiter Wally has allowed his self-hatred to turn to cynicism by telling the same lies to black high school seniors that white recruiters tell. This masking through psychic negation becomes Wally's fervent cry—or one of them—to Reuben: "They did unto me. Now I'm doing unto others. Chopping myself into smaller and smaller bits" (*Reuben,* 107). His cynicism is redoubled upon itself and returned to him. Wally has also murdered a white man in a Chicago washroom. Like Bigger Thomas in Wright's *Native Son,* he is relieved by the random killing, feeling his life affirmed by it, and deriving an existential rejuvenation from it. Wally also has in common with Bigger a fundamental dissociation with nurturance and with women's bodies more specifically; he cannot bear his girlfriend Felicia's logorrhea, and is estranged from the memory of his grandmother, the very scent of the elderly woman reconstructing what seems to be Wally's only pleasant memory: "His grandmother's house didn't stink. It was as if she'd taken a blanket she'd slept under for years, a blanket older than Wally, and stretched it over roof, doors, windows, shutting their three rooms away from the treacherous streets. You couldn't see the blanket, it was thinner than skin but it stayed where she draped it, holding in the warmth, the care, she lavished on him, her love inseparable from the smell of her body soaked into each of the blanket's fibers" (*Reuben,* 106). Wally's grandmother's scent, the same scent of the house and the blanket, remarks upon the Kongo scent of the elders, a balm to which younger relations try to come near; it is *funk* in a sense truly uncorrupted by American vernacular. Robert Farris Thompson remarks at length on the derivation of the word "funk" and its value:

> The black nuance seems to derive from the Ki-Kongo *lu-fuki,* "bad body odor," and is perhaps reinforced by contact with *fumet,* "aroma of food and wine," in French Louisiana. But the Ki-Kongo word is closer to the jazz word "funky" in form and meaning, as both jazzmen and Bakong use "funky" and *lu-fuki* to praise persons for the integrity of their art, for having "worked out" to achieve their aims. In Kongo today it is possible to hear an elder lauded in this way: "like, there is a really funky person!—my soul advances toward him to receive his blessing." Fu-Kiau Bunseki, a leading native authority on Kongo culture, explains: "Someone who is very old, I go to sit with him, in order to feel his *lu-fuki,* meaning, I would like to be blessed by him." For in Kongo the smell of a hardworking elder carries luck. This Kongo sign of exertion is identified with the positive energy of a person. Hence "funk" in black American jazz parlance can mean earthiness, a return to fundamentals.[10]

But rather than that the odor from his grandmother and her surroundings enriches him, Wally's self-hatred makes the memory of that love an embarrassment that further estranges him from virtually everyone: from his former lovers and from other African Americans as he goes into their homes in search of their sons as recruits, and from those recruits. He cannot hear the value of Reuben's "lie," the fantasy he tells of the woman whose son is torn into pieces by some unknown force and eventually reassembled by her, a story he tells in answer to Wally's metaphoric dismemberment, the psychic negation

10. Robert Farris Thompson, *Flash of the Spirit,* 104–5.

of his own body. It is to Wally "a child's story, if you thought about it" (*Reuben,* 107), for Reuben ordinarily told stories with disastrous endings, or without endings at all. The story is indeed a child's story, but not in the way Wally means; it serves as a return to his grandmother and a further balm to his cynicism. Reuben tells the story as much for himself as for Wally, however, for it recapitulates for him his lost connection with Flora, who in her recollection of her first meeting with Reuben, first imagined him as childlike. But as she moved through that memory, Flora understood that "we definitely weren't dealing with mamas and little boys no more" (*Reuben,* 82).

Reuben's story of recovery might have served well Wally's continuing battle with the masculine fear of bodily fragmentation through considering Bimbo, Wally's childhood friend with whom he remains close. Bimbo, whose interesting name comes from his having been raised "soft," that is, with many sisters (but fiercely protective of them), was nevertheless during their teen years the devout libertine with whose sexual conquests Wally strove to keep pace. A later auto accident has left Bimbo a quadriplegic, however, and although as a successful rhythm-and-blues crooner he still surrounds himself with as many women as before, he is unable to enjoy them physically, or to do more than he can in a wheelchair. Wally, partly in an effort to avoid Bimbo's pain, but partly to reassure himself against the horror of such an existence, jogs around Bimbo's estate in an effort to keep fit. They once ran together, but that is now the impossibility that plagues Wally as well as it does Bimbo, for Bimbo has asked Wally to help him die. Wally cannot bring himself to free Bimbo, and instead reminisces about their childhood, the dares, the exploits. Away from Bimbo's palace on Shore Road, he remembers the old days, but images of the comparatively bookish Reuben intrude; to disrupt these images and break the monotony, "the stony silence of lying dead two thousand years" (*Reuben,* 181), he turns on some of Bimbo's soulful, sensual music, and tries to forget. In this effort, however, Wally only manages once again to miss the crucial element in his relationships with others. He cannot see the powerful and enduring reservoirs of manly purpose in each body despite the physical challenges they face. Reuben's tricksterism—his bookishness and his willingness to subvert the legal system on the community's behalf— and Bimbo, who now wants to honor a spirited life by leaving it, rep-

resent aspects of courage that Wally has in short supply. This is
nowhere more evident than in the ringing of the phone that disrupts
his reverie, that "sneaks in somewhere between the lines" of Bimbo's
song (*Reuben,* 182), bringing it and Wally down.

The caller is Reuben; he has been arrested for impersonating an
attorney, and is asking Wally's help. Wally's reluctance to go near a
police station is understandable as he, the murderer of a white man
in a Chicago washroom, is still at large. Both men have endured
colossal guilt—Wally for the murder and Reuben, not for imperson-
ation, though his littleness in this regard is an ingredient of his
dream, but for his inability to save Flora from her death at the hands
of the fraternity boys. Both men lead lives that have been determined
by a malevolent whiteness, and while this has nourished Wally's cynicism toward all relationships, it has fashioned Reuben's smallness
even more definitively, as even an element as healing as an imaginary or dreamlike return to Africa contains images of helplessness,
emasculation, and slavery; Reuben, via an earlier conversation with
a particularly unkind Wally, compares himself in his dream to an
Egyptian dung beetle:

> You hear the captive women. But you see nothing. . . . The
> ashy perfume of women singing is cool, dry hurt buried in their
> throats, like seed, like dead men wrapped in swaddling clothes,
> like the promise you made to Flora, who begs you to hurt them,
> to save her son, Reuben. You goddamned crackpot.
>
> Deep in the hold. Above you in fading purple dust you hear
> the bellying of wind in the sail, a single mast, bent like a scim-
> itar, bellying, slicing, scattering the fleet so each boat, the *Niña,*
> the *Pinta,* the *Santa María,* scoots like a bug over the current,
> at the whim of the wind. Wildly tacking. Edging toward one
> shore then leaning to the other. Chips zigzagging on a Ouija
> board. Opposites attracting, opposites driving the switchblade
> sails toward home. Not your home. You know, though you are
> blind as a bat in your cave, that they've stolen you and stolen
> the women from home and the only way home again is on a
> beetle's back, a journey like this, as far from home as this, the
> scattered pieces of you rolled in a ball, the ball rolling as this
> broad river rolls toward the sea, your gimpy-legged funeral
> barge inching forward, scratching its mark in sand till wind
> seals the wound. (*Reuben,* 204)

Thus begins Reuben's dark night of the soul in that the prison in which he is now placed puts him proximate to his brother, who will never be free. It also fixes him at an unbridgeable distance from Flora, as she represents the captive women Reuben cannot save. But he can perhaps secure a freedom for himself through the act of recovering Cudjoe, who is not Flora's son, but Kwansa's, and therefore obliquely Flora's in that the recapture of Reuben's own youth is "the son he never had." Reuben, despite his chronic misgivings, is spiritually able through this act and through the invocation of Thoth, and phenomenologically, through conversations with Muybridge, to finally embrace the self. In much the same way as with Hurston's Supernature, Reuben's fundamental bond with and acknowledgment of broad spiritual power admits something of a restoration of order. His embrace of the self is consonant with Kwansa's embrace of Toodles, Kwansa's female lover. She has given to Kwansa the support she has needed to deal with Cudjoe's biological father, Waddell, who leverages the entire misogynist apparatus of the state against his son's mother. Toodles' eventual murder of Waddell is swift and sudden retribution for his crimes against women, reprieving both Kwansa and Toodles from heterosexism's bondage. In this tableau the gifts given to others are also gifts the givers give to themselves. Just as important as this gift is Reuben's recovery of Cudjoe. While Cudjoe is an aspect of Reuben's youth—the missing son who can be returned to Reuben himself as well as to Kwansa—Toodles acknowledges that Kwansa's next love would have to be someone who "got something going for they ownself, something special you couldn't get nowhere else" (*Reuben,* 48). While she understands that "the pieces of Kwansa are scattered all over Homewood" (*Reuben,* 208), the gathering of those pieces in Cudjoe's return is an act of reciprocity that for both Kwansa and Reuben bridges all incommensurabilities. The embrace that Toodles holds for Kwansa becomes indistinct from that which Reuben desires for himself through Cudjoe and discovers briefly in Flora.

With respect to issues of masculinity and whiteness, Wally's and Toodles's entrances into the text through violence make their own trenchant statements. Waddell's desire to control Kwansa by appropriating their son mirrors the control that slaveholders had against female slaves and the children they sired with them, and in this mirroring is reflected Kwansa's ultimate frustration in finding a name for her son that, as Reuben cautions, is not a "slave name." Though Wally kills a nameless, faceless white man in Chicago, that namelessness and facelessness represents the fundamental shape of man—Muybridge's negative, the proper space of habitation for any existential expression of manhood without regard to race. But race has made it a space of dominance, a space of white masculine privilege to which black men are not admitted, and Wally, again mirroring Wright's Bigger, kills to feel and wants to kill "in the next city and the next till the hate was gone" (*Reuben,* 119). But it is Wally's guilt and his fundamentally frustrated selfhood as contoured by racism that makes the hatred irreducible, ineradicable. Waddell, particularly through his use of the law to oppress women, easily assumes an illegitimate privilege. Through his abuse of a black woman and the theft of her child, Waddell inhabits the space of the masculine as it was first corrupted by whiteness and dominance. Toodles, in literally shoving him out of that space, announces that it should be ill-fitting for black men. Finally (and ironically), it is a physically challenged black maleness in both Reuben and Bimbo that reshapes and redefines that space for a healthy development of masculinity, and not through physical demand or need, but rather through ethical and communitarian responsibility.

Brotherhood in Chaos: *Philadelphia Fire*

Though *Reuben*'s theme of recovery seeks a return in *Philadelphia Fire,* that return is in fact ultimately and dramatically frustrated. Though we are not invited to think of the child Cudjoe in *Reuben* as the adult Cudjoe of *Fire,* at the grounds of twinning and spectatorial artistry mentioned previously, there is perhaps, in consideration of both novels taken together, a brief ideational return to romanticism even in Wordsworthian terms of the child's "being father to the man": what is sanguinary in terms of black recovery in *Reuben* is largely absent in *Fire.* Another consideration of the name Cudjoe, however, more applicable to the protagonist of *Fire,* perhaps reveals the difference between the child and the adult, as little else would seem to contribute so heavily in explaining the character's lack of integrity. Cudjoe is also the name of the eighteenth-century warrior, the chief of the Jamaican Maroons, who were runaway slaves fighting the

British for their freedom. A skilled guerrilla warrior, Cudjoe successfully terrorized planters who wanted to expand slavery by opening up Jamaica's northeastern coast. Richard Price notes, however, the unevenness of this leader's career as liberator. He would not hesitate to be brutal, even to his own men, and could often be fawning toward the very whites he was fighting against. At a meeting toward peace in 1739, upon facing the British emissary for the planters, Colonel John Guthrie, Cudjoe, even though supported by large numbers of his own men, prostrated himself, kissing Guthrie's feet. His men, perhaps not knowing what else to do, followed suit.[11]

The Cudjoe of *Fire* is similarly uneven. His motives are never quite clear, and to the extent that they are, they are rarely moral. This Cudjoe is at first self-exiled from the Philadelphia neighborhood he once knew. Mykonos, the Greek island in the Aegean on which he lives at the opening of the novel, is a significant venue for a man whose sense of himself has been altered, wasted by the injustice and decay of the postmodern metropolis; after Cudjoe returns to his lost Philadelphia, Wideman locates him both in and as the belly of the beast:

> If the city is a man, a giant sprawled for miles on his back, rough contours of his body smothering the rolling landscape, the rivers and woods, hills and valleys, bumps and gullies, crushing with his weight, his shadow, all the life beneath him, a derelict in a terminal stupor, too exhausted, too wasted to move, rotting in the sun, then Cudjoe is deep within the giant's stomach, in a subway-surface car shuddering through stinking loops of gut, tunnels carved out of decaying flesh, a prisoner of rumbling innards that scream when trolleys pass over rails embedded in flesh. (*Fire,* 20–21)

Philadelphia, its name also derived from Greek (and Egyptian) origins, is a city of a more recent history, but its present is marked by neglect, homelessness, and despair; again, if the city is a man, this time "sprawled unconscious drunk in an alley, kids might find him, drench him with lighter fluid and drop a match on his chest" (*Fire,* 21), which is the fate of J. B., the last of the voices in *Fire.* As the

---

11. Richard Price, *Maroon Societies: Rebel Slave Communities in the Americas,* 260–61.

American city's decay deepens, the contrast is made with Mykonos itself, whose Greek name means "white island"; the Cyclades, the archipelago of which Mykonos is a part, were named for the Cycladic, the Bronze Age culture known for its white marble idols. Though these representations of whiteness may suggest Cudjoe's initial preference for the Philadelphia to which he has returned, perhaps just as striking is the Mykonos legend, one that speaks to the durable manhood that Cudjoe is desperate everywhere to represent: the island itself, while being mostly a mass of granite, is said to be the great rock hurled by Hercules in his battle against the Titans. As true cities on hills, the islands are themselves the peaks of submerged mountains, giving man his ultimate conquest of summits. But while at this ground masculinity's reign is crucial to a questing Cudjoe, he focuses his affection upon the presence and history of the Greek bootlegger Zivanias, who was named for the moonshine his grandfather cooked, and traveled from island to island selling his own home-grown brew until a storm of which the seasoned seaman had ample knowledge beforehand kills him on one of his runs. The nobility of such a death is, to Cudjoe, inescapable.

Of Zivanias, Cudjoe "was slightly envious. He would like to be named for something his father or grandfather had done well. A name celebrating a deed. A name to stamp him, guide him" (*Fire,* 3). Cudjoe wants desperately to court the honored name and to become part of something else, but inexorably, Zivanias, in his death at sea, is himself irrecoverably fragmented, as he is "out there sea-changed, feeding the fish" (*Fire,* 5). As a writer Cudjoe's consolation is the quest to recover masculine possibility by finding the Philadelphia boy missing in the conflagration that was the MOVE disaster of 1985. Both the boy's loss and the name given to him by his mother when she joined the group—Simba Muntu, "lion man" in Yoruba dialect—signifies an irony that shapes the fragility of masculinity that is older than any of the stories of its indestructibility and shapes as well for Cudjoe a sense of the masculine that he hopes to locate in a culture somewhat more familiar to him.

On May 13, 1985, at approximately 5:30 p.m., Philadelphia police and firefighters, led by Mayor W. Wilson Goode, detonated an explosive device at MOVE headquarters, starting a fire that killed eleven of its occupants, five of them children. MOVE was short for "The Movement," a countercultural, multiethnic, grassroots collective living in a middle-class section of the city, on Osage Avenue. MOVE, very much a "back-to-nature" collective in the middle of a large urban area, with disputes with neighbors and law enforcement stretching back over the preceding decade and spread into other parts of the city, had attracted both regional and national attention. Believing that all life is sacred, even that of stray animals and vermin, MOVE became a source of unrest. MOVE did not use heat or electricity; they ate their food, including their meats, raw; they did not cut their hair; and, after their leader, they all took the last name "Africa." As Hizkias Assefa and Paul Wahrhaftig have chronicled the crisis, MOVE's habits, among others, of "[MOVE'S children] rooting in [neighbors'] trash for food, . . . leaving garbage outside, collecting animals and giving them raw meat, cutting flea collars off neighbors' pets, and feeding pigeons and building coops for them caused friction between MOVE and its neighbors." Goode, Philadelphia's first African American mayor, had already established credibility as city manager, having implemented a plan for dealing with urban crisis situations, but according to Assefa and Wahrhaftig, the plan was neglected during Goode's campaign. Crisis-management liaisons in Philadelphia complained that they had had more contact with the office of the former mayor, Frank Rizzo, who presided over a long period of racist policy and police brutality directed principally toward Philadelphia's black citizens, and toward MOVE in particular, than with anyone in Goode's office. The result of the breakdown of communications between MOVE and the Goode administration was the bombing of the group's headquarters on Osage Avenue, which caused a fire that police and firefighters allowed to spread until it got out of control. The fire also destroyed sixty-one homes, damaged 110 others, and left 250 people homeless. Of those in the MOVE compound, only one woman and one child had survived. Even today the legacy of the disaster lives on in malfeasance, neglect, displacement, intimidation, and forced evictions; as of this writing, residents of the rebuilt houses on Osage Avenue and adjacent Pine Street had either been bought out by the city or were being forced out. The houses were scheduled to be razed because of shoddy construction.[12]

12. Hizkias Assefa and Paul Wahrhaftig, *The MOVE Crisis in Philadelphia: Extremist Groups and Conflict Resolution,* 102–3, 112–13; "Residents Leaving Doomed Philadelphia Houses," *New York Times,* Sunday, September 3, 2000.

Cudjoe's dream of his last morning on Mykonos is a conflation of phantasms: a dark-haired woman, who "will rise naked from the sea . . . crowned by a bonnet of black snakes, arms and legs splashing showers of spray, sun spots and sun darts tearing away great chunks of her so he doesn't know what she is" (*Fire,* 6), is memorially conjoined with his grandmother's favorite souvenir, a landscape in a musical glass ball filled with water and snowflakes which match the salt he tasted when he tried to commune with the dark-haired woman. This synaesthesia brings him to memories of his grandmother, whose dying, disintegrating body, like the disintegration of Zivanias, suggests an integral part of him, comprising his entelechy, his motivations, his emotional and sexual selves:

> Her husband of forty years dead, her flesh turning to water. Sweat is what gives you life. He figured that out as life drained from her. Her dry bones never rose from the bed. You could lift her and arrange her in the rocking chair but life was gone. He'd wiped it from her brow, her neck. Dried the shiny rivers in her scalp. Leg is . . . arm is . . . He learned the parts of a woman's body caring for her, the language of sweat and smell they spoke. Why was he supposed to look away from her nakedness when his aunts bathed her? He loved her. Shared her secrets. If he sat in the rocker keeping watch while she slept, she would not die. (*Fire,* 7)

But the dark-haired woman in Cudjoe's dream is actually a Greek woman he has met several times in the café in which he tends bar in Mykonos. On this last morning, "she will teach him the Greek for body parts. Hair is . . . eyes are . . . nose is . . . ," but he will be far more distant from her tutelage of *female* reclamation of his psychic fragmentation than he is from Zivanias' physical disintegration and what it holds for him: as she speaks, "the Greek words are escaping him even as he hears them" (*Fire,* 6). Cudjoe's later incest fantasy between his close friend and editor Sam and Sam's daughter Cassandra involves him as well as he imagines her for himself, but he hears Sam's admonitions against her defilement. The narration moves quickly ahead in free indirect discourse to the tragedy-in-prolepsis of Cassandra's death in a fiery crash in Mexico nine months later. Cudjoe's odd meditation on the brevity of life causes him to wonder whether Sam would not himself want to savor his daughter sexually, with "his heart in his throat like Cudjoe's. His old pecker nudging

his shorts like Cudjoe's" (*Fire,* 65). To this point, it is a Cudjoe himself fragmented in spirit and without redemption who hears a call to
recover not only an element of black manhood he understands to be
imperiled but also to seize a materiality, a palpable (if irremediably
male) meaning from the fragility of all life.

Back in the Philadelphia he left behind, Cudjoe decides that his
quest for Simba demands the supports of a youthful masculinity, an
erect posture, and exercise. He determines to be "a better Cudjoe inside this whipped flesh. Lean, fierce, a fighter, someone who could help
the lost boy" (*Fire,* 72). The ensuing irony of lunch with his old
friend Timbo, however, hurls this desire for the fit, fighting body into
frustration. Timbo, who now works for the mayor's office, will have
the city pay for a sumptuous lunch with his old buddy at an exclusive
restaurant. Now educated and coarsened by urban racism, its step-
child radical chic, and the bitter facts of contemporary politics, Timbo
plays the class game with deftness; he shades his history when he
omits his actual birthplace, "a farm a long ways inland from the
New Orleans he liked to claim when questions about a birthplace
were really questions about family, about pedigree and pretensions
to civilization" (*Fire,* 73). Timbo strikes an intriguing figure in
Fire—that of black peasant success among the urban bourgeoisie—
in complicating his membership in this group, which is ordinarily
presumed to have subverted black spiritual and communitarian values. The complication is manifest in his cynicism, which implicates
the university-as-citadel and what was its radical experiment with
liberalism that so characterized the sixties:

> The old days. Sure I remember them. And some of them were
> good. None of us had a dime but we was living good, better
> than we knew at the time. Academic welfare. Way I look at it
> now they was testing us. Put a handful of niggers in this test
> tube and shook it up and watched it bubble. Was we gon blow
> up or blow up the school or die or was some weird green shit
> gon start to foaming in the tube? Or maybe the whole idea was
> to see if we'd come out white. . . . How many of us in our class
> at the University? No more than nine, ten total. Set us down in
> the middle of a place Negroes never been before, wasn't ever
> spozed to be. Then shook up the tube. (*Fire,* 76)

Timbo's indignation is well documented in the history of an urban
integrationist liberalism that itself became fragmented and exploita-

tive. He refers to the advantage he and others similarly situated, including Cudjoe, managed to inherit, the opportunity to mine Philadelphia's economic resources as "our black Camelot" (*Fire,* 77). Whether Timbo is thinking of the Camelot of Arthurian legend or that of the Kennedys, he understands that both were short-lived. But while he acknowledges his and Cudjoe's survival, noting the sumptuous meal before them, he recognizes that his boss, as a black mayor in a white-controlled city, may also have been given rather a short tether. "Election's coming," Timbo warns. "Goodies might all be gone tomorrow. Get it while it's hot" (*Fire,* 76).

Timbo speaks glibly of new city projects, such as the one that imaginatively returns to Cudjoe's Greece, with universities and their students as centerpieces. "When redevelopment's finished," he says, the city guarantees "a nice, uncluttered view of the art museum. That's the idea. Open up the view. With universities just a hop skip down the way what we're trying to create here is our own little version of Athens, you dig? Museum's the Acropolis up on the hill" (*Fire,* 78). Timbo relates a trip to Rio, on which he was hosted by a business associate whose sumptuous villa had "more servants than I got cousins" (*Fire,* 79), but moves then to his drive to this estate, through the other Rio and its extreme poverty. The demographic of Rio's *favelas*—the pockets of privation spread around the hills above Ipanema Beach—is another inversion of the urban paradise on the hill. Timbo recalls the area as a human dumping ground, but also as a place to avoid getting on one's shoes: "Most of them just plain-ass living on the ground. The ground, man. Stinks like bad meat. Don't matter all the car windows closed. Stink sneaks in. You feel dirty, like stink's painting you a nasty color" (*Fire,* 79, 80). Like Wally in *Reuben,* Timbo has lost his moral compass, its crystal first cracked by sometimes unconscious but usually injudicious social and political mediations. The choices he makes, however, are the choices that were first fashioned by the machinations of whiteness that sought to determine his fate. His boss the mayor, a victim of his own class-bound unwillingness to communicate, is defended by Timbo as he and Cudjoe discuss the fire: "How the mayor spozed to stand up and talk to white folks when he can't control his own people" (*Fire,* 81)? Timbo's message becomes one of control, a control that will preserve the interests of the privileged, and a dark stichomythia aids Cudjoe in his understanding the mechanism of this final solution:

Sooner or later, one way or another, them and their dreadlocks
had to go.
   The fire.
   The fire. (*Fire*, 81)

Timbo's echoing of Cudjoe's realization easily recalls Kurtz's "The
horror! the horror!" in Conrad's *Heart of Darkness,* wherein Mar-
lowe earlier offers the admonition that Kurtz, to his ultimate peril,
has ignored: "The conquest of the earth, which mostly means the
taking it away from those who have a different complexion or slightly
flatter noses than ourselves, is not a pretty thing when you look at it
too much."[13] The colonizer's plunder is justified by his self-deception,
his belief in the saving function of imperialism. *Fire's* colonized,
who know this, return the gaze to the black imperial—the colonizer
identified not by difference, but by his suddenly dismaying sameness.
   As the agent of fragmentation in the present, Timbo leaves the
realpolitik of poverty management and, as he remembers the friends
and acquaintances that he and Cudjoe shared as young men, displays
the fragmented even in his recollections, being mired in an always-
already of bodily disintegration:

> A shooting gallery of faces as Timbo ticks off their signs: bad
> breath, big tits, the stuttering, dickhead motherfucker. Mr. Prim
> and Proper, Miss Fine Ass, Woody Woodpecker square-headed
> no dancing turkey. The Crab Lady. The Dog Man. . . . Cudjoe
> thinks up a god so prodigal it can't help creating everything it
> thinks. Runaway creation, people spilling from its orifices as it
> laughs and farts and slaps its thigh and marvels at the perver-
> sity, the fecundity of its mind, the permutations and combina-
> tions it can spin off the basic human clay. One leg, three legs,
> no legs at all. Legs where arms should be. A phantom leg after
> the real one blown off by a land mine. Legs tangled, twisted,
> one shorter than the other, legs like flippers, perfect deadly
> legs, legs undersized and elephantized, suppurating and skin
> flaking away, black ones on red people, green ones on white,
> and as fast as the god dreams them, here they come pouring
> from a cornucopia, flooding the earth, a rickety, crooked, mis-
> shapen pair, a joke, a whim, the only set of legs some sorrowful
> motherfucker will own all the days of his life. (*Fire*, 85)

13. Joseph Conrad, *Heart of Darkness,* 57.

Timbo's recollections of times and persons past are spread before Cudjoe and before us as a sort of macabre buffet, as the values of progress and uplift have moved inexorably toward the satisfaction of the privileged. Cudjoe shortly begins to wonder what has happened to the zeal for that physical, bodily masculinity that he was earlier sure would save Simba; sitting in the midst of the charnel-house that is black Philadelphia, its inferno that is Osage Avenue, he wonders what he can even say to him if he should find him (*Fire,* 92).

Though the city on one hand represents to Cudjoe the body of a decaying man, on the other hand it remains a great venue, a market-place of ideas that Cudjoe, again seeking the humanitarian within him, wishes to rescue in seeking Simba—or any child. If Caliban's quest for power is presumed to end with the seizure of Prospero's books, then for Cudjoe that quest may be further fulfilled, in the con-temporary situation, by what the bearer of such knowledge can teach. In "man-high letters" (*Fire,* 88), Cudjoe spies the graffiti of "Kaliban's Kiddie Korps," a gang of disaffected youth whose slogan is "Money Power Things." Untutored as to critical thinking and choice, each member of the gang is the invisible manchild of the postmodern city, identified only by the individual graffito that strug-gles for primacy above the others. Directionless and often danger-ous, they roam the city streets "unnoticed. . . . Like dead trees, dead rivers, poisonous air, dying blocks of stone" (89). In the forgotten city, the mood is one of defensiveness and defiance among the youngsters, who feel their elders prepared to betray and destroy them. But Cudjoe seeks to bridge this gap between old and young by proving that children can learn art, and revitalize themselves and the city with their new language. His vehicle is Shakespeare's *The Tempest,* and he believes that by directing a version of this play, he can imbue his troupe of pre-teenagers with a sense of self-worth that can be embraced through a reading of Caliban's struggle as a form of nationalist culture. In much the same way that he wishes to be the superhero who rescues Simba, he wants to rescue these children by being the "someone to teach them to be other than what they are. Lost behind snotty, dingy curtains" (*Fire,* 127).

Cudjoe's singular frustration, however, is that his production can never achieve the protonationalist meaning he wishes, and he here invokes a sense of the incommensurable that is both within and be-yond the text. In describing the production to an interlocutor, Cudjoe revisits Miranda's "abhorred slave" speech (I.ii. 352–62), which, despite Miranda's whiteness, resituates the chasm on whose sides man and woman are opposed. Cudjoe's continued description of the relation between Caliban and Miranda descends to the prurient and scatological (*Fire,* 140), but this appears actually to describe an enforcement of difference, this time *because* of Miranda's whiteness. Cudjoe's immediate dropping of the defense of aggressive black male sexuality, however, allows his seeing the larger picture as one in which both Caliban and Miranda are victims of a larger history that momentarily transcends her difference in whiteness but deftly reinscribes it, thus giving political highlight to her difference in gender:

> Someday, when your prince comes, then you may people this property with property. More. Makes more. In the meantime, go to Vassar. Travel, if you must, during school vacations but not on the Frontier because there are barbarians sleeping at the gate. If we wake them, we must teach them manners. Manners maketh man. Teach them to speak when spoken to. Are you following me, children? The dangerousness of this speech about speech shoved in a woman's mouth. It's informed by a theme older than Willy or Willy's time. Eternal triangle and wrangle. The Garden where three's a crowd. Monkey in the middle. Who's in, who's out, who says so? (*Fire,* 140)

Willy is of course a reference to Shakespeare, but in the arena of discourse on race an additional associative reference to Du Bois seems to be invited. Du Bois (known as "Willie" to those closest to him) invoked race as being the twentieth century's defining issue, though he understood that injustice born of difference was a problem infecting every moment in every century. What Du Bois exercised through the voice of Caliban was only the anguish against any inhumanity: "Daddy Caliban learned enough to pick out meaty curses. Like starving prisoners in concentration camps straining kernels of corn from do do. It happened. At Andersonville, for instance. It happens today, every day, round the world, round the clock, where the wind blows and the cradle rocks, prisoners catching hell, captive populations beaten into submission. Or death. Kid stuff. Elementary. Old as nursery rhymes" (*Fire,* 141). To further attempt to bring Miranda to awareness, Cudjoe's rewriting of the play returns to the sexual contract as the element of gendered injustice that ensures greater gains for her father, Prospero, than for Miranda herself, but the writing begins to interpret the ways in which incommensurability is ensured and injustices are preserved: "Her father needs her to corner the future, her loins the highway, the bridge, sweet chariot to carry his claim home. Her womb perpetuates his property. Signs, seals, delivers. Spirit needs flesh. Word needs deed. And Caliban understands the connections. Wants out. Wants in. All her civilization whispered in his ear. Her words on the tip of his tongue" (*Fire,* 141).

As Cudjoe's interlocutor warns him, the divide between Miranda and Caliban is the way of the world; determined are their roles, irreducible is their distance, and as Hamlet himself said, "the play's the thing":

> Yeah, but that's another story, another country, it doesn't fit here. You can't rewrite *The Tempest* any damn way you please. Schoolmarms. Freedom riders. All the dead weight of their good intentions. You can't put that on stage. How's Caliban supposed to sass Miss Ann Miranda without him get his woolly behind stung good and proper by that evil CIA covert operations motherfucker, Ariel? Round-the-clock surveillance, man. Prospero got that island sewed up tight as a turkey's butt on Thanksgiving. Play got to end the way it always does. Prospero still the boss. Master of ceremonies. Spinning the wheel of fortune. Having the last laugh. Standing there thinking he's cute telling everybody what to do next. And people can't wait to clap their hands and say thanks. (*Fire,* 144)

As if this were not impasse enough, a doubling of irony completes the fashioning of this frame, laying waste to possibilities for a sexual, political union as Cudjoe envisions it: first, the play is ultimately rained out, never to be performed; in Shakespeare's *Tempest,* the play *opens* with a storm, during which Prospero proceeds to give Miranda the truth of her origins, to tell her who she is.[14] Further, the actor playing Miranda in Cudjoe's production would of course be a child—a black child—whose slightly older sister, a girl that would probably have been Miranda's age, has already become the prey of a neighborhood Caliban, as she is the mother of twins. Life, as Cudjoe perhaps only vaguely understands, sometimes less imitates art than only laughs mirthlessly at it.

14. *Hamlet,* I.ii.15–64.

The oppositional black text—the text wrought by the seeker after justice to reduce injudicious binarisms—is not quite realizable in *The Tempest,* but has possibilities in The Book of Life, as in the last book of *Fire,* J. B.'s section, this book falls to him. J. B. is not just a voice unconnected to the historical events about which Wideman is writing. As Cudjoe's interviewee Margaret Jones relates, J. B. is the self-styled Reverend King, the representation in the text of John Africa, MOVE's leader. Born Vincent Leaphart in 1931, John Africa, a skilled carpenter, had another job for which he became famous in Powelton Village, the first of the Philadelphia neighborhoods MOVE called home. Illiterate, perhaps dyslexic, John Africa by his mid-thirties had no more than a grade-school education. A young community college instructor, Donald Glassey (the "Richard Corey" of *Fire*), struck up a friendship with John, and as John laid out his philosophy, Glassey began to take notes. White, upper-middle-class, and idealistic, Glassey represented a portion of the curious assortment of individuals that coalesced into MOVE. Most of its members were black and poor; some were young, others middle-aged. Some were educated, some not. For all of them, Glassey compiled "The Guideline," which later became known simply as "The Book," an eight-hundred-page typescript document outlining the whole of John Africa's thinking. Despite the fact that much of this philosophy was questionable—apparently the hierarchy of the collective preached violence, and MOVE members were later caught with firearms and explosives by federal agents—John Africa had many disciples. Eventually, however, one of his most trusted, Glassey himself, had been caught by law enforcement, and for a reduced sentence and witness protection, he agreed to become an informant, testifying against John Africa and MOVE in a trial regarding a confrontation with Philadelphia police in 1978. His whereabouts are today unknown. MOVE resumed operations after John Africa was acquitted in 1981, but he was one of those who died in the Osage Avenue fire that fateful May afternoon.[15]

By the time J. B.'s meandering voice assumes command of the text, the conflagration on Osage Avenue has already begun, and as a signifier of Donald Glassey's betrayal of MOVE, a guilt-ridden

15. Assefa and Wahrhaftig, *MOVE Crisis,* 10, 11; Michael Boyette with Randi Boyette, *"Let It Burn!": The Philadelphia Tragedy,* 31–36, 69–74, 208.

Richard Corey is rushing through town with King's dictated text. He perhaps gets this name from Edward Arlington Robinson's poem "Richard Cory," about a man who, distraught by the disparity between his wealth and the poverty of his neighbors who admire him, takes his own life. In *Fire,* Corey's suicide allows the briefcase to come into J. B.'s possession, but the bombing of Osage returns J. B. to considerations of a blighted Philadelphia, another false promise of the New Jerusalem, now compromised even unto its origins: "Image a city called the City of Brotherly Love. Consider the pretension of that greeky compound, tinker with the sound till it becomes brothel-ly, City of Brothelly Love. Imagine old tumbleweed, tumbledown James Brown, J. B., living there. What was the name of the first city? At this very moment someone at the University is achieving academic prominence puzzling out the answer to that question. Was it Jericho?" (*Fire,* 169). Jericho's otherwise impenetrable wall was finally shattered by the blare of the trumpets of Joshua's army—what might be Caliban's "thousand twangling instruments." But J. B. carries a card that invites passersby to give him handouts. It reads: "I am a vet. Lost voice in war. Please help." While J. B. would be a veteran of every war against the elements of the city that might spell his demise, his voice—cast more as an interior monologue than any of the voices in the book—is lost in the din of his daily battle for survival. Philadelphia's moral decay, now revealed as the "real" behind its insubstantial name, feeds ruminations on sex, diminishes discourses on brotherhood, and reinvigorates ideas of male prowess and the violence necessary to achieve those. The most immediate failure is that of the abstracted, isolated intellectual whose forays into a truly ancient history reveal no remedy. If they can, they do so too late for a Philadelphia already on fire.

His initials stand for "James Brown," but when the rhythm-and-blues icon of the same name gained prominence, J. B.'s friends mocked his identity. There is an inevitable irony in the difference between the singer's worldwide fame and the homeless man's abject obscurity, both joined by the very common name they share, an irony highlighted here also in the singer's achievement of fame via his difficult road to it. In the same vein, the J. B. of *Fire,* the sudden bearer of the black oppositional text, "remembers all the smoke from burning cities he's ever sucked up the four-lane blues highway of his nose" (*Fire,* 156). Brown the soul singer, nicknamed the

"Godfather of Soul" for the earthy, grassroots sexuality of his music, lyrics, and stage presence, was called this also for the defiance of some of his lyrics during his popularity in the sixties and seventies, another significant era of black political awakening. Wideman extends this soul/blues mood through J. B.'s ruminations on the state of the now-burning Philadelphia, on how things came to such a pass:

> Who's zooming who? The mayor born in Georgia? The old South. Red mud country, slow-talking roots. Rumor has it the paddy-boy director of public safety a cracker, too. Imported from Bull Connorsville, given a voice lift, a polyester leisure suit, a slinky, retarded teenage mistress from an Italian slum in South Philly (why can't we write about these things—they're not true, are they?) and carte-blanche, white power to whip whatever heads needed to roll. Carte blanche and the black mayor's dark blessing, chocolate oreo cookie above the director's vanilla brow, so who's gonna get in their way? Zooming whom? (*Fire*, 157)

While Wideman's use of free indirect here makes it difficult to know whether J. B.'s interior monologue persists or it is in fact Wideman who makes the pronouncement that Northern racism reflects its Southern source, or even that Philadelphia's black mayor is co-opted by white political influence, the parenthetical similarly frames either or both The Book of Life and *Fire* itself as being the black oppositional text. But this confluence of voices and authors is present in even the framing of the paragraph by its identical opening and closing question, "Who's Zooming Who?" As the title song of an album by Aretha Franklin, known as "Lady Soul" for her many successive hits with Atlantic Records in the sixties, it subtextually joins both Brown and Franklin as soulmates, marking their performances celebrating black difference, black dissatisfaction and anger, and sociopolitical critique as complementary. It contextualizes within the sphere of black popular culture the sixties' and seventies' history of burning American cities as the result of uprisings against injustice.

The sheer vastness and weight of such tragedy, however, distorts the possibility of critique for J. B.; there is indeed little that a homeless man with no resources or connections can do. His speculative analysis of the power structure that caused the conflagration in the first place seems to him to be impotent and wasteful; it is reduced by him to being "an irresponsible way of looking at things" (*Fire,* 157). He begins to feel that by breaching the wall of fire and seeking those trapped inside the burning building on Osage, he may perhaps be of some use, but he remembers instead that the despairing world is so much larger than he, that it is the stuff of media, the ordinary, the everyday, the vernacular of humankind. Even Aretha's challenge grows more faint as it assumes a different stance:

> Lists of lists. Lists listing. Lists passing in the night. Lists while I woo thee. J. B. can't recall the items or the lists listing the items. Only flashes of commercials, of blood. News reviews of massacres. A year of terror. Us versus Them. Who's zooming who? Shattered, bloodstained glass strewn in an airport lounge. Mile after square mile of broken glass littering the countryside. Lebanon Soweto West Bank Belfast San Salvador Kabul Kampuchea. Spin the globe and touch it wherever it stops. You'll get blood on your finger. (*Fire,* 160)

The tone of the song's refrain is changed from "who's being fooled" to "who's getting strafed," and in the absence of answers to either question, the solution is flight. But to where, with the whole world aflame? J. B.'s initials, while announcing the presence of singer James Brown, suggests also another J. B. in the homeless man's aborted attempt to enable himself toward responsibility and heroism—James Baldwin. In *The Fire Next Time,* Baldwin's answer to the horror of American racism and injustice is conscientious citizenship, conveyed through love. Baldwin writes that the newness of "new Negroness" is in fact the inauguration of every black resistance to repression, as such resistance again and again delays an entire country's satisfaction and complacence. This is "the torment and necessity of love" that can awaken America, the "enormous contribution that the Negro has made to this otherwise shapeless and undiscovered country" (*Ticket,* 370). This is love, Baldwin writes, that practiced through resolve, conscience, and unity will save the world. But the J. B. of *Philadelphia Fire* sees that the fire is already here, it is already everywhere, and the only impulse to heed is flight. As he understands, he cannot elude this fire—indeed, he is *in* it, as street kids— like the ones that Cudjoe felt challenged to save through art—have found a homeless man lying drunk in an alley, doused him with gasoline, and set him ablaze.

Metaphorically and otherwise, the sacred, oppositional Book of Life disappears. A significant defense against oppression, a salutary, defiant black manhood, troped through Baldwin, James Brown, Du Bois, and Caliban through Shakespeare—"godfathers of soul" all—watches the shining city, the city on the hill, as it burns its slow, agonizing way into the earth. Simba, never having been found by Cudjoe, becomes part of a gang, and recounts in a new text—the new, postmodern dissonance, the lyric of rap—the effect of the bombs hitting 6221 Osage Avenue: "They tried to shoot us, bomb us / Drown us burn us / They brought us here, but they can't return us" (*Fire,* 165). But their retaliatory pastime—their "payback"—involves attacking whites in the city's downtown, where they reopen the chasm of sexism to recover a sense of the black masculine obliterated by racism's power: "Cop a feel. Run your hand up the bitches' clothes. . . . Off the dudes' money. . . . We gone before they catch their breath. Long gone. Biff. Bam. Thank you, ma'am. Cop and blow" (*Fire,* 164). The war waged by Simba's newly found crew against white Philadelphia is only another manifestation of J. B.'s worst fear. Though the oppositional text has given way to the oppositional lyric in *Fire,* thus honoring the slave lyric, the work song, the blues, the Spirituals as the more accessible, even portable means of transmitting information about the black Holocaust and the holocausts to come, its recrudescence in Simba's lyric closes the novel with a sense of horror. As Paul Gilroy suggests, the goal of freedom, otherwise obscured by overwhelming racism, was finely articulated in the sixties and seventies by the soul and rhythm-and-blues lyrics of black popular culture. The current stage of the evolution of lyrical black public culture, however, particularly in hip hop and gangsta, yields something of its own incommensurability, of an aberrant communitarian politics, less a focus on freedom than on the body and the pleasures of the self. The signs and silences of the codings of the eroticized self contained within these cultural productions, Gilroy writes, "represent the end of older notions of public interaction that helped to create and were themselves created by the forms of densely coded, verbally mediated intersubjective dialogue that nurtured racial solidarity and made the idea of an exclusive racialized identity a credible, operable one" (*Sphere,* 60). Though Simba's lyric is not yet the lyric of corporeal insularity but rather retains an element of identity that is believable and usable, its development from and proximity to the acts of sexualized violence in which he and his gang engage seem to chart a point on this evolutionary map. In this eerily prophetic sense, Wideman collides the Brown lyric "I'm black and I'm proud" with Aretha's "Who's zoomin' who?" Cudjoe's own contribution to the oppositional text, the book he intended to write about the boy's disappearance and recovery, is also lost due to his failure to find Simba, who, like the shining city on the hill now in flame, is himself lost. Unlike *Reuben, Fire* displays an incompleteness on the part of the artist, a failure to maintain the static in service to the fluid, to find the new articulation of the law to free the body. Cudjoe now faces the fire, the fire *this* time, and he is swallowed up by the community's howls of execration, the anger of black Philadelphians who, having sorely noted this failure, come for him.

7

WHEN AND WHERE WE ENTER

Closing the Gap in Morrison's *Beloved*
and Naylor's *Mama Day*

You are mine.

—Toni Morrison, *Beloved*

In Hattia M'Keehan's 1858 novel *Liberty or Death; or, Heaven's Infraction of the Fugitive Slave Law,* the tragic tale is told of the escaping slave Margaret Garner's slaying of her daughter Mary as
United States marshals charged with upholding the Fugitive Slave
Law were closing in. Gazella, the fictionalized Margaret, having
been taught to read from an earlier age by her mistress's mother, displays all the charm, bearing, and eloquence of the educated bonds-
woman, with "complexion almost fair—for in her veins ran but a
tincture of African blood. Comely was she in feature—expression
benignant, enlightened and thoughtful." As if the white antebellum
author's concern with the slave's degree of whiteness—a marker of
justification for her actions toward freedom—were not enough, the
reader is informed that Gazella's husband and the father of her four
children "to the south had been sold" (*Liberty,* 9), a change which
effectively writes out of the text the role of Robert Garner, Margaret's
husband and the leader of the party of seventeen escapees who sought
freedom across the Ohio River. Edgar Allen, though "a negro of
more than ordinary sagacity" (*Liberty,* 45), appears only briefly in a
later chapter to lead the escape party including Gazella and her chil-

182

dren across the frozen Ohio, and is never heard from again. Although Henry Field James's *Abolitionism Unveiled; or, Its Origin, Progress, and Pernicious Tendency Fully Developed* (1856) does describe "Sam," a figure of Robert who decides to lead the escape, even down to the detail of defending Margaret by firing at the closing posse, it does not do so without "Sam" having been duped into fleeing his Eden of the plantation by a satanic abolitionism (*Abolitionism*, 240–45).

But more interesting than either *Abolitionism Unveiled* or *Liberty or Death* is *Chattanooga* (1858), a version of the Garner story in which black male agency is ignored in its entirety. Its author, John Jolliffe, was Margaret Garner's defense counsel at her trial; he was also a Quaker and thus a staunch opponent of slavery, having the reputation of taking the most difficult cases involving escaping slaves. Huldah, in this text the fictive Margaret, is again the young, beautiful, and near-white subject of the sentimental, but unlike M'Keehan's Gazella is pliant and unassuming. Abe, the old slave (at forty) chosen for her, cannot escape associations with the simian: he is described as thick, heavy-set, and possessive of "arms that extended nearly to his feet" (*Chattanooga,* 50). Huldah escapes, however, with Grey Eagle, the Indian noted several times as having grace of movement, which features his independence, having "deliberately chosen . . . to wander through the forest as his fathers for ages had wandered, and to enjoy the dignity and freedom of his position, as a hereditary chief of his tribe, and as a Cherokee" (*Chattanooga,* 62). The absence of a figure of black male agency is remarkable in that few persons during the case would have had the opportunity to know both Garners as intimately as did Jolliffe, not only their attorney, but because of this, also a shaper of their legend.

Steven Weisenburger's excellent history of the Garner affair shows that both Margaret and Robert shortly became victims of the vagaries of both literature and journalism: while interest in the case quickly diminished, leaving it to distortions in dimming memories, Robert's seems rarely to have appeared as more than a footnote. The racism of the era's newspaper culture, writes Weisenburger, never deemed worthy of record the black *man's* firsthand report of the Margaret Garner tragedy. Though Margaret's act supplied enough drama, Robert—without whom the party might not have been formed and the escape never attempted—was scarcely noticed by the press.

Court transcripts excerpted for newspaper accounts reveal the numerous logical inconsistencies, any one of which would today challenge entirely the validity of a capital case. Not the least of these regards the fact of Robert Garner himself, who, though unfree and therefore not counted as a person to be protected by law, enters the case as a deponent being "of lawful age, being duly sworn," and making remarks "on his oath." Such was the equivocal status of human property—only a small example of what Orlando Patterson calls "natal alienation," the utter disregard from birth for one's humanity based on one's status as chattel. It creates his status as a non-being on the one hand, as he is forced to swear as a deponent against his own interest in a capital case, having attained "the lawful age" so to achieve, on the other.[1] The victim of legalistic, journalistic, and literary distortion, the real Robert Garner nevertheless demonstrated his agency and the commitment to freeing his party unto the most crucial moment: as Margaret, trapped, struggled in that barn with her terrible decision, he fired rounds from his pistol at the surrounding slavecatchers, being willing to risk all for liberty even when the game was up.

In the novel *Beloved*, Toni Morrison returns to Robert Garner something of his agency in the person of Paul D via the revisionist modernist sensibility to be found particularly in Hurston. In an earlier chapter I discussed Hurston's "hermetically sealed" South as being a landscape in which black folk culture flourished without intervention from an intrusive, industrializing North or without the need for Southern blacks to escape thereto. But although *Jonah's Gourd Vine* argues a liminal recognition of class consciousness in John Buddy's beginnings as one who lived "over the creek," his stepfather, Ned, exhibited a subservience mirroring that of the bondsman. The milieu of the sawmill in *Mules and Men*, at least as much as the environs of Toomer's *Cane*, pictures black labor as being exploitative and dangerous. Each of these works describes the peonage of the postbellum period, a period whose source is another hermetically sealed milieu, the era of slavery itself. In slavery's nether realm brutality becomes the currency of power and one of the principal

---

1. Steven Weisenburger, *Modern Medea: A Family Story of Slavery and Child Murder from the Old South,* 72; *Provincial Freeman,* February 23, 1856, n.p.; Orlando Patterson, *Slavery and Social Death: A Comparative Study,* 13.

means toward capital. As Louis Althusser and Etienne Balibar write, the time of economic production is a condition whose concept "must be constructed out of the reality of the different rhythms which punctuate the different operations of production, circulation and distribution"; it is a time that has its own rhythm, a saturating cadence that is neither clock nor calendrical time, but rather an infamous "time of times," a time marked by the ceaseless repetition of labor and the fact of production. Inexorably, in slavery the engine of this time is violence, the least movement of whose subjects is labor. For Eric Williams, slavery, which "made the American South and the Caribbean islands," always was but "a part of that general picture of the harsh treatment of the underprivileged classes . . . and the indifference with which the rising capitalist class was 'beginning to reckon prosperity in pounds sterling, and . . . becoming used to sacrificing human life to the deity of increased production.' " Chief among the slave's daily duties to the self was the resistance of an always-encroaching sense of nonbeing, a resistance, as the character Dana remarks in Octavia Butler's novel *Kindred,* to slavery as "a long slow process of dulling" (*Kindred,* 183). While "no authentic human relationship was possible where violence was the ultimate sanction," writes Orlando Patterson of the relationship between master and slave, one can also include within this the difficulty of establishing one's relationship to oneself, as Sethe experiences in *Beloved.*[2] Though she kills her infant daughter in order to prevent her return to slavery, Sethe is in fact saving her child from what she herself endures as impossible existence, as existence in contradiction with itself: her natal alienation, the condition of domination and dishonor that from birth defines the status of every enslaved person. Paul D, while committed to helping Sethe to reclaim her self from the guilt and the horror of her act, is also engaged in the difficult task of reclaiming his self.

Mr. Garner, owner of Sweet Home, gives the male slaves on his plantation respect as men. He listens to them, values their opinions, and even lets them dictate the pace of work—but the facts of their enslavement and that they are considered no more than chattel once they leave the plantation secure his ultimate control of them. He

2. Louis Althusser and Etienne Balibar, *Reading Capital,* 101; Eric E. Williams, *Capitalism and Slavery,* 5; Patterson, *Social Death,* 12.

ordinarily risks more severe sanctions for violating the code of social control common among slaveholders by calling the Sweet Home
male slaves men, as he is always willing to take a beating from his
peers for doing so. But despite his pronouncements and power, Paul
D, Paul F, and Paul A Garner, Halle Suggs, and Sixo manage to acquit themselves as strong men in other ways. In Garner's formulation of black manhood, the determining one in slaveocracy, they
move and live and have their being; before Sethe's arrival they were
"all in their twenties, minus women, fucking cows, dreaming of
rape, thrashing on pallets, rubbing their thighs and waiting for the
new girl" (*Beloved,* 11). The respect they gave to one another, however, was manifest in their having Sethe make *her* choice. Each man
offers a different and intriguing representation of manhood. Sixo,
for example, will risk all each weekend for his all-too-brief visit
with the Thirty-Mile Woman, and after his return Sunday night the
others will spend the entire next day concealing his fatigue from
Garner. Such devotion makes Sixo unique, incomparable even to the
constancy of nature's other wonders: "Now *there* was a man, and
that was a tree," the novel's chorus remarks. "Himself lying in the
bed and the 'tree' lying next to him didn't compare" (*Beloved,* 22).
Sixo's behavior and commitment establish him not as object but as
subject; however difficult it becomes to maintain the difference, he
takes his place among other men rather than among things.

Of her strong and capable son Halle, the wise Baby Suggs had
said, "A man ain't nothing but a man, but a son? Well, that's *somebody"* (*Beloved,* 23), and though this seems a curious locution, Baby
is actually mindful of the complexities of men; their definition at this
time depends crucially on the fact of slavery itself, its ravages on the
body and the possible absence of that body through anything from
sale, to escape, to death. Baby's thought also again mirrors what
Hortense Spillers remarks about the issue of the black masculine in
the fact of the Middle Passage and after: that the African American
male "has been touched . . . by the *mother, handed* by her in ways he
cannot escape. . . ."[3] The idea of the divide between expressions of
black manhood and a maternal ethos, prominent in *Cane,* returns,
thus guiding a reconsideration of Garner's valuation of the Sweet
Home men as men, coming as it does from a restrictive white paternalism. After Halle's witnessing of Sethe's violation, however—an

3. Spillers, "Mama's Baby, Papa's Maybe: An American Grammar Book," 80.

event that undoes both his strength and his sanity—Paul D becomes Sethe's counterpart in her struggle toward self-recovery, and is honored as the man who steps in to replace Halle after his fall.

Paul D has come to Cincinnati eighteen years after so many tragedies—long after Halle's breakdown and death at witnessing Sethe's abuse by the brutal Schoolteacher, and as yet unbeknownst to him, the murder of Beloved. Nevertheless, he strives to mingle laughter with tears. "Emotions sped to the surface in his company," *Beloved*'s narrator says of Paul D, "and wouldn't you know he'd be a singing man . . . singing as he mended the things he had broken the day before" (*Beloved,* 39–40). The little blues lyrics he sings tell the story of a difficult, enslaved life, made only marginally easier by his first years of freedom. They were remnants of songs learned during some of his darkest hours on the prison farm in Alfred, Georgia, or during the Civil War years, "nothing like what they sang at Sweet Home, where yearning fashioned every note" (*Beloved,* 40). Paul D is rendered as a prototypical bluesman who, like Tea Cake Woods, is capable of rendering a balm to those in need, but in helping Sethe to heal, his songs are also geared toward the remaking of his self. This remaking takes its form as well in his mending the small household items he has damaged in his wake, becoming a synthesis of lyric and labor captured in Jon Michael Spencer's notion of a "therapy-of-remembering" that was accessible only through the blues singer or through the *houngan* of Voudou, who with his immediate access to Damballah, was the guide to healthy communal and family relations, among other things.[4] While the overburdened Sethe begins to think that it is with Paul D that she might be able to resume her life and achieve some happiness in the bargain, it has not been without extreme difficulty that Paul D has managed his own life in freedom. The therapy of remembering seems best for having brought him body and spirit to 124 Bluestone Road and anchoring him there, for if a life with Sethe is possible, it may relieve the dreaded memory of the Georgia prison farm, after which "he had shut down a generous portion of his head" (*Beloved,* 41). At seeing Sethe alive after her ordeal, through such impossible odds, that closed part of him does reopen, and the possibility of their obliterating the suffering of both by sharing it becomes available to him.

The men of Sweet Home share travail in a way similar to that of

---

4. Jon Michael Spencer, *Blues and Evil,* 14.

communities of women in bondage. As much as Sethe loved Halle, she carries within her the pain of his having seen her violation by Schoolteacher's boys; Halle is destroyed from within because he could not stop the boys from taking Sethe's milk, or Schoolteacher from chronicling the act. Paul D, who saw Halle for the last time with his face smeared with butter, could not speak with Halle for both Halle's insanity and Paul D's mouth being restrained by an iron bit. These stark yet common images of slavery depict broad and apparently unbridgeable divisions between Halle and Sethe, Halle and Paul D, and ultimately create the shared wounds to be healed by the mutual work of Sethe and Paul D. In Paul D's anguish male strength and courage, unlike trees, shrink at inhuman horror. "Let me tell you something," he admonishes Sethe in her bitter resentment of Halle. "A man ain't a goddamn ax. Chopping, hacking, busting every goddamn minute of the day. Things get to him. Things he can't chop down because they're inside" (*Beloved,* 69). Part of Paul D's more personal anguish comes from this comparison with trees, as black men were routinely tied to them to be whipped, or hung from them; for this reason, a part of himself is also bound up with the "tree" on Sethe's back, the scars raised by one of Schoolteacher's boys said to look like a chokecherry tree to Sethe's rescuer and her daughter Denver's namesake, the white Amy Denver. Paul D, struggling as he might to bridge the gaps between Sethe and herself and between Sethe and himself, is remarkably relatively unencumbered by the ordinary barriers of gender. Though "not even trying," we are told, "he had become the kind of man who could walk into a house and make the women cry. Because with him, in his presence, they could. There was something blessed in his manner" (*Beloved,* 17). After Sethe tells him of the scars, he bends over her without lust, "his body an arc of kindness," and begins to touch the scars with his cheek. In this moment he seeks, rather than simple physical gratification, something transindividual with Sethe: in his caressing the scars, "he learned that way her sorrow, the roots of it; its wide trunk and intricate branches," but the apparently incommensurable distance between them will have to be reconciled another way as the scars have barred Sethe from all sensation, despite the fact that Paul D "would tolerate no peace until he had touched every ridge and leaf of it with his mouth" (*Beloved,* 17–18).

The tree is the barrier between them, but it is also the medium through which he reads her pain, a pain of which, as a slave, he has his irreducible share. For Paul D to read Sethe in this way is to begin to love her, and it is also to find some of this love for himself. As opposed to the form of the escaped slave narrative in which the generative, usually male narrator is incisively literate, Paul D cannot read. He is otherwise literate, however, possessing the lens of feeling that allows him to read the pain of Sethe's back, of Halle's terrible witness, and of his own horror. Imagined in Benedict Anderson's sense, Paul D's community cannot be assembled by the print culture of his time; as Stamp Paid smoothes out the newspaper clipping that tells of the murder, what Paul D recognizes though he cannot read the text is the drawing of Sethe accompanying it. "That ain't her mouth," he insists, and at this discrepancy and at her very appearance in the paper, he can discern that the text could never have reported favorably of her "because there was no way in hell a black face could appear in a newspaper if the story was about something anybody wanted to hear" (*Beloved,* 155). The distortion of Sethe's mouth represents Gayatri Spivak's idea of the subaltern black figure who cannot speak in her own defense,[5] and Paul D's prescience here, a reading and a knowing beyond reading and knowing, produces the inexorable return to both the historical Garners: to Margaret, whose tragic act could not be understood if the pain of slavery could not, and to Robert, who was written out of every community and every history. The Foucauldian valuation of pain as marker of its own record on the body also makes visible Sethe's and Paul D's shared sensibilities. The distortion of Sethe's mouth that Paul D discerns in the newspaper drawing is linked to the bit that distorted his own mouth, making him unable to speak to Halle after Halle's witness of Sethe's defilement. Indicative of the common sexual exploitation of black women by white men, the taking of Sethe's milk by Schoolteacher's boys is linked to the suffering of Paul D in the coffle in Alfred, Georgia, where the guardsmen's ritual exploitation each morning of their black captives—fellatio at gunpoint—was only one of many atrocities to be survived.

As both Mary Helen Washington and Wilson Moses write, women

5. Benedict Anderson, *Imagined Communities: Reflections on the Origin and Spread of Nationalism,* 30–36; Gayatri Spivak, *A Critique of Postcolonial Reason: Toward a History of the Vanishing Present,* 255.

as escaped slave narrators had to name their sexuality in ways that male narrators did not. Even contemporary critical perspectives tend to emphasize the typically gendered scenario of sexual exploitation as it appeared to be foregrounded in antebellum narratives; for example, Harriet Jacobs's sexuality is "the source of much of her torment, and much of the attention that has recently been given to her narrative focuses on her reaction to sexual oppression as a component of the American social order" (Sundquist, 71). But Jacobs herself both critiques and highlights this tableau by describing for her audience the sexual demands that could be put upon slave men as well. Late in her narrative *Incidents in the Life of a Slave Girl* (1861), Jacobs tells the story of Luke, who she remembers after having already escaped New York. After the death of his master, Luke passes as property to the master's son, who, through drink and general dissipation, is gradually deprived of the use of his limbs. If Luke resisted beatings in the slightest, the master would send for the local constable, stronger and more robust, to carry out the task, and from this Luke understood that punishment from his weakening master was to be preferred to beatings by proxy. As Jacobs writes:

> The arm of his tyrant *grew weaker,* and was finally palsied; and then *the constable's services were in constant requisition.* The fact that he was *entirely dependent* on Luke's care, and was obliged to be tended *like an infant,* instead of inspiring any gratitude or compassion towards his poor slave, seemed only to *increase* his irritability and cruelty. As he lay there on his bed, *a mere degraded wreck of manhood,* he took into his head the strangest freaks of despotism; and if Luke hesitated to submit to his orders, the constable was immediately sent for. Some of these freaks were of a nature too filthy to be repeated. When I fled from the house of bondage, I left poor Luke *still chained to the bed* of this cruel and disgusting wretch. (*Incidents,* ch. xl; emphasis added)

The most remarkable feature of this aside by Jacobs is its daring to illustrate to a genteel, Northern, principally female audience the depredations upon the black male body that were possible for Southern white men of leisure and property to effect. The italicized portions of the previous excerpt, as well as Jacobs's detail that

Luke had previously been owned by the master's father (thus suggesting at least a different invasiveness to the black male body, the "kicks and cuffs" that Luke later describes as being an ordinary event of his everyday servitude), are meant to indicate that as Luke's situation worsens, his bond to his master becomes stronger and more indissoluble; that is, the relative space of safety that Luke might assume to avoid beatings and forcible sex dramatically decreases. (This transition corresponds to the master's being depicted as merely a "prey to vices" early in Luke's story, and a "cruel and disgusting wretch" at its end.) This is a critique of male sexual slavery that represents itself as an inversion of Jacobs's master trope in *Incidents,* the "loophole of retreat" through which she flees her owner, the imperious and lustful Dr. Flint: the progressively smaller and more confined her surroundings, the greater her space of resistance in deceiving her predator, winning thereby both freedom and a bodily security. In a way similar to Luke's diminution of space and the correlative increase in cruelty in *Incidents,* Paul D's sexual exploitation is but one feature of his captivity in the Georgia coffle. As he relates his ordeal to Sethe, he is held in a five-by-five-foot cell that is dug upright some five feet into the earth, but still more like a coffin than anything else, with forty-five other men each with their own similar spaces, and "with anything that crawled or scurried welcome to share that grave calling itself quarters" (*Beloved,* 106). If Jacobs's "loophole" is an inversion of women's sexual exploitation, it also highlights the fundamentally gothic nature of the textual figuration of that exploitation—violation and/or death as end results of the impossibility of escape—and both Jacobs in her recollection of Luke and Morrison in her rendering of Paul D's ordeal claim this unspeakable episode of bondage for men. As Elaine Scarry writes, the condition of torture is described by the enlargement of the torturer's world and the diminution of that of the tortured via the medium of pain.[6] Torture as an aspect of existence is embedded in the fact of slavery; if as a psychic consequence of pain the tortured subject experiences a diminution of his world because even the common objects of that world become instruments of torture, the experience of the slave approximates this in the gratuitous punishment he experiences

6. Elaine Scarry, *The Body in Pain: The Making and Unmaking of the World,* 355n192.

as an ordinary course of existence. Fighting the reduction to this state is what Paul D and the other forty-five men in the coffle are engaged in daily, though it seems inevitably a battle to be lost:

> They sang of bosses and masters and misses; of mules and dogs and the shamelessness of life. They sang lovingly of graveyards and sisters long gone. Of pork in the woods; meal in the pan; fish on the line; cane, rain and rocking chairs.
>
> And they beat. The women for having known them and no more, no more; the children for having been them but never again. They killed a boss so often and so completely they have to bring him back to life to pulp him one more time. Tasting hot meal cake among pine trees, they beat it away. Singing love songs to Mr. Death, they smashed his head. More than the rest, they killed the flirt whom folks called Life for leading them on. Making them think the next sunrise would be worth it; that another stroke of time would do it at last. Only when she was dead would they be safe. (*Beloved,* 108–9)

Paul D is able to share these things with Sethe in meaningful ways because he has endured them and is able to articulate the experiences, but he cannot, at least for the present, share Sethe's chief anguish, that of having murdered her daughter. His leaving Sethe for what he feels to be her horrible crime not only widens the chasm between them, but further complicates the idea of love as a value. What appears to be one strange valuation of love is expressed by Ella, one of the conductors on the underground railroad who aids Sethe shortly after Denver's birth. "If anybody was to ask me," she muses sadly while looking at the tiny baby's face, "I'd say, 'Don't love nothing'" (*Beloved,* 92). Sethe, in discussing with Paul D the now-older Denver's reluctance to accept his moving in, provokes this feeling from him: it was "very risky," he thought, for a former slave woman to love anything, especially her own children. "The best thing, he knew, was to love just a little bit; everything, just a little bit, so when they broke its back, or shoved it in a croaker sack, well, maybe you'd have a little love left over for the next one" (*Beloved,* 45). Baby Suggs, the mother of Sethe's dead husband Halle, carries with her vestiges of love as vivid and as poignant as the colors she collects: she has among them her first name, a reminder of the only man she ever claimed as husband: that he called her "Baby" as an endearment. But in allowing this appellation, she chooses what love is

possible in this perilous time. The renaming is less his sexist label-
ing of her than it is the means by which his reuniting with her may
be made easier.

The ironical and asynchronous movement of Morrison's text further complicates the idea of love, and adds to the fragmentary nature
of this among other values; for example, Paul D learns of Beloved's
murder only after several painful visitations to the truth. Sethe is
somehow involved in several shadings of truth, including her telling
Paul D that the little girl had died, though not how; later, that she has
had to go to jail, but not why. But in the most ironic and poignant of
these, Stamp Paid has shown him the newspaper clipping whose text
Paul D cannot read, but whose drawing of Sethe he can; at this
ground Paul D, who can trust only that news about blacks condemns
them, thus has the consciousness that Sethe's deeds, however heinous, are in fact bridgeable if she can speak to them. Hardened by
his experiences, he carries a heavy heart metaphorized by the tobacco tin rusted shut and lodged in his bosom. Beloved, the ghost,
the trace of the dead daughter, is the composite of hard recollections
that both Sethe and Paul D must confront; Beloved's seduction and
eventual conquest of Paul D represent for him the love, even the love
for the self, fragmentary at best, that he must seek to replace his
pain. At a diegetic ground, the sex they have is ultimately desexual-
ized, making the erotic descriptions themselves fragmentary; as she
exhorts him to "touch me on the inside part" the suggestion is ambiguous, in one instance genital, but in another, spiritual. It is a command that also is really a matter of reflexivity: she also tells him to
call her by her name, which in one utterance of it is "be loved"
(*Beloved*, 117). That the assaults upon his spirit via his body are
what has hardened Paul D to begin with makes all the more intriguing
Valerie Smith's remark that Paul D's sexual relations with Beloved
can be read as "a bodily cure."[7] Sethe, who carries within herself an
oppressive guilt at having murdered her youngest daughter, has that
guilt best manifested in the daily humiliations she experiences at
Beloved's hands. Compared to the beatings she received that formed
the chokecherry tree on her back, Beloved's domination of her
mother actually purifies. Not only is Beloved constructed as an act
of Supernature seeking harmony, but for both Sethe and Paul D, she

---

7. Philip Page, "Circularity in Toni Morrison's *Beloved*," 31–39; Valerie Smith,
"'Circling the Subject': History and Narrative in *Beloved*," 342–55.

becomes a definition for the achievement of love: the several, painful visitations to the truth.

As Harriet Jacobs invokes again and again in *Incidents,* it is "that demon Slavery" that sunders even the most basic human emotions, and *Beloved*'s heroic task is to represent the aftermath of slavery as an assembling of fragments for as whole and as vital a humanity as is possible. While Jacobs's telling of her story in the era of the Fugitive Slave Law makes evident the fragmentation of her presentation of self—for the success of her antislavery message to her audience she must appear variously in the text as innocent child, abused child, woman, wronged woman, mother—*Beloved*'s setting in the era of Reconstruction, which choice forces a new appreciation of the term's layered meanings, generates the reader's consistent consideration of Sethe's often repeated neologism *rememory.* While Sethe conflates the words "memory" and "remember," inherent in her every utterance of the word is another tension so savagely violent for both its psychic and physical implications. *Re-membering,* as a reassembling of the body made horrifically legible by the marking that sundered it, is the seemingly impossible yet fundamental task in which both Sethe and Paul D are crucially engaged. Homi Bhabha discusses Lacanian temporality as "time-lag," and for Bhabha, *Beloved*'s time-lag serves as the anagogic space in which exists the possibility of the reordering of both community and history as against the depredations of slavery, a "not-there" which produces "historical revision in diaspora" and by its very nonlinear structure "subverts the synchronous Western sense of time and tradition" (*Location,* 199). But the embedded meaning of this incommensurable space is to be found in the memory of both male and female bodies, in Elaine Scarry's discussion of the relation of the body to war. "[The presence of learned culture] must at least in part be seen as originating in the body," she writes, "attributed to the refusal of the body to disown its own early circumstances, its mute and often beautiful insistence on absorbing into its rhythms and postures the signs that it inhabits in a particular space at a particular time." Intrigue inheres in the comparison between Bhabha's notion of the "not-there" as a function of temporality with Scarry's description of the minutiae of bodily function as indices to cultures in bodies:

> The extent to which in ordinary peacetime activity the nation-state resides unnoticed in the intricate recesses of personhood,

penetrates the deepest layers of consciousness, and manifests
itself in the body itself is hard to assess; for it seems at any
given moment "hardly" there, yet seems at many moments,
however hardly, *there* in the metabolic mysteries of the body's
hunger for culturally stipulated forms of food and drink the external objects one is willing habitually to put into oneself;
hardly there but *there* in the learned postures, gestures, gait, the
ease or reluctance with which it breaks into a smile; *there* in the
regional accent, the disposition of the tongue, mouth, and throat,
the elaborate and intricate play of small muscles that may also
be echoed and magnified throughout the whole body, as when a
man moves across the room there radiates across his shoulder,
head, hips, legs, and arms the history of his early boyhood years
of life in Georgia and his young adolescence in Manhattan.[8]

Though Bhabha's formulation is inclusive of a discussion of pain unto
the wrenching of Western time into asynchronous temporality, Scarry's
references are far more specific to pain that is both psychic and physical, and both point graphically to every aspect of re-membering, from
the healing sought from both Sethe's and Paul D's violation to the
thrice-layered pain of Sethe's biting through her tongue to bear a savage beating: the last layer is manifest in her inability to voice her violation as speaking subject, a condition Paul D is able to recognize from
the distortion of her mouth in a newspaper drawing.

Paul D's sense of his masculinity within the context of his enslavement was always imperiled, and this peril is similar to what
Sethe feels she must convey to Beloved before she leaves: "that anybody white could take your whole self for anything that came to
mind. Not just work, kill or maim you, but dirty you. Dirty you so
bad you couldn't like yourself anymore. Dirty you so bad you forgot
who you were and couldn't think it up" (*Beloved,* 251). Paul D
specifically recalls what it means to be called a man by the slave-
holder Garner, and in a strenuous effort of memory he labors to
bring himself beyond the confines of bondage: "What would he have
been anyway," he muses, "before Sweet Home—without Garner? In
Sixo's country, or his mother's? Or, God help him, on the boat?" (*Beloved,* 220). In an effort to imagine himself in a time and milieu
perhaps like that of Hurston's Moses, beyond the reach of the always-
already realm of capitalist time, Paul D is ultimately stopped by

8. Scarry, *Pain,* 109.

capitalism's first hour, slavery's dreadful beginning, the Middle Passage. But two other constituents of his thought are also powerfully present: his mother, who again recalls the irreducible connection between black maleness and the maternal, as well as it recalls the elusive figure of the maternal in Wideman's novels, the mother as crucible of incommensurability in Toomer's *Cane,* and also Sixo, who though he had never smiled throughout his life laughs hysterically and defiantly at the hour of his death with the knowledge that the Thirty-Mile Woman will bear their child. Even Sixo's risky thirty-mile treks for the sake of loving this woman seem meant less for individual pleasure than for the ontic significance that both Sixo and Paul D give it in the logic of human effort against human negation. Of the Thirty-Mile Woman, Sixo had shared with Paul D her role at the horizon of his process of memory; indeed how she became this horizon, as she helped him to reshape his place in history: "She is a friend of my mind. She gather me, man. The pieces I am, she gather them and give them back to me in all the right order. It's good, you know, when you got a woman who is a friend of your mind" (*Beloved,* 272–73). With this as a strength, Paul D can help render to Sethe her relation to her self, and Sethe can reciprocate, helping him mend the shards of his being. Others may follow the example, attempting to give one another a healing present through the mutual gifts of the bodily imaginary: not pained and distorted voices, but women; not trees, but men.

Mama Day's Witnesses to Love

Gloria Naylor's novels are linked by character and/or by situation from *The Women of Brewster Place* to *Mama Day,* and George Andrews makes his first appearance at the end of *Bailey's Café,* the novel preceding *Mama Day,* as the infant son of a prostitute whose birth inspires hope in all of the café's regulars who are, by the poignant claims their stories make, the community's most disenfranchised. George compels us to imagine a contemporary black maleness that can locate its provenance in no specific place, but nevertheless claims for itself an inheritance in much the way that slave narrators generally begin their tales of bondage with the phrase "I was born." George's difficulty in locating his past ultimately becomes ours: he *was* born in Bailey's café, but neither is Bailey the owner's real name, nor does the café itself have a location: it is the oasis of memory, a liminal refuge from human catastrophe. "Bailey" himself, as he introduces the novel, informs the reader of his travels, which includes recollections of the error of human exclusion, from its relatively innocuous to its most devastating, everything from the class consciousness of the black elite to the nuclear holocausts of Hiroshima and Nagasaki. The building itself exists only in the imaginations of those for whom real spaces of safety were difficult to come by; as the proprietor himself says of his clientele, "if they can't figure out that we're only here when they need us, they don't need to figure it out" (*Bailey's,* 28). In *Mama Day,* however, the café acquires more of a fixed space as George takes Cocoa north to Harlem along Riverside Drive and identifies the café as being the place outside of which he was found by the owner as an infant lying on a stack of newspapers. If no man is an island, as the English writer John Donne demanded, but rather that "every man is a piece of the continent, a part of the main," then in at least two ways, George Andrews's connection to his community is interestingly ironized: in *Mama Day,* he points out his separation from his community in *Bailey's Café* by telling Cocoa that he was a foundling; at the same time, the café itself has a location, occupying liminal space. That space is now on Manhattan Island, known popularly as the Big Apple, the center of all things, with both its history and its personality being blithely unconnected to the other four counties that compose New York City. Unlike the great cities of antiquity, New York, as Michel de Certeau writes, "has never learned the art of growing old by playing on all its pasts. Its present invents itself, from hour to hour, in the act of throwing away its previous accomplishments and challenging the future." This description argues for fitting George's life as well; as Mrs. Jackson, the headmistress at the Wallace P. Andrews Shelter for Boys consistently reminded him and others as he was growing up, "Only the present has potential, *sir*," the remark itself a clarion call for self-reinvention. The school itself was located in Richmond County, or Staten Island, to the west of Manhattan, a place often dismissed by Manhattanites as being a repository for landfill, but in fact having its own rich history, particularly as regards black self-reinvention. In the nineteenth century, free blacks in Maryland's oyster trade were barred from becoming oystermen by white captains who refused to sign them on. Staten Island's southern shore, known as Sandy Ground, thus became a major site for the oyster trade, as it was settled by African Americans in the 1830s who had migrated from as far as Maryland and Virginia after slavery had been abolished in New York State in 1827. Every free opportunity to make a living in Sandy Ground was the fulfillment of a nourishing present and an always-contiguous future; the past need never again have true bearing. Also at the ground of the notion of reinvention, the 1830s would be the same decade in which Frederick Douglass escaped from Maryland's eastern shore, with freedom—and masculine self-reinvention—at stake.[9]

George's background recalls the "islands" of sensibility that suggest the very structure of part one of *Cane,* as Karintha, trapped by the twin wardens of gender and environment, must develop the thickest armor in order to control the tenor of sexual demand upon her. This first section dramatically erects these structural boundaries within which women must either rely on their own unique resources or die Becky's death, or endure Esther's or Louisa's psychological disintegration. If the elements of George's birth are sustained in *Mama Day,* however, then in *Bailey's Café* George's mother was both black and Jewish, and in this George would closely resemble Toomer's Fern as an emblem of the split subject. In many of Toomer's women resides the thin line between a canny individualism and a melancholic isolation. As there are aspects of both in George, thus casting for him a sophisticated androgyny, there are lines of division even unto his political choices: as an African American who is also a registered Republican, he represents himself as being virtually a breed apart. A football fan who, for his weak heart, had never played as a child, he supports the New England Patriots rather than either the hometown New York Giants or Jets; though he believes he has "a special affinity for underdogs" (*Mama Day,* 125), there seems here a deeper manifestation of dislocation from the man who as a foundling was himself misnamed: his team was originally known as the Boston Patriots, a team that in its first decade of existence moved nomadically around the Boston area without a home

---

9. Michel de Certeau, "Walking in the City," 151–52; Eugene L. Meyer, "Not Forgotten," 11–14; Bayly E. Marks, "Skilled Blacks in Antebellum St. Mary's County, Maryland," 543–44.

field of its own.[10] Football is by far George's most cherished sport, and as a man who for his physical infirmity could never play the game, he is forced to approach it virtually from the perspective of intellect. In the machismo- and even class-coded world of contact sport, particularly football, this approach suggests a fundamental effeteness in him that is reflected in the limitation forced upon him by an arrhythmic heart, but George Andrews also strives for a conventional manhood that evinces itself not by rejecting, but by even embracing the severest physical limitation: "Baseball and basketball were a linear display of skill and strength: if you thought fast and were strong and flexible, you could endure. But football took that extra ounce from a man: when your physical frame is being beaten and slammed, you can simply become too tired to think, to move. And sometimes your guts can even give out. So you keep going because you keep going. It produces a high that's possible only when a man has glimpsed the substance of immortality" (*Mama Day,* 124). For George, the athlete-warrior *makes* his manhood by continuing toward the goal of winning despite pain, despite even the threat of death. George's struggle with mortality is only partly the most fundamental aspect of this demand that he places upon himself; it is indistinguishable from his sense of his masculinity and his vague history, which began as an infant abandoned on a stack of newspapers. Notions of the ephemeral and the anonymous that appear to govern George Andrews's life begin here, in the painful randomness of his mother's career as a sex worker, and in the lack of fixity in communitarian culture, this time *not* as illustrated in the physical structure of the newspaper as represented by Benedict Anderson but in both the passing vitality of its content as news and its inability to record all human tragedy, thus inevitably regarding its omissions as banalities. While the historical Robert Garner was virtually written out of history by the newspaper culture of his era, the fictional George Andrews lies helpless atop a stack of them. While Paul D remarks that nothing good about black life ever appears in newspapers, much of the worst, particularly in George's case, also does not.

Though George can be said to be unable to trace a past, he can remember the Andrews Shelter where he grew up and the way in which he was raised. Though it was Mrs. Jackson who repeated the

10. David Harris, *The League: The Rise and Decline of the NFL,* 123–24.

phrase that he was to find useful throughout his life, the dynamic in which she most often utters it to her charges is tinged with an irreducible irony, as George explains: "I knew I'd hear her until the day I died. 'Only the present has potential, *sir.*' I could see her even then, the way she'd jerk up the face, gripping the chin of some kid who was crying because his last foster home hadn't worked out, or because he was teased at school about not having a mother. . . . I could still feel the ache in my bottom lip from the relentless grip of her thumb and forefinger pressed into the bone of my chin—'Only the present has potential, *sir'* " (*Mama Day,* 23; original emphasis). The children George describes, whether from their failed foster homes or from enduring cruelties from their peers at school, are engaged in *marronages,* which were slave escapes, but sometimes they were only brief respites from the toil and horror of plantation life to which they must inevitably return. Mrs. Jackson and her assistant Chip, who would invariably be seen "chewing on his bottom right jaw and spitting as if he still had the plug of tobacco in there Mrs. Jackson refused to let him use in front of us," seem paired vaguely as slave-master and overseer; in this regard Mrs. Jackson—director of the Andrews Shelter for Boys—recalls Andrew Jackson, whose illicit proprietary claims on Indian lands in the 1820s paved the way for the expansion of chattel slavery on the North American continent. Before Jackson's raids on Florida began in 1816, the Seminoles, refusing to honor a treaty requiring them to cede their land, also sheltered or enslaved escaping black slaves. Southern slaveholders, outraged that their property was fleeing into Florida, pressed for intervention; black escapees, who blended with the Seminole population, made their *marronages* to another isolated space; this venue, a peninsula rather than an island, figures eventual doom for both Indian and fugitive black, as the military presence advances.[11] Albery Allson Whitman's 1885 epic poem *Twasinta's Seminoles, or, The Rape of Florida,* having the ring of the Romantic Supernatural, finds the pleasures of the remaking of the self at land's end, the last such paradise in which such remaking is possible:

> Negro, or Arab, Zulu if one choose,
> Unmoved be thou reproached for all but fear!

11. Howard Zinn, *A People's History of the United States, 1492–Present,* 127–29; Michael Rogin, *Fathers and Children: Andrew Jackson and the Subjugation of the American Indian,* 194–95.

By the unhindered waters learn to muse,
With nature's liberal voices in thy ear;
Dwell on her nobler aspects that appear,
And make companions of all one may find:
Go rove the mountain forests far and near,

And hear the laughter of the open wind;
Then ask, what earth affords like freedom of the mind!
(canto II, str. IX, ll. 73–81)

Ironically, Mrs. Jackson denies George and the other boys at the Andrews Shelter any illusion of a future; the present of the Whitman poem is ephemeral at best, as the future of freedom in the Negro's compact with nature is foreshortened by approaching government forces. The idea of a return to nature as being the saving grace of mankind, prevalent among the English Romantic poets, finds expression here in Whitman's poem, as even for those Romantics, being in the presence of such natural beauty was generally not without its proximate peril—in the case of Wordsworth and Coleridge, that peril was the French Revolution. While the literacy-to-freedom trope of the slave narrative mapped the escapee's success, the human compact with nature that was often the last vestige of strength in pan-African expression again becomes the new literacy. For Jean Toomer, an idyllic if horrific age of black cultural formation was rushing toward its demise in the modern present; for Zora Neale Hurston, the black folk culture of her present had to be held inviolate from modernism. For the modern exile George Andrews, a generous helping of this new literacy is, paradoxically, what is required.

Ophelia Day, the woman with whom George falls in love, hails from the fictional Willow Springs, one of the Sea Islands off the coast of South Carolina and Georgia. Ophelia—or Cocoa or Baby Girl, as she is known back home—is descended from the slave woman Sapphira Wade, who has wide influence and wields great power in Willow Springs even in the present, as her bill of sale, registered August 3, 1819, indicates:

Sold to Mister Bascombe Wade of Willow Springs, one negress answering to the name Sapphira. Age 20. Pure African stock. Limbs and teeth sound. *All warranty against the vices and maladies prescribed by law do not hold forth;* purchaser being in full knowledge—and affixing signature in witness thereof—

that said Sapphira is half prime, inflicted with sullenness and entertains a bilious nature, having resisted under reasonable chastisement the performance of field or domestic labour. Has served on occasion in the capacity of midwife and nurse, not without extreme mischief and suspicions of delving in witchcraft. (*Mama Day,* flyleaf, emphasis added)

Sapphira's "vices and maladies" are of course only her natural inclination against enslavement, but even as such the bill of sale's caveat also indicates the powerlessness of slavery's inhumane forces in ever diminishing or eradicating this inclination. It would perhaps be difficult for contemporary sensibilities to imagine a will so indomitable as to successfully withstand "reasonable chastisement" in consistently resisting most of a typical slave's duties, but Sapphira's strength recalls some of Hurston's most resolute women. Sapphira's "pure African stock" and her facility with the occult recall as well Hurston's pan-African Supernature and its location of spiritual power in places and times beyond the reaches of the West's demands of capital. Having won her freedom just four years later, there is understandable confusion in her later generations of just how this was done; as an opening narrative voice says, "Sapphira Wade don't live in the part of our memory we can use to form words" (*Mama Day,* 4).

Sapphira was "the original conjure woman," and as the guiding spirit of the Days and of all of the other inhabitants of Willow Springs, she also echoes Morrison's Beloved in her similar capacity as the conscience of love and re-membering that Sethe and Paul D must confront. Most specifically, however, she is the force who, through her conduit, Ophelia's great-aunt Miranda Day, brings George and Ophelia together in a unique and enduring way—a way in which the sundering rituals of the contemporary world are themselves definitively undone. Willow Springs, as Cocoa remarks to George during their courtship, is an island whose jurisdiction is in no state, whose history after Sapphira's defeat of Bascombe Wade becomes entirely its own. Its master narrative is of nature and therefore of freedom, as suggested by Albery Whitman's poem, and it manages to achieve this narrative during the same years in which the narrative of Jacksonian tyranny, one of the great narratives in the history of mass displacement on the mainland, is taking shape. This determination of nature's element toward the principle of freedom is at the heart of the interplay between Miranda's efficacy as conjure woman and the natural and scientific explanations she gives for her conjurations; as conjure is for many a questionable means of control over nature, and freedom is a felt quality that cannot be contained, the interplay also lends this undecidability to the text that it is left to George, finally, to mediate. George's islands are places of the irreducible "now," places that allow him no history, no memory; his ineluctable participation in them resembles the time of the slave, the capitalist, Althusserian "time of times" from which relief seems impossible. "To lack memory is to be a slave of time, confined to space," remarks W. J. T. Mitchell; "to have memory is to use space as an instrument in the control of time and language."[12] But George's ability to remake the self— his apparent talent for the autochthonous, born of his particular circumstance of having the past abstracted from him, is perhaps his principal virtue.

Not only does George gain from the transformation of space in his eventual move south, but Cocoa also benefits from George's showing her around New York, the City of Exiles. The modern valuation of life beyond Willow Springs is that there is a wide world beyond it, a world that does not have to be an object of suspicion or stereotype. Cocoa, who earlier often referred to ethnic others as food, among other things, loses this prejudice after George shows her around town, and while George's continuing education will later take place at Willow Springs, Cocoa becomes overwhelmed by the vastness of Manhattan Island, and realizes how small her life had become. Moreover, she is overwhelmed by the degree to which George has already remade himself: he behaves as a perfect gentleman, appearing to want no more than that Cocoa enjoy herself. Much of the beginning of the text's narration is also characterized by George's and Cocoa's engagement in crossing monologues, each referring to aspects of the other, though without directly addressing the other. Taken together, they represent a narrative dislocation that resembles the asynchronous time of *Beloved* and lends to the tension, tenderness, and humor of their budding relationship without becoming sentimental. "Nothing I had met in that world had prepared me for your possibility," Cocoa says in one instance (*Mama Day,* 99), as George seems already to have transcended what a world of faster

12. W. J. T. Mitchell, "Narrative, Memory, and Slavery," 207.

pace has to offer. But the phrase "your possibility" has a double edge to it: George is far from perfect, in not entirely having transcended his sexism, as Cocoa soon learns. His passion for football for which he is often willing to sacrifice time with her and his reductive explanation of her anger as being caused by her menstrual cycle reveal that he invariably regards women as objects. Additionally, however, and by comparison ironically, the point of romance in Cocoa's remark is made without recourse to the unreliability of sentiment in "your possibility": it announces George on one hand as having an agency prepared to bridge differences and Cocoa on the other as one prepared at least to appreciate the effort.

Once in Willow Springs, George has his measure taken by the island's various characters: first by Miranda and Abigail, Cocoa's grandmother, and then by others such as Ambush Duvall, the comical Dr. Buzzard, and the philandering Junior Lee, who lives with the perennially jealous Ruby. In most cases George is more than equal to the task, as he does everything from beat the cheating Buzzard at cards to help in repairing the bridge between Willow Springs and the mainland. But the fight between Cocoa and George—as they both agree, their "worst fight ever" (*Mama Day,* 230, 232)—becomes the occasion for Junior Lee's assault on Cocoa and, as a result, Ruby's effort at retribution against Cocoa through conjure. As it happens, the worst fight ever between George and Cocoa is about black identity, about the African American presentation of self. More specifically, it is about Cocoa's choice of coloration in her makeup and that the choice of a darker shade than her light skin tones support reflects the ways in which she perceives others have always regarded her—as other than a black woman. Entering this unfortunate war of words is the mention of Shawn, George's white former girlfriend. While neither party in a marital spat can be expected to behave without recourse to nasty remarks, what has also widened the chasm between George and Cocoa in this moment is the specter of whiteness itself. In comparing herself with Shawn in fights with George, Cocoa has always feared this specter, offering it as yet another remove from who she really is. This condition makes the second phase of Ruby's conjuration all the more interesting: as Cocoa later puts on makeup after Miranda rescues her from the first phase, which was the delirium she contracted from Ruby's braiding her hair, her every brushstroke now distorts her face, or appears to do so as she looks in the mirror. All the while, of course, with its winds bending the trees and waves lashing the shore, a hurricane has been building.

The trope of the coastal storm that has become a staple of Caribbean and eastern U.S. African American writing, representing *marasa* consciousness, occurs here as well. *Marasa* consciousness, as described in the previous chapter, represents movement, particularly displacement—through migrant labor, rural-urban drift, exile and emigration, and radical sociopolitical change. One can add *marronage* to this list, as this event depends on the kind of upheaval that eventually leads to flight. Such was the case with the *marronage* of the feisty Sapphira Wade, who, as legend has it, sought to escape bondage by going due east through the woods in Willow Springs, and upon reaching the edge of the island, tried to return her spirit if not her body across the Atlantic to Africa. Every December twenty-second, Sapphira's trek to the eastern side of the island is commemorated by Candle Walk, the yearly ritual of Willow Springs in which the Days and everyone else on the island participate with fervor. As each of Candle Walk's pilgrims "lead on with light"—symbolizing Sapphira's movement to the shore with no more than candlelight to guide her—they reenact her singular and passionate drive toward freedom. Year after year, however, the spirit of Willow Springs moves slowly toward decline, as is evidenced by the kinds of commercialism creeping across the bridge from the mainland to devalue its rituals—including the confusion of Candle Walk rituals with those of Christmas arriving three days later, which, as Miranda muses to herself, "ain't never caught on too much here" (*Mama Day,* 108). There is also more specific decline, as the neighborliness of Willow Springs is disrupted by Ruby's jealousy. She has killed before for Junior Lee's undivided attention, and now Cocoa, as a result of Junior's aggressive flirtations, is the object of her wrath. As Abigail tracks poetically the world course of the storm, beneath her musings are the soul's record of the immemorial injustices wrought against it in this hemisphere:

> It starts on the shores of Africa, a simple breeze among the palms and cassavas, before it's carried off, tied up with thousands like it on a strong wave heading due west. A world of water, heaving and rolling, weeks of water, and all them breezes die but one. *I cried unto God with my voice, even unto God with*

my voice. Restless and disturbed, no land in front of it, no land
in back, it draws up the ocean vapor and rains fall like tears. . . .
A roar goes up and it starts to spin: moving counterclockwise
against the march of time, it rips through the sugar canes in
Jamaica, stripping juices from their heart, shedding red buds
from royal poincianas as it spins up in the heat. Over the broken
sugar cane fields—hot rains fall. But it's spinning wider, spinning wider, spinning higher, groaning as it bounces off the
curve of the earth to head due north. *Thou holdest mine eyes
waking; I am so troubled that I cannot speak. I have considered
the days of old, the years of ancient times. (Mama Day,* 249–50;
original emphasis)

As Sapphira—both the Sapphire who had dominated and emascu-
lated Bascombe Wade in the cause of her freedom, and the zephyr,
spirit of the wind—had embraced the east after making her way to
the edge of the island, now do hurricane gales, developed from the
harmattan breezes off Africa's west coast, come in liberation. Miranda,
who becomes the agent of this effort, now alertly cuts Cocoa's hair,
which had been braided by the malevolent Ruby, and later, with a little help from the storm, causes lightning to strike Ruby's trailer—
twice, killing her.

As is the case in Hurston's understanding of conjure, the work of
supernatural forces is guided by balance. Little Caesar Duvall, the
child born to Ambush and Bernice, is killed in the storm, but curiously there is much conjecture by the neighbors as to exactly how.
Bernice, devastated, yearns to bring the boy back to life. Her effort
to take Little Caesar to the "other place," the house built by Miranda's and Abigail's father, John-Paul Day, is given a gentle demurrer
by Miranda, who understands the limits of her own power. "More
crushing, just a bit more crushing than that baby's death," the old
woman muses to herself, "is the belief that his mama came to her
with" (*Mama Day,* 261). John-Paul, having been born the "seventh
son of a seventh son," was bestowed with a second sight and a talent
for certain control of natural forces that was inexplicably conferred
upon his daughter Miranda, but even more than this was given to
Miranda in her youth, as she took care of the family, and of the entire island, as nurse and midwife. Other islanders remarked about
her "gifted hands," and late in life Miranda understands and accepts
the gift, having assisted in birthing most of the people living on the

island to this point. She adopts the same view as would her stoically philosophical father as she sighs to herself that she's "everybody's mama now" (*Mama Day,* 89). Balance in other areas becomes a key to reading the novel's climax; after Miranda's rescue of Cocoa from a phase of the death-dealing conjuration by cutting her braids, Cocoa begins to revive, and upon seeing her shortened hair, remarks that she would restyle it, trimming the ends and marcelling it in body waves—"a sort of 1920s style that you saw in old photographs of those swanky women when Harlem was in its heyday" (*Mama Day,* 273). Here a doubled irony ensues: Cocoa's interesting return to a time when Harlem was in vogue centers her in one of the era's fundamental anxieties. Its preference for lighter-complexioned African Americans was a notion often satirized by Toomer, Hurston, and other writers of the era, and specifically it recalls the women of *Cane,* who meet with tragedy because of the distortions race performs within the self. Contrasted with *Cane*'s women is Hurston's Janie, whose development of black female self-expression is remarkably undeterred by her light skin. Additionally, the photographs depicting women of the Harlem Renaissance would have been in black and white, a medium leaving some room, though certainly not enough, for the subtleties of color. George, who for his anchorage in the present holds no such fantasy, feels the broad distance between himself and his wife becoming even more difficult to traverse. "You refused to share my optimism," Cocoa muses, noting his dissatisfaction with things as they are.

In returning to Cocoa's delusional gaze of herself in the mirror, she is comforted by the fact that Abigail does not see what she sees. The image in the mirror, therefore, is not real. But what is real is the series of welts that seem to move across Cocoa's body, the grotesque colonies of worms that are eating her body from the inside. The imbalance of Cocoa's racial consciousness is depicted by this wasting, and is further characterized by the colors that ensue from it: the welts themselves, once red, are now "like clear water blisters" (*Mama Day,* 281); her urine is "thick and brown" (*Mama Day,* 287), as if not only blood but also dark flesh—the "black inside"—is part of the bodily detritus. In another of Cocoa's delusions, the worms further take on the characteristics of whiteness, seeming the color of and even becoming the beads of water in her shower; George recognizes one of the worms only after mistaking it for a drop of his semen

(*Mama Day,* 298), and at one point remembers looking at Cocoa in bed, with much of her face "turning a sickly pale . . ." with "still the face of a cadaver" (*Mama Day,* 288). It may seem odd that such a stark symbolic progression, a whiteness-as-grotesquerie, appears to be conquering the black body of Cocoa, for while having been somewhat naïve about the complexity of culture until having met George, she has otherwise appeared as a confident and self-assured woman, nurtured by family and community structures that bespeak a local cultural and racial independence. But as Ann duCille suggests, the demons of racial self-doubt in the public sphere are both ubiquitous and insidious; despite consistent nurturance from her mother and the considerable force of that personality, duCille's active childhood fantasy life became for her "less a wish to flee my own black flesh than a desire to escape the limitations that went with such bodies. . . . Even as a girl of seven or eight I was at once aware of and frightened by the burdens that seemed to me natural by-products of living in a black woman's body."[13]

George and Miranda are united not only in their sense of purpose, the saving of Cocoa, but also in their shared sense of loss. George's mother's death was probably from drowning in Long Island Sound; Miranda's sister Peace died in The Sound off the western edge of Willow Springs, and her niece, also named Peace, was lost to the bottom of a well. But George has already been put off by the charlatanry of Dr. Buzzard, and is now even less disposed toward attempting to save Cocoa through conjure. Miranda challenges George to do it her way, however—to enter the henhouse near the other place with John-Paul's walking stick and the old ledger with Sapphira's bill of sale, whose ink is now blurred with age, and bring back from a particular nest, that of "an old red hen setting her last batch of eggs," whatever he finds there with his own hands. George, whom we know to have been misnamed, is carrying the ledger in which Sapphira's name is all but obliterated, which connection signifies the only thing that then remains—the force of the individual spirit. In a way similar to Paul D's "reading" of the way Sethe was maligned, Miranda, though the name of her foremother is unintelligible to her, can nevertheless through her dreams read the spirit that can save. John-Paul's walking stick, once the old man's and now his daughter's signature, bears

13. Ann duCille, *Skin Trade,* 13.

powerfully the sign of Damballah: as we are told of the stick's orna-
mentation, "the long, sleek bodies of them snakes [were] carved so
finely down its length that when he turned it they seemed to come
alive" (*Mama Day,* 88). But the already weakened George is disori-
ented by the hen's fierce attack, and in the fray he breaks the eggs
that are in the nest, and kills the hen in a confusion of frustration, fatigue, and self-defense: "I tried grabbing her from behind," he relates in the moments before his death. "My right hand, my left
hand—both hands attacked with her beak and spurting fresh blood"
(*Mama Day,* 301). Bleeding hands would be all that George would
have to return to Miranda, and all that he could use to save Cocoa. In
his final act of love George achieves this balance, as all incommen-
surables are laid to rest.

Miranda understands that George had chosen his way over hers to
save Cocoa, but though she never entertains the notion, even she
cannot tell us whether George exercised a choice that was entirely
free. Even George, the eternal skeptic, was earlier unable to keep his
own faith in mechanized modernity from being dwarfed by the
forces of nature as he felt the beginnings of the storm. "That was
power," he recalls of his early engineering exploits that produced
machinery powerful enough to light every home in New York, "but
the winds coming around the corners of the house was God" (*Mama
Day,* 251). Though he has never disregarded God to the point of
atheism—rather calling himself "a comfortable amnesiac"—he reveals that what has always guided his sensibilities regarding his existence is the insistence on valuing only the present instilled in him
by Mrs. Jackson. It is this tenet that has reminded him of his infini-
tesimal place in this universe, a place that is given this proper perspective in the presence of such raw, unmitigated power. "You yearn
for company then," he says, "any company, to have some minor evidence of your worth reflected back at you" (*Mama Day,* 252), and
though he is with the entire family, he goes only to the bedside of his
dying wife. Cocoa in her helplessness does for George in this instance what Paul D does for Sethe: she allows him to appreciate his
own fundamental worth. George reciprocates, finally, with the greatest possible gift—that of the whole self.

George should perhaps not be advanced simply as a Christ-figure,
but at the ground of the development of the modern male interces-
sor, he appears to fashion the courage of this kind of sacrifice through

a reversal of the failed sacrifice of the spectatorial artist in "Kabnis" to issues of race and reconciliation. In chapter three I discussed the ending of "Kabnis" in terms of the denial of the presence of Father John's struggle, his ability to bear witness, and the Christian symbolism that surrounds and structures that denial. As intriguing as is Hurston's conflation of African and Western religious symbolism, particularly in *Jonah's Gourd Vine,* is the opening of "Kabnis," in which Kabnis, after having returned to the South from the North, alone in his cabin and terrified of the Southern horror of sudden death, is frightened by the nearby scratching of a hen. He chases it down, decapitates it, and "wipes blood on his hands onto the coarse scant grass" (*Cane,* 82), which resembles the Kongo practice of honoring the presence of the dead. But Kabnis, erring even to the point of denial and sacrifice, is unaware of the significance of this act; moreover, it has little effect as symbol as it is performed in fear and in despair of coming to terms with his history. He cannot honor what he aches to flee. The hen in pitched battle with George, however, spills *his* blood, allowing what becomes George's transcendent function. Though Miranda berates the fallen George as having had to try saving Cocoa his way, she has forgotten an earlier colloquy with Abigail about George's fitness to create a future with Cocoa: "No," she cautions Abigail, "he said, 'She has all I have.' That means sharing. If he got a nickel, she's got a part in it. He got a dream, he's gonna take her along. If he got a life, Abigail, he's saying that life can open itself up for her. You can't ask no more than that from a man" (*Mama Day,* 136).[14] George's final moments are much like the Passion, which like the saving of Cocoa was engineered to inaugurate a new history. If his ultimate value is determined only in the potentiality of the present, then only his laying on of his bloodied hands could be Cocoa's salvation. She is freed in a uniquely modern sense and from more than a physical death, if that were not enough. The fact of her racial doubt and shame, excised and healed by the inner grace of one impelled to remake himself in each contingent moment, becomes past as well.

14. Thompson, *Flash of the Spirit,* 134–35; Gary Storhoff, "'The Only Voice is Your Own': Gloria Naylor's Revision of *The Tempest,*" 35–45.

CONCLUSION

[Legislators who have changed offenses punishable by lynching from voting to assaulting white women] encourage or lead the mobs which do the lynching. They belong to the race which holds Negro life cheap, which owns the telegraph wires, newspapers, and all other communication with the outside world. They write the reports which justify lynching by painting the Negro as black as possible, and those reports are accepted by the press associations and the world without question or investigation. . . . Over a thousand black men, women and children have been thus sacrificed the past ten years. Masks have long since been thrown aside and the lynchings of the present day take place in broad daylight. The sheriffs, police and state officials stand by and see the work well done.

—Ida B. Wells, from *The Reason Why the Colored American Is Not in the World's Columbian Exposition*

"Americans are imbued," writes Nicholas Lemann, "with the notion that social systems proceed from ideas, because that is what happened at the founding of our country. The relationship of society and ideas can work the other way around, though: people can create social systems first and then invent ideas that will fulfill their need to feel that the world as it exists makes sense." This was demonstrably the case with the 1893 World's Columbian Exposition in Chicago, which, through its pageantry and splendor, was expected to be the international fair that would display American progress through science, technology, and cultural influence, and thus announce the approaching twentieth century with a distinctly American voice. The United States was quickly emerging as a world power, and by the end of the decade it would indisputably realize this goal through, among other events, the Spanish-American War. The fair's many planners, investors, and builders, however, envisioned the Exposition to represent even more than power: the fair was intended to symbolize, indeed reconstruct, America as Utopia, a venue in which Western progress reached its zenith, projecting a world washed clean by Columbian streams. As Robert Rydell recounts, in the Exposition's Midway, the fair's "honky-tonk" sector, "evolution, ethnology, and popular amusements interlocked as active agents and bulwarks of hegemonic assertion of ruling-class authority"; through this and other displays of American capitalist expansion, the Columbian Exposition "became the standard with which every subsequent fair would be compared."[1] As a function of edifying amusement, representations of the world's ethnicities were brought together and displayed as elements to be studied, yet dismissed; desired, yet averted; feared, yet controlled.

The Midway, a long, narrow, crowded avenue of such racial exhibits, ended at the White City, the microcosmic urban paradise of the American century with which it was contrasted structurally and thus liminally. The world of color was relegated to the Midway, while the White City left no doubt as to who were its preferred inhabitants. Particularly egregious among the exhibits along the Midway were those depicting Asiatic, African, and African American life and culture; as Asiatic and pan-African scholars were not allowed to participate in their construction, these were the places where racist representations flourished. The usurpation of physical space by the White City and its massive focal center, the Court of Honor—a pavilion dedicated to millennial achievement, commerce, and power by pan-European males—severely limited similar symbolic representation by both women and nonwhites. Influential women of the era, including Susan B. Anthony, had unsuccessfully petitioned Congress for the inclusion of women's contribution to world civilization at the exposition. Though other later efforts met with success, representations of black and brown women in the Women's

1. Nicholas Lemann, *The Promised Land: The Great Black Migration and How It Changed America,* 24; Robert Rydell, *All the World's a Fair: Visions of Empire at American International Expositions, 1876–1916,* 40, 71.

Building were limited to exhibits depicting an evolution of pristine Western white womanhood from beginnings in a presumed savagery. The exhibitions of African and Asiatic peoples generally were so recessed and remote as to stir the outrage of prominent African Americans, including Frederick Douglass and anti-lynching crusader Ida B. Wells, who cowrote the pamphlet *The Reason Why the Colored American Is Not in the World's Columbian Exposition*. For Wells and Douglass, the black presence in their counterstatement to the exposition had a face as much male as female; for them, the importance of gender difference was by the makers of the exposition as profoundly undercut as was race. As Gail Bederman writes, *The Reason Why* became the document that "inverted the White City's depiction of 'Negro Savagery' as the opposite of manly civilization," suggesting instead that "manhood and civilization were more characteristic of black Americans than of white."[2] Through this discursive medium of civilized manhood, Wells and Douglass force the recognition of black women. While noting that black men are far more consistently the *victims* of savagery—are far more often lynched by whites because of the presumption of rape—Wells also acknowledges that "the women of the race have not escaped the fury of the mob"; a Douglass deeply disturbed by the Midway's caricatures remarks that "we earnestly desired to show some results of our first thirty years of acknowledged manhood and womanhood" (*Reason*, 50, 77). Each commentator thus emphasizes that freedom and citizenship are not issues that can be limited to one gender alone. In this emphasis they expose the ethical and intellectual bankruptcy of the exposition, and demonstrate that for black men and women, who *share* these injustices and misrepresentations, freedom and citizenship are superordinate goals requiring their combined efforts.

The Columbian Exposition's construction of a racially sterile utopia also provided both Wells and Douglass the opportunity to inveigh against what we in the United States today consider a contemporary issue, an issue they understood to have a history with beginnings nearly immemorial: the often capricious incarceration of black men. Even though the writers are aware that black men are imprisoned at a rate simply overwhelming that of black women, they

2. Gail Bederman, *Manliness and Civilization: A Cultural History of Gender and Race in the United States, 1880–1917*, 38.

insightfully produce statistics that show that both black men and women are jailed—and with far more punitive sentencing—than white men and women (*Reason,* 69), thus making even more difficult the broadening and securing of black community. Black incarceration is a significant feature not only of the multifaceted twentieth-century "problem of the color line" later articulated by Du Bois but also of this young twenty-first century; in 1893, Wells and Douglass acknowledged that the devastation caused by this feature had already long preceded them. It is in *The Reason Why* that the man most passionately driven to preserve the spirit in the black body spoke as one with the woman most fervently committed to preserving its substance. Together they fashioned a blended voice, a discourse of equity, that continued a call against injustice by challenging the hypocrisies of the modern age.

If the White City stands as metaphor for the industrialized Northern metropolis, then the avenue beyond its gates, the Midway, stands as the crucible of black culture, however corrupt that figuration, that the city is so desperate to exclude. The Great Migration of blacks from the agrarian South to the industrialized North closes this gap, and in the closing attenuates all binaries and seeks to render to blacks more of their birthright, the nation; but this movement by itself does not fully articulate the gendered and racial isolation of African Americans, and in particular it does not address the fragmentation of black men in the theater of the modern. If the Midway's slow but indefatigable movement comes to rest in Harlem, then the city within a city, black dissent within white complacency, is possible. But it is probably important that Toomer and Hurston, parties to this dissent though with separate voices, did not limit themselves, even physically, to Harlem: Toomer, a seeker after knowledge and inner peace through various spiritual media, also negotiated the tension between the South of his forebears and the North of his own time. For Hurston, the black Midway truly seems never to meet the maw of the White City, but challenges its presumed, accepted notions of culture from within agrarian, Southern boundaries. Both phases of representation are not only part of the Harlem aesthetic but also transcend it, expressing through the often tragic ends of their black male characters possibilities for new and vibrant senses of the black masculine and of black life beyond the nineteenth-century novel of reaction. In doing this, they have also left indices for contemporary black writers, Morrison, Wideman, and Naylor being examples among others, who have chosen the romantic realism of Toomer and Hurston as an instrument to aid in the reinterpretation of the black masculine in a postmodern age. In their pages are many of the situations, though in new contexts, that continue to challenge black maleness and make sharper and more focused a black female response.

Audre Lorde's simple yet compelling question: "If society ascribes roles to black men which they are not allowed to fulfill, is it black women who must bend and alter our lives to compensate, or is it society that needs changing?"[3] goes to the heart of the issue concerning the continuing necessity for black feminism. As did the black women's Club movement, which began at the end of the nineteenth century and just three years after the Columbian Exposition and the appearance of its counterstatement, *The Reason Why,* only an intellectually honest black feminism can be expected to see this issue as a dilemma that it must not only confront but absorb and make a component of political praxis. After the later literary experiments of Toomer and Hurston, other troubled yet thoughtful perspectives appeared on the African American landscape with respect to maleness and identity, and many others continue to appear, as they yet revive the same questions and articulate similar dilemmas. But it might otherwise be hoped that there is a measure of success in Toomer and Hurston which endures: that if black men's engagement in the struggle for lasting and salutary self-expression involves societal change, as Lorde suggests, there is for them something of a record of what to affirm, and what to deny.

3. Audre Lorde, *Sister Outsider,* 61.

BIBLIOGRAPHY

Abrams, M. H. *Natural Supernaturalism: Tradition and Revolution in Romantic Literature.* New York: W. W. Norton and Company, 1971.

Althusser, Louis, and Etienne Balibar. *Reading Capital.* London: Verso, 1979.

Anderson, Benedict. *Imagined Communities: Reflections on the Origin and Spread of Nationalism.* New York: Verso, 1991.

Andrews, William. *To Tell a Free Story: The First Century of Afro-American Autobiography, 1760–1865.* Chicago: University of Illinois Press, 1986.

Assefa, Hizkias, and Paul Wahrhaftig. *The MOVE Crisis in Philadelphia: Extremist Groups and Conflict Resolution.* Pittsburgh: University of Pittsburgh Press, 1990.

Baker, Houston A., Jr. *Afro-American Poetics: Revisions of Harlem and the Black Aesthetic.* Madison: University of Wisconsin Press, 1988.

———. *Blues, Ideology and African-American Literature: A Vernacular Theory.* Chicago: University of Chicago Press, 1984.

———. *The Journey Back: Issues in Black Literature and Criticism.* Chicago: University of Chicago Press, 1980.

———. *Modernism and the Harlem Renaissance.* Chicago: University of Chicago Press, 1987.

Baldwin, James. *The Price of the Ticket: Collected Nonfiction, 1948–1985.* New York: St. Martin's/Marek, 1985.

Barnes, Gilbert H., and Dwight L. Dumond, eds. *Letters of Theodore Dwight Weld, Angelina Grimke Weld, and Sarah Grimke.* Gloucester, Mass.: Peter Smith, 1965.

Barthes, Roland. *Image, Music, Text.* Translated by Stephen Heath. New York: Hill and Wang, 1977.

Bederman, Gail. *Manliness and Civilization: A Cultural History of Gender and Race in the United States, 1880–1917.* Chicago: University of Chicago Press, 1995.

Bell, Bernard W. *The Afro-American Novel and Its Tradition.* Amherst: University of Massachusetts Press, 1987.

Benston, Kimberly W. "'I Yam What I Am': Naming and Unnaming in Afro-American Literature." *Black American Literature Forum* 16, no. 1 (Spring 1982): 3–11.

Berzon, Judith. *Neither White nor Black: The Mulatto Character in American Fiction.* New York: New York University Press, 1978.

Bhabha, Homi R. *The Location of Culture.* New York: Routledge, 1994.

Blake, Susan L. "The Spectatorial Artist and the Structure of *Cane.*" *CLA Journal* 17, no. 4 (June 1974): 516–34.

Bourne, Randolph. "The Handicapped—by One of Them." *Atlantic Monthly* 108, no. 3 (September 1911): 320–29.

———. *The State.* 1918. Rprt., New York: Resistance Press, 1947.

Bowen, Barbara E. "Untroubled Voice: Call-and-Response in *Cane.*" *Black American Literature Forum* 16 (Spring 1982): 12–18.

Boyce Davies, Carole. *Black Women, Writing and Identity: Migrations of the Subject.* New York: Routledge, 1994.

Boyette, Michael, with Randi Boyette. *"Let It Burn!": The Philadelphia Tragedy.* Chicago: Contemporary Books, 1989.

Brawley, Benjamin. *The Negro in Literature and Art in the United States.* New York: Duffield, 1929.

Brickell, Herschel. "A Woman Saved." Review of *Seraph on the Suwanee,* by Zora Neale Hurston. *Saturday Review of Literature,* November 6, 1948, 19.

Bruce, Dickson D. *Black American Writing from the Nadir: The Evolution of a Literary Tradition, 1877–1915.* Baton Rouge: Louisiana State University Press, 1989.

Butler, Octavia E. *Kindred.* Boston: Beacon Press, 1988.

Byrd, Rudolph P. *Jean Toomer's Years with Gurdjieff: Portrait of an Artist, 1923–1936.* Athens: University of Georgia Press, 1990.

Cable, George Washington. *The Silent South.* 1889. Rprt., Montclair, N.J.: Patterson Smith, 1969.

Caldeira, Maria Isabel. "Jean Toomer's *Cane:* The Anxiety of the Modern Artist." *Callaloo* 8, no. 3 (1985): 544–50.

Callahan, John F. *In the African-American Grain: Call-and-Response in Twentieth-Century Black Fiction*. Middletown, Conn.: Wesleyan University Press, 1988.

Carper, Noel Gordon. "The Convict-Lease System in Florida, 1866–1923." Ph.D. diss., Florida State University, 1964.

Chapman, Abraham, ed. *Black Voices: An Anthology of Afro-American Literature*. New York: Mentor, 1968.

Chase, Patricia. "The Women in *Cane.*" In Therman B. O'Daniel, ed., *Jean Toomer: A Critical Evaluation* (Washington, D.C.: Howard University Press, 1988).

Christ, Jack M. "Jean Toomer's 'Bona and Paul': The Innocence and Artifice of Words." In Therman B. O'Daniel, ed., *Jean Toomer: A Critical Evaluation* (Washington, D.C.: Howard University Press, 1988).

Christian, Barbara. *Black Women Novelists*. Westport, Conn.: Greenwood Press, 1990.

Clark, VèVè A. "Developing Diaspora Literacy and *Marasa* Consciousness." In Hortense Spillers, ed., *Comparative American Identities: Race, Sex, and Nationality in the Modern Text* (New York: Routledge, 1991).

Conrad, Joseph. *Heart of Darkness*. In *Youth: A Narrative, and Two Other Stories*. London: William Blackwood and Sons, 1902.

Cooper, Anna Julia. *A Voice from the South*. 1892. Rprt., New York: Oxford University Press, 1988.

Crunden, Robert M. *Body and Soul: The Making of American Modernism*. New York: Basic Books, 2000.

Davis, Arthur P. *From the Dark Tower: Afro-American Writers, 1900–1960*. Washington: Howard University Press, 1982.

de Certeau, Michel. "Walking in the City." In Simon During, ed., *The Cultural Studies Reader* (New York: Routledge, 1993).

de Jongh, James. *Vicious Modernism*. New York: Cambridge University Press, 1990.

Deren, Maya. *The Voodoo Gods*. London: Thames and Hudson, 1953.

Douglas, Ann. *Terrible Honesty: Mongrel Manhattan in the 1920s*. New York: Farrar, Straus, and Giroux, 1995.

Douglass, Frederick. *Autobiographies: Frederick Douglass*. New York: Library of America, 1994.

Dubek, Laura. "The Social Geography of Race in Hurston's *Seraph on the Suwanee.*" *African American Review* 30, no. 3 (Fall 1996): 341–65.

Du Bois, W. E. B. *The Philadelphia Negro.* 1899. Rprt., Millwood, N.Y.: Kraus-Thomson Organization, 1973.

——. *The Souls of Black Folk.* 1903. Rprt., New York: Library of America, 1986.

duCille, Ann. *The Coupling Convention: Sex, Text, and Tradition in Black Women's Fiction.* New York: Oxford University Press, 1993.

——. *Skin Trade.* Cambridge, Mass.: Harvard University Press, 1996.

Eagleton, Terry, Frederic Jameson, and Edward Said. *Nationalism, Colonialism and Literature.* With an Introduction by Seamus Deane. Minneapolis: University of Minnesota Press, 1990.

Ershkowitz, Miriam, and Joseph Zikmund, eds. *Black Politics in Philadelphia.* New York: Basic Books, 1973.

Ferguson, SallyAnn. "Folkloric Men and Female Growth in *Their Eyes Were Watching God.*" *Black American Literature Forum* 21, nos. 1–2 (1987): 185–97.

Fierce, Milfred C. *Slavery Revisited: Blacks and the Southern Convict Lease System, 1865–1933.* New York: Africana Studies Research Center, 1994.

Fischer, William C. "The Aggregate Man in Jean Toomer's *Cane.*" *Studies in the Novel* 3 (Summer 1971): 190–215.

Foley, Barbara. "Jean Toomer's Sparta." *American Literature* 67 (December 1995): 747–75.

——. "Jean Toomer's Washington and the Politics of Class: From 'Blue Veins' to Seventh-Street Rebels." *Modern Fiction Studies* 42, no. 2 (1996): 289–321.

——. "In the Land of Cotton: Economics and Violence in Jean Toomer's *Cane.*" *African American Review* 32, no. 2 (Summer 1998): 181–98.

Foner, Eric. *Reconstruction: America's Unfinished Revolution, 1863–1877.* New York: Harper and Row, 1988.

Foucault, Michel. *Discipline and Punish: The Birth of the Prison.* New York: Pantheon Books, 1977.

——. *The History of Sexuality.* Vol. 1. New York: Pantheon Books, 1978.

Gates, Henry Louis, Jr. *The Signifying Monkey.* New York: Oxford University Press, 1988.

Gatewood, Willard H. *Aristocrats of Color: The Black Elite, 1880–1920.* Bloomington: Indiana University Press, 1990.

Gilroy, Paul. "'After the Love Has Gone': Bio-Politics and Etho-Poetics in the Black Public Sphere." In Gilroy et al., eds., *The Black Public Sphere* (Chicago: University of Chicago Press, 1995).

Goede, William J. "Portrait of the Negro Artist as a Young Man." *Phylon* 30 (1969): 73–85.

Goldfield, David R. *Black, White and Southern: Race Relations and Southern Culture, 1940 to the Present.* Baton Rouge: Louisiana State University Press, 1990.

Gossett, Thomas F. *Race: The History of an Idea in America.* New York: Oxford University Press, 1997.

Griffin, Farah Jasmine. *"Who Set You Flowin'?" The African-American Migration Narrative.* New York: Oxford University Press, 1995.

Griggs, Sutton E. *Imperium in Imperio.* 1899. Rprt., Miami: Mnemosyne, 1969.

Harper, Phillip Brian. *Are We Not Men? Masculine Anxiety and the Problem of African-American Identity.* New York: Oxford University Press, 1996.

Harris, Trudier. *Exorcising Blackness: Historical and Literary Lynching and Burning Rituals.* Bloomington: Indiana University Press, 1984.

Hemenway, Robert. *Zora Neale Hurston: A Literary Biography.* Chicago: University of Illinois Press, 1977.

Holloway, Karla F. C. *The Character of the Word: The Texts of Zora Neale Hurston.* Westport, Conn.: Greenwood Press, 1987.

hooks, bell. *Black Looks: Race and Representation.* Boston: South End Press, 1992.

———. "Zora Neale Hurston: A Subversive Reading." *Matatu* 3, no. 6 (1989): 5–23.

Howard, Lillie P. "Marriage: Zora Neale Hurston's System of Values." *CLA Journal* 21, no. 2 (1977): 256–68.

Huggins, Nathan Irvin. *Harlem Renaissance.* New York: Oxford University Press, 1971.

Hurston, Zora Neale. "Characteristics of Negro Expression." In Nancy Cunard, ed., *Negro: An Anthology* (1934; rprt., New York: Frederick Ungar, 1970).

———. *The Complete Stories.* With an Introduction by Henry Louis Gates, Jr., and Sieglinde Lemke. New York: HarperCollins, 1995.

———. *Dust Tracks on a Road: An Autobiography.* 2nd ed. Edited and with an introduction by Robert Hemenway. Urbana: University of Illinois Press, 1984.

———. *Jonah's Gourd Vine.* New York: J. B. Lippincott, 1934.

———. *Moses, Man of the Mountain.* New York: J. B. Lippincott, 1939.

———. *Mules and Men.* Philadelphia: J. B. Lippincott, 1935.

———. "The 'Pet Negro' System." *American Mercury* (May 1943): 593–600.

———. *Seraph on the Suwanee.* New York: Scribners, 1948.

———. *Tell My Horse.* Philadelphia: J. B. Lippincott, 1938.

———. *Their Eyes Were Watching God.* New York: Harper and Row, 1937.

Jackson, Blyden. *A History of Afro-American Literature, 1746–1895.* Baton Rouge: Louisiana State University Press, 1989.

Jacobs, Harriet. *Incidents in the Life of a Slave Girl, Written by Herself.* Boston, 1861.

Jahn, Janheinz. *Neo-African Literature: A History of Black Writing.* New York: Grove Press, 1968.

James, Henry Field. *Abolitionism Unveiled, or, Its Origin, Progress and Pernicious Tendency Fully Developed.* Cincinnati: E. Morgan, 1856.

Jameson, Fredric. *The Political Unconscious.* New York: Cornell University Press, 1981.

Johnson, Barbara. "Thresholds of Difference: Structures of Address in Zora Neale Hurston." In Henry Louis Gates, Jr., ed., *"Race," Writing and Difference* (Chicago: University of Chicago Press, 1986).

Johnson, James Weldon. *Along This Way.* 1933. Rprt., New York: Da Capo, 1973.

———. *The Autobiography of an Ex-Coloured Man.* 1912. Rprt., New York: Vintage, 1989.

Jolliffe, John. *Chattanooga.* Cincinnati: Wrightson, 1858.

Jordan, June. "On Richard Wright and Zora Neale Hurston: Notes toward a Balancing of Love and Hatred." *Black World* 23 (August 1974): 4–8.

Jordan, Winthrop D. *White over Black: American Attitudes toward the Negro, 1550–1812.* Baltimore: Penguin Books, 1973.

Kerman, Cynthia Earl, and Richard Eldridge. *The Lives of Jean*

Toomer: A Hunger for Wholeness. Baton Rouge: Louisiana State University Press, 1987.

Kimmel, Michael. *Manhood in America: A Cultural History.* New York: Free Press, 1996.

Krasny, Michael J. "Design in Jean Toomer's *Balo.*" *Negro American Literature Forum* 7 (Fall 1973): 103–4.

Kubitchek, Missy Dehn. "'Tuh de Horizon and Back': The Female Quest in *Their Eyes Were Watching God.*" *Black American Literature Forum* 17, no. 3 (1983): 19–33.

Lacan, Jacques. "The Mirror Stage as Formative of the Function of the I as Revealed in the Psychoanalytic Experience." In Alan Sheridan, trans., *Ecrits: A Selection* (New York: W. W. Norton and Company, 1977).

Lemann, Nicholas. *The Promised Land: The Great Black Migration and How It Changed America.* New York: Alfred A. Knopf, 1991.

Leverenz, David. *Manhood and the American Renaissance.* Ithaca, N.Y.: Cornell University Press, 1989.

Levy, Eugene. *James Weldon Johnson, Black Leader, Black Voice.* Chicago: University of Chicago Press, 1973.

Lewis, David Levering. *W. E. B. Du Bois: Biography of a Race, 1868–1919.* New York: Henry Holt, 1993.

————. *When Harlem Was in Vogue.* New York: Oxford University Press, 1981.

Lewis, R. W. B. *The American Adam.* Chicago: University of Chicago Press, 1955.

Lionnet-McCumber, Francoise. "Autoethnography: The An-Archic Style of *Dust Tracks on a Road.*" In Henry Louis Gates and Kwame Anthony Appiah, eds., *Zora Neale Hurston: Critical Perspectives Past and Present* (New York: Amistad, 1993).

Locke, Alain. *The New Negro.* New York: Albert and Charles Boni, 1925.

Lorde, Audre. *Sister Outsider.* Trumansberg, N.Y.: Crossing Press, 1984.

Lott, Eric. *Love and Theft: Blackface Minstrelsy and the American Working Class.* New York: Oxford University Press, 1993.

Marks, Bayly E. "Skilled Blacks in Antebellum St. Mary's County, Maryland." *Journal of Southern History* 53, no. 4 (November 1987): 537–64.

McHale, Brian. *Postmodernist Fiction.* New York: Methuen, 1987.

McKay, Nellie Y. *Jean Toomer: Artist*. Chapel Hill: University of North Carolina Press, 1984.

Meyer, Eugene L. "Not Forgotten." *Preservation: Magazine of the National Trust for Historic Preservation* 54 (July–August 2002): 11–14.

M'Keehan, Hattia. *Liberty or Death; or, Heaven's Infraction of the Fugitive Slave Law*. Cincinnati, 1858.

Mitchell, W. J. T. "Narrative, Memory, and Slavery." In Margaret J. M. Ezell and Katherine O'Brien O'Keefe, eds., *Cultural Artifacts and the Production of Meaning* (Ann Arbor: University of Michigan Press, 1994).

Morrison, Toni. *Beloved*. New York: Alfred A. Knopf, 1987.

Moses, Wilson J. "Writing Freely? Frederick Douglass and the Constraints of Racialized Writing." In Eric J. Sundquist, ed., *Frederick Douglass: New Literary and Historical Essays* (New York: Cambridge University Press, 1990).

Munson, Gorham. "The Significance of Jean Toomer." *Opportunity* 3 (September 1925): 262–63.

Naylor, Gloria. *Bailey's Café*. New York: Harcourt Brace Jovanovich, 1992.

———. *Mama Day*. New York: Ticknor and Fields, 1988.

Neal, Mark Anthony. *What the Music Said: Black Popular Music and Black Public Culture*. New York: Routledge, 1999.

Nielsen, Aldon Lynn. *Reading Race: White American Poets and the Racial Discourse in the Twentieth Century*. Athens: University of Georgia Press, 1988.

North, Michael. *The Dialect of Modernism: Race, Language and Twentieth-Century Literature*. New York: Oxford University Press, 1994.

Olney, James. "'I Was Born': Slave Narratives, Their Status as Autobiography and as Literature." In Charles T. Davis and Henry Louis Gates, Jr., eds., *The Slave's Narrative* (New York: Oxford University Press, 1985).

Page, Phillip. "Circularity in Toni Morrison's *Beloved*." *African American Review* 26, no. 1 (1992): 31–39.

Pateman, Carole. *The Sexual Contract*. Stanford, Calif.: Stanford University Press, 1988.

Patterson, Orlando. *Slavery and Social Death: A Comparative Study*. Cambridge, Mass.: Harvard University Press, 1982.

Pondrom, Cyrena N. "The Role of Myth in Hurston's *Their Eyes Were Watching God." American Literature* 58, no. 2 (May 1986): 181–202.

Price, Richard. *Maroon Societies: Rebel Slave Communities in the Americas.* Garden City, N.Y.: Anchor Press, 1973.

Pryse, Marjorie, and Hortense J. Spillers, eds. *Conjuring: Black Women, Fiction and Literary Tradition.* Bloomington: Indiana University Press, 1985.

Radano, Ronald M. "Soul Texts and the Blackness of Folk." *Modernism/Modernity* 2, no. 1 (1995): 71–95.

Rampersad, Arnold. *The Art and Imagination of W. E. B. Du Bois.* Cambridge: Harvard University Press, 1976.

Retamar, Jose Fernandez. *Caliban and Other Essays.* Translated by Edward Baker. Minneapolis: University of Minnesota Press, 1989.

Riley, Roberta. "Search for Identity and Artistry." *CLA Journal* 17, no. 4 (June 1974): 480–85.

Rogin, Michael. *Fathers and Children: Andrew Jackson and the Subjugation of the American Indian.* New York: Alfred A. Knopf, 1975.

Rydell, Robert W. *All the World's a Fair: Visions of Empire at American International Expositions, 1876–1916.* Chicago: University of Chicago Press, 1984.

Scarry, Elaine. *The Body in Pain: The Making and Unmaking of the World.* New York: Oxford University Press, 1985.

Scruggs, Charles. "Jean Toomer: Fugitive." *American Literature* 47 (1975): 84–96.

———. "The Photographic Print, the Literary Negative: Alfred Stieglitz and Jean Toomer." *Arizona Quarterly* 53, no. 1 (Spring 1997): 61–89.

———. *Sweet Home: Invisible Cities in the Afro-American Novel.* Baltimore: Johns Hopkins University Press, 1993.

———, and Lee Vandemarr. *Jean Toomer and the Terrors of American History.* Philadelphia: University of Pennsylvania Press, 1998.

Serumaga, Robert. "A Mirror of Integration." In Cosmo Pieterse and Donald Munro, eds., *Protest and Conflict in African Literature* (New York: Africana Publishing Corporation, 1969).

Smith, Valerie A. "'Circling the Subject': History and Narrative in *Beloved.*" In Henry Louis Gates, Jr., and Kwame Anthony

Appiah, eds., *Toni Morrison: Critical Perspectives Past and Present* (New York: Amistad, 1993).

————. *Self-Discovery and Authority in Afro-American Narrative.* Cambridge, Mass.: Harvard University Press, 1987.

Snead, James A. "Spectatorship and Capture in *King Kong:* The Guilty Look." In Valerie Smith, ed., *Representing Blackness: Issues in Film and Video* (New Brunswick, N.J.: Rutgers University Press, 1997).

Spencer, Jon Michael. *Blues and Evil.* Knoxville: University of Tennessee Press, 1993.

Spillers, Hortense J. "Mama's Baby, Papa's Maybe: An American Grammar Book." *Diacritics* 17, no. 2 (Summer 1987): 64–81.

Spivak, Gayatri Chakravorty. *A Critique of Postcolonial Reason: Toward a History of the Vanishing Present.* Cambridge, Mass.: Harvard University Press, 1999.

Stampp, Kenneth M. *The Peculiar Institution: Slavery in the Ante-Bellum South.* New York: Alfred A. Knopf, 1956.

Stepto, Robert B. *From Behind the Veil: A Study of Afro-American Narrative.* Chicago: University of Illinois Press, 1991.

Storhoff, Gary. "'The Only Voice Is Your Own': Gloria Naylor's Revision of *The Tempest."* *African American Review* 29, no. 1 (Spring 1995): 35–45.

Sundquist, Eric J. *The Hammers of Creation: Folk Culture in Modern African-American Fiction.* Athens: University of Georgia Press, 1992.

Tate, Claudia. *Psychoanalysis and Black Novels: Desire and the Protocols of Race.* New York: Oxford University Press, 1998.

Taylor, William R. *Cavalier and Yankee: The Old South and American National Character.* Garden City, N.Y.: Anchor Books, 1963.

Thompson, Robert Farris. *Flash of the Spirit: African and Afro-American Art and Philosophy.* New York: Random House, 1983.

Tickner, Lisa. "Men's Work? Masculinity and Modernism." *Differences* 4, no. 3 (1992): 1–37.

Tillich, Paul. *The Courage to Be.* London: Yale University Press, 1952.

Tocqueville, Alexis de. *Democracy in America.* 1835. Edited by J. P. Mayer and Max Lerner. Translated by George Lawrence. New York: Harper and Row, 1966.

Toll, Robert C. *Blacking Up: The Minstrel Show in Nineteenth-Century America.* New York: Oxford University Press, 1974.

Toomer, Jean. *The Blue Meridian.* In Darwin T. Turner, ed., *The Wayward and the Seeking: A Collection of Writings by Jean Toomer* (Washington, D.C.: Howard University Press, 1980).

————. *Cane.* 1923. New York: W. W. Norton and Company, 1975.

————. *Natalie Mann.* In Darwin T. Turner, ed., *The Wayward and the Seeking: A Collection of Writings by Jean Toomer* (Washington, D.C.: Howard University Press, 1980).

————. *The Sacred Factory.* In Darwin T. Turner, ed., *The Wayward and the Seeking: A Collection of Writings by Jean Toomer* (Washington, D.C.: Howard University Press, 1980).

Turner, Darwin T. *In a Minor Chord.* Carbondale: Southern Illinois University Press, 1971.

————, ed. *The Wayward and the Seeking: A Collection of Writings by Jean Toomer.* Washington, D.C.: Howard University Press, 1980.

TuSmith, Bonnie. *Conversations with John Edgar Wideman.* Jackson: University Press of Mississippi, 1998.

Wagner, Jean. *Black Poets of the United States: From Paul Laurence Dunbar to Langston Hughes.* Translated by Kenneth Douglas. Chicago: University of Illinois Press, 1973.

Walker, Alice. *In Search of Our Mothers' Gardens.* New York: Harcourt Brace Jovanovich, 1983.

Walker, David. *An Appeal, in Four Articles: Together With a Preamble, to the Coloured Citizens of the World, But in Particular, and Very Expressly, to Those of the United States of America.* With an Introduction by James Turner. 1829. Rprt., Baltimore: Black Classic Press, 1993.

Warren, Kenneth W. *Black and White Strangers: Race and American Literary Realism.* Chicago: University of Chicago Press, 1993.

Washington, Mary Helen. *Invented Lives: Narratives of Black Women, 1860–1960.* Garden City, N.Y.: Doubleday, 1987.

Waskow, Arthur I. "The 1919 Race Riots: A Study in the Connection between Conflict and Violence." Ph.D. diss., University of Wisconsin, 1964.

Watt, Ian. *The Rise of the Novel.* Los Angeles: University of California Press, 1957.

Weisenburger, Steven. *Modern Medea: A Family Story of Slavery and Child Murder from the Old South.* New York: Hill and Wang, 1998.

Wells, Ida B., et al. *The Reason Why the Colored American Is Not in the Columbian Exposition: The Afro-American's Contribution to Columbian Literature.* In *Selected Works of Ida B. Wells-Barnett,* compiled and with an introduction by Trudier Harris (New York: Oxford University Press, 1991).

White, Walter Francis. *A Man Called White.* New York: Viking Press, 1948.

Whitman, Albery Allson. *Twasinta's Seminoles; or, The Rape of Florida.* 1885. Rprt., Miami: Mnemosyne, 1969.

Wideman, John Edgar. *Brothers and Keepers.* New York: Holt, Rinehart and Winston, 1984.

———. *Philadelphia Fire.* New York: Henry Holt, 1990.

———. *Reuben.* New York: Henry Holt, 1987.

———. *Two Cities.* Boston: Houghton Mifflin, 1998.

Williams, Eric E. *Capitalism and Slavery.* New York: Russell and Russell, 1961.

Williams, Raymond. *The Politics of Modernism: Against the New Conformists.* London: Verso, 1989.

Wollen, Peter. "Fashion/Orientalism/The Body." *New Formations* 1 (Spring 1987): 5–33.

Yarborough, Richard. "Race, Violence, and Manhood: The Masculine Ideal in Frederick Douglass's *The Heroic Slave.*" In Eric J. Sundquist, ed., *Frederick Douglass: New Literary and Historical Essays* (New York: Cambridge University Press, 1990).

Zamir, Shamoon. *Dark Voices: W. E. B. Du Bois and American Thought, 1888–1903.* Chicago: University of Chicago Press, 1995.

Zinn, Howard. *A People's History of the United States, 1492–Present.* New York: HarperCollins, 1999.

INDEX

Abolitionism, 4–5
Abolitionism Unveiled; or, Its Origin, Progress, and Pernicious Tendency Fully Developed (James), 183
Africa, 109–10; black cultural capital from, 10, 16; influence of, 42, 47–48, 58–60, 120. *See also* Pan-African symbolism; Religion, African
Africa, John (Vincent Leapheart), 176
African Americans. *See* Black men; Black women
Agency, 112, 117–18; of black characters, 94; of black men, 11, 99, 103, 183–84, 204
Agrarian culture, 11, 16; in *Cane,* 13, 50; Toomer's experience with, 22–23. *See also* Folk culture
Althusser, Louis, 185
Anderson, Benedict, 189
Anderson, Sherwood, 13, 29
Appeal (Walker), 1
Art, high modernism in, 7–8
Artists, 9
Assefa, Hizkias, 168
Atonement, 119, 121, 124
Auld, Sophia, 3–5
Auld, Thomas, 4–5
Authors, race differences among, 9
Autobiographies, 1; Hurston's, 93, 122 *(See also Dust Tracks on a Road);* Toomer's, 35, 38–40, 48, 55–56. *See also Narrative of the Life* (Douglass)

Autobiography of an Ex-Coloured Man, The (Johnson), 75–76, 148–49
"Avey," in *Cane* (Toomer), 33, 53–55, 61, 76; narrator of, 38, 40–41, 52–54, 56–57, 70

Bailey, Harriet, 4
Bailey's Café (Naylor), 18, 196–98
Baker, Houston, 2–3, 24, 26; on form and mastery, 64–66; on mask, 142–43
Baldwin, James, 179
Balibar, Etienne, 185
Baraka, Amiri, 64
Barthes, Roland, 10–11
Beauty, in *Cane,* 23–25
"Becky," in *Cane* (Toomer), 49, 87; Barlo character in, 43–44, 46; machines as oppressive in, 31–33; narrator in, 35, 38–40
Bederman, Gail, 213
Bell, Bernard, 6–7
Beloved (Morrison), 17–18, 184–89, 194–96, 203; love in, 192–94
Benedict, Ruth, 93, 145
Benston, Kimberly, 30–31
Berzon, Judith, 37
Bhabha, Homi, 194–95
Bibb, Henry, 1
Binarisms, 53, 63, 87, 105; black, 11, 59, 69; European vs. U.S., 8–9; in Hurston's stories, 109, 126–28, 157; Toomer and, 29, 37, 61; twins as, 156–58

Black characters, 8, 94, 105
Black Consciousness movement, 149
Black culture, 58, 93, 119; influences
    on, 24, 51. *See also* Folk culture,
    black
Black folk humor, 97–98, 126
Black men: ambiguities of, 77, 88; in
    Cane, 23–26, 37–38, 44–49, 54,
    71, 79; corruption of, 116,
    122–23, 138–39, 178; criticisms
    of, 17–18, 94, 115; devaluation of,
    144; duality of, 126–27; exploita-
    tion under slavery, 190–91; failure
    to transmit folk culture, 62–63, 70;
    fragmentation of, 14, 86–87, 119,
    122–23, 131, 144, 160–62, 170,
    214; gender relations of, 23, 115,
    119; heroic status in literature,
    6–7, 14; Hurston's portrayals of,
    16–17, 93, 117, 138; identity of,
    11, 41; impotence of, 51–52, 56;
    incarceration of, 213–14; legacy of
    slavery on, 185–86; limitations of,
    44, 96, 149; in literature, 1–2, 149;
    mothers of, 186, 196; as necessary
    to black South, 93–94; in
    patriarchy, 106, 115; power of, 3,
    127; restoration of order through,
    119–21; stereotypes of, 1–2,
    98–100, 106; subordination of, 96,
    148–49. *See also* Men
Black women, 4, 140, 202; abuse of,
    117, 119, 164, 186–88; black men
    and, 11, 17–18, 94, 163; in *Cane,*
    23–24, 37, 198; complexion of,
    36–37; exploitation under slavery,
    189–90; nurturance by, 160–61;
    suffering of, 131–32, 159, 188–89;
    Toomer's portrayal of, 23, 26, 48.
    See also Women
Blacker the Berry, The (Thurman),
    146
Blake, Susan L., 26, 33
"Blood-Burning Moon," in *Cane*
    (Toomer), 31–32, 44–48, 50, 71,
    73, 126
"Blue Meridian, The" (Toomer), 62,
    85

Blues, the, 18–19, 42, 50, 129–30,
    177–78, 187
Boas, Franz, 93, 145
Body, 21, 153, 155, 165, 170; auton-
    omy of, 3, 186; black, 120, 143,
    162; of black men, 120, 190–91;
    of black women, 159, 207–8; in
    culture, 194–95; deformity of,
    150–52, 163; disintegration of,
    135, 169, 172–73, 207–8; pain as
    marker on, 187–89; wholeness of,
    120, 194
"Bona and Paul," in *Cane* (Toomer),
    38, 55–56, 63–64, 70–76
Book of Life, in *Philadelphia Fire,*
    176–80
Bourne, Randolph, 29, 150–53
Bowen, Barbara, 42
"Box Seat," in *Cane* (Toomer), 56,
    61, 69–70, 75, 84, 86
Brickell, Herschel, 94
Brooks, Van Wyck, 29
Brothers and Keepers (Wideman),
    155–56
Brown, Sterling, 10
Bruce, Dickson, 7
Butler, Octavia, 185

Callahan, John, 88
Cane (Toomer), 85, 146, 184; arche-
    types from *The Tempest* in, 66–70;
    author as narrator in, 77–79; black
    folk culture in, 22–24; black men
    in, 37–38, 90–91; differences be-
    tween parts one and two, 49, 53;
    historicized setting of, 83–85; lo-
    cale of stories of, 49, 52–55; loss
    of redemption by black men in,
    12, 77, 89, 91, 117; masculinity in,
    33, 69–70, 186; the maternal in,
    186, 196; race, class, and gender
    differences in, 63, 66, 69; race and
    complexion in, 37, 207; relation
    among sections of, 22, 44–48, 50,
    65, 71, 89; site of incommensura-
    bility in, 64, 89–90; song in, 61,
    63–64, 66, 69; success of, 90;
    women in, 37, 198; writing of,

13–14. *See also* specific story
titles
Capitalism, 134, 195–96, 212; cor-
ruption of black men by, 116, 119;
in *Seraph on the Suwanee,* 101–2
"Carma," in *Cane* (Toomer), 35, 38,
40
Cavalier planters, 100–102
"Characteristics of Negro
Expression" (Hurston), 16, 93, 140
Chase, Patricia, 38
Chattanooga (Jolliffe), 183
Chesnutt, Charles, 6–7
Chicago, 52, 63, 71–72
Christianity, in Toomer's stories, 33
Cities, 8, 147, 173; black culture in,
147, 170–71, 214; critiqued in
African American writing, 17,
146, 150; in *Philadelphia Fire,*
166–67, 177; urban culture as cor-
rupting, 126, 133–34
Clark, VèVè, 157
Class, 52, 60, 66, 185; and black
elite, 52, 65–66, 69, 79, 147,
150–51; in black society, 27–29,
43; influence of, 2, 5; in "Kabnis,"
79, 81; and poverty management,
171–73; race and, 7, 49; Southern
aristocracy, 100–102
Class conflict, 58–59
Class consciousness, 3, 110, 120,
170, 184; of black writers, 6–7;
and racial self-doubt, 10–11; in
Their Eyes, 134–35, 139, 141
Class difference, 66–67, 69, 101–2
Color, race and gender typed, 74–75
"Colored 400," 12
Community, 18, 32, 189, 197; black,
120–21, 150–51; healing of,
120–21, 124, 187; Hurston and,
15–16, 16, 109, 140–41; response
to violence against women, 140,
144; responsibility to, 123, 127,
134–35, 165
Conjure, 109; in *Mama Day,* 202–8
Contending Forces (Hopkins), 6
Cooper, Anna Julia, 148
Covey, Edward, 1, 3

Crime, 51–52
Crisis, The, 9, 22
Crunden, Robert, 29
Cudjoe, 165–66
Cult of masculinity, of Douglass, 1
Culture, 72, 129, 147, 212; body in,
194–95; in Harlem, 8–9; urban,
126, 133–34, 147; white appropri-
ation of, 129–30. *See also* Black
culture; Folk culture
Cunard, Nancy, 93

Damballah (Wideman), 150
Dark Princess (Du Bois), 70, 148
Davies, Carole Boyce, 128, 158
De Jongh, James, 9, 50
Defiance, 1, 50, 71, 180
Depression, influence of, 149
Deren, Maya, 157
Dew, Thomas R., 1
"Dictie" theme, in *Cane,* 49, 53, 69
Disenfranchisement, black rage at, 5
Dixon, Thomas, 6
Dominance: by black men, 15–16,
26, 35; control of cities, 171–72;
male, 95, 97–98; race and, 45, 165;
through violence, 139, 141–43
Double consciousness, 65, 70–71,
120, 126–28, 134, 157
Douglas, Ann, 8
Douglass, Anna Murray (wife), 4
Douglass, Frederick, 1–5, 113,
213–14
Du Bois, W. E. B., 9, 13, 26; on black
elite, 65, 147–48; on black song,
63–65; and Booker T. Washington,
10–11; on double consciousness,
65, 70, 120, 127; race conscious-
ness of, 120, 174; *The Souls of
Black Folk* by, 26, 50, 63–64
DuCille, Ann, 95, 106, 208
Dunbar, Paul Laurence, 59, 146
Dust Tracks on a Road (Hurston), 15,
120, 141; as autoethnography,
145–46; time in North omitted
from, 93, 145–46
Dyer Anti-Lynching Bill (1922), 83
Eagleton, Terry, 2

"Earth-Being" (Toomer), 55–56
Eatonville, Florida, 14–15, 134–35
Economics, 25–27, 45, 48, 94. *See also* Capitalism
Eldridge, Richard, 13
Equality: gender, 6, 113; social, 1–2, 6; South's arguments against, 5
"Esther," in *Cane* (Toomer), 33, 47–48, 87; compared to "Blood-Burning Moon," 45–46; narrator of, 41–44
Ethnography, Hurston's, 114, 118, 140–41

Family: houses' effects on, 25–26; Hurston questioning, 15–16; interracial, 34–35; in *Mama Day,* 206–7; sanctity of home, 127–28
Fashion, high modernism in, 7–8
Father: absent, 63–65, 72, 141; black vs. white, 64–65
Fear, 80–83, 140
Feminism: abolitionism and, 4–5; black, 4, 18, 215; black men's response to, 148, 149; Hurston's influence in, 95; response to Hurston's stories, 95–96, 139–40
"Fern," in *Cane* (Toomer), 23, 48–49, 198; narrator in, 35, 38, 40, 44; similarities with "Esther," 42–43
Fire Next Time, The (Baldwin), 179
Fischer, William C., 71
Fitzhugh, George, 1
Foley, Barbara, 52, 83–85
Folk culture, 58, 60, 65, 120, 184, 201; black, 8, 16, 85–87, 109; black males' failure to transmit, 62–63, 70; loss of black, 22–23, 33, 35, 49; modernism and, 62–63; Toomer and, 33, 35, 62
Folklore, 15, 85–87, 121
Foner, Eric, 127
Form and mastery, 64–66
Formal realism, 10
Frank, Waldo, 13, 27, 29, 68n15
Franklin, Aretha, 178–79
Free labor, 3

Freedom, 3, 5, 76–77, 180, 213; drive toward, 182–84, 205–6; nature as, 202–3; and reinvention of self, 198, 200–201; trains symbolizing, 124–25
Freud, Sigmund, 107
Fugitive Slave Law, 182–84, 194
Funk, 161

Garner, Margaret and Robert, 182–84, 189
Gates, Henry Louis, 69, 113
Gender, 18, 32, 64–65, 119, 134
Gender difference, 49, 110–11, 120, 128, 174
Gender equality, 6, 113
Gender relations, 196; in *Cane,* 23–24; dominance in black, 15–16, 26; Hurston's, 137–38; in Hurston's stories, 110–14; interracial, 32, 34, 76; in *Mama Day,* 18; race and, 73, 115–16, 130–31, 204; in *Seraph on the Suwanee,* 95–98; in slavery, 186, 188; in *Their Eyes,* 111–16, 135–37
Gender roles, 16, 29
Georgia, "Kabnis" set in, 77
Gilroy, Paul, 180
Glassey, Donald, 176
Goede, William, 79
Goldfield, David, 97
Goode, W. Wilson, 167–68
Gossett, Thomas, 99
Great Migration, 8, 48, 56; as threatening to whites, 51, 100
Griffin, Farah Jasmine, 51
Griggs, Sutton, 7
Grimke, Sarah, 12
Guilt, 99, 109, 163, 165, 177, 193; race and, 73–74, 76, 90
Gurdjieff, Georges, 13–14, 85, 90
Guthrie, John, 166

Hanvey, Dorothy, 48
Harlem, culture in, 8–9, 214
Harlem Renaissance, prose of, 10–11
Harper, Frances E. W., 6–7
Harper, Philip Brian, 103

Harris, Trudier, 51
Healing, 210; in *Beloved,* 187, 193,
    195–96; of community, 120–21,
    124, 187
Hemenway, Robert, 15, 107–9, 114,
    119, 129, 145
Herskovits, Melville, 93
Hiding Place (Wideman), 150
"High John de Conquer" (Hurston),
    104
High modernism, 7–8
Holloway, Karla, 114
Home, 25–26, 93, 128
hooks, bell, 106
Hopkins, Pauline, 6
Huggins, Nathan, 9–10
Hughes, Langston, 9, 10, 50
Hurston, Lucy (mother), 15–16, 140
Hurston, Rev. John (father), 15–16,
    125, 137
Hurston, Zora Neale, 119, 137; alle-
    giance to community, 140–41;
    background of, 11–12, 14–17,
    122, 125, 131–32; on black men,
    117, 119; essays in *American
    Mercury,* 96–97, 104;
    ethnographic work by, 114, 118,
    140–41; on folk culture, 86–87,
    201; on forces of nature, 117–18;
    grandmother of, 131–32, 137; in-
    fluence of, 92, 95; influence of
    Africa on, 19, 121, 159; influences
    on, 11, 121, 141; and mother's
    dying wishes, 15–16, 140; motives
    for writing, 94, 104–5; omitting
    time in North from autobiography,
    145–46; race and, 120, 207; on the
    South, 11, 94, 105, 184, 214;
    structural ambiguity in texts,
    124–25, 128–29. *See also Dust
    Tracks on a Road; Moses, Man of
    the Mountain; Seraph on the
    Suwanee; Their Eyes Were
    Watching God*

Idealism, 215
Identity, 55, 146, 158; black, 42–43,
    204; of black men, 24, 29;
    construction of, 2–3; racial, 64,
    71, 76, 80–81, 113–14; Toomer's
    as black man, 33, 41, 59
Imperialism, 8
Imperium in Imperio (Griggs), 7, 10
Incarceration, of African Americans,
    213–14
Incidents in the Life of a Slave Girl
    (Jacobs), 113–14, 190–91, 194
Industrialism, 22–23, 45
Ingraham, Linton S., 21–22, 84
Intellect, vs. sexuality, 59–60
Iola Leroy (Harper), 6–7

Jackson, Andrew, 200, 202
Jacobs, Harriet, 113–14, 190, 194
James, Henry Field, 183
Jazz, 50, 53, 58, 75–76
Jea, John, 1
John (or Jack), as folk hero, 85–87
"John Redding Goes to Sea"
    (Hurston), 93
Johnson, Barbara, 112
Johnson, James Weldon, 52, 75,
    147–49
Jolliffe, John, 183
Jonah's Gourd Vine (Hurston), 94,
    138, 184; black men in, 122–23;
    as semi-autobiographical, 122;
    symbolism in, 123–27, 142
Jordan, June, 14–15
Jordan, Winthrop, 99

"Kabnis," in *Cane* (Toomer), 14, 38,
    77–84, 157, 210; Father John in,
    85–91; Toomer as, 70, 90
"Karintha," in *Cane* (Toomer),
    23–27, 33, 50; men in, 38, 40–41,
    49, 54; in *Natalie Mann,* 27–28;
    similarity to "Avey," 53–55
Kerman, Cynthia Earl, 13
Kindred (Butler), 185
Knowledge, limits of, 33

Labor, 3–4; black, 50–51, 55, 71;
    exploitation of black, 120, 133,
    184; masculinity and, 51,
    100–101; in slavery, 185

Language, uses of, 49, 112
Larsen, Nella, 146
Leadership, 109, 115
Legal system, 98, 144, 150–53, 163
Lemann, Nicholas, 211
Leverenz, David, 4
Liberalism, 170–71
Liberty or Death; or, Heaven's Infraction of the Fugitive Slave Law (M'Keehan), 182–83
Lionnet-McCumber, Francoise, 145–46
Literacy, 201
Literary realism, 5
Literature: African American, 10–11, 17–18, 46, 92, 94, 121, 146, 149, 205–6; high modernism in, 7–8; plantation tradition in, 5–7. *See also* specific titles and authors
Locke, Alain, 13
Lorde, Audre, 215
Lott, Eric, 69
Lovelace, Rev. C. C., 124–25
Lynchings, 50, 51, 71; fear of, 52, 82–83, 88; and struggle to survive in the South, 81–82

Macfadden, Bernarr, 21
Machines, 55, 124, 209; in *Jonah's Gourd Vine,* 122, 126–27; as oppressive, 31–32, 47; power of, 22, 26–27, 122; train symbolizing, 58, 128–29
Mama Day (Naylor), 17–18, 196–210
Manliness, 2, 12, 21
Marasa principle, 157, 205
Marriage, 102, 114; in *Jonah's Gourd Vine,* 127–28; in *Seraph on the Suwanee,* 95–96, 98; in *Their Eyes,* 132–33. *See also* Gender relations
Marrow of Tradition, The (Chesnutt), 6–7
Marxism, 52, 119
Masculinity/maleness/manhood: coming to terms with, 12, 18; components of, 198–99; effects of education on, 147–48; power and, 100–102, 149; race and, 14, 84–85, 98–99; search for meaningful, 156, 167; sources of, 51, 102; white, 2, 64, 100–101; white vs. black, 106–7, 213. *See also* Black men; Men
Masculinity/maleness/manhood, black: ambition in, 133–35; of black elite, 147–48; competence of, 53, 109; corruption of, 93, 164; critiques of, 132, 150; gender relations and, 147–48, 186; in literature, 10, 147; pan-African symbolism in, 18–19, 159; race relations' effects on, 96–97, 180; recovery of, 17, 19; representations of, 17, 69–70, 215; in slavery, 3, 186, 195; sources of, 2, 186
Maternal, the, 4, 64–65, 186, 196
McClure, John, 27–28
McHale, Brian, 149, 156
Men, 111; bewilderment of, 90–91. *See also* Black men
Middle class, 5
Midway (World's Columbian Exposition), symbolism of, 212–14
Migration, 126, 160; and black culture, 62–63, 214; corruption by, 138–39; movement and, 124–25, 205. *See also* Great Migration
Minstrel shows, 61–62
Miscegenation, 64, 79–80, 90
Mitchell, W. J. T., 203
M'Keehan, Hattia, 182–83
Modernism, 11, 18, 53, 62, 88; in *Cane,* 22, 50–52, 63; folk culture and, 62–63; "Young America" group and, 29–30
Modernity, 31–32, 149, 160, 209
Morrison, Toni, 17–18, 215. *See also* *Beloved*
Moses, Man of the Mountain (Hurston), 18, 107–12, 118, 158; compared to *Their Eyes,* 114–15

Moses, Wilson, 189–90
Mothers, 4, 64–65, 186, 196
MOVE (The Movement), 167–68, 176–77, 179
Mules and Men (Hurston), 86–87, 140–41, 184
Munson, Gorham, 29, 33, 41, 77
Music, 72–73, 132; in *Beloved,* 187, 192; in *Cane,* 61, 63–64, 66, 69, 82; in *Philadelphia Fire,* 177–79, 180; symbolism of, 75–76; whites taking over black, 129–30
Muybridge, Eadweard, 152–55
Mythology, Hurston and, 118, 159

NAACP, re-created in "Kabnis," 83
Names/naming, 34, 158, 160, 167; in *Beloved,* 192–93; race and, 30–31, 62; in *Reuben,* 154–55
Narrative of the Life (Douglass), 1, 3, 113
Natalie Mann (Toomer), 27–31, 34, 62
Nation, health of, 114–15. *See also* Community
Native Son (Wright), 160
Naturalism, 149
Nature: forces of, 117–18, 141–43, 157, 203, 209 (*See also* Supernature); as freedom, 202–3
Naylor, Gloria, 17–18, 196–210, 215
Negro (Cunard), 93
"Negro Artist and the Racial Mountain, The" (Hughes), 9
"Negro in Art: A Symposium, The" (Du Bois), 9
New Jerusalem, in African American writing, 46, 159–60, 177
New Negro, 9–10, 14, 23, 47, 179
New York: Hurston omitting from autobiography, 93, 145–46; *Mama Day* in, 197–98. *See also* Harlem
New York Call, Toomer's articles in, 52
Nielsen, Aldon Lynn, 8
"Nigger," use of term, 30–31
North, 5, 214; black life in, 16–17; corruption from, 22–23, 138–39;

Hurston omitting from autobiography, 93, 145–46; Hurston's mistrust of, 125–26
North, Michael, 62
Novel of reaction, 6–7, 11
Novels. *See* Literature

"Of Our Spiritual Strivings," in *The Souls of Black Folk* (Du Bois), 65–66
"Of the Coming of John," in *The Souls of Black Folk* (Du Bois), 70, 72
Old Negro, 10
Olney, James, 5
O'Neill, Eugene, 9
Oppositional black text, 176–78, 180–81
Oratory, 87–88, 122

Page, Thomas Nelson, 6
Pan-African symbolism, 18, 107, 121–22, 130, 202; Hurston's use of, 124, 159; retribution in, 17, 117, 131
Pateman, Carole, 102
Paternalism, 6, 80, 96–97, 103, 186
Patriarchy, 102, 105–6, 134–35
Patterson, Orlando, 184–85
"'Pet Negro' System, The" (Hurston), 96–97, 104
Philadelphia Fire (Wideman), 17, 149–50, 158, 165–75; Book of Life in, 176–80; J. B.'s book in, 176–79; *Tempest* in, 173–76
Philadelphia Negro, The (Du Bois), 147
Picasso, Pablo, 8
Pinchback, Pinckney Benton Stewart, 12, 14–15, 20–22, 34–36
Plantation tradition, 5–7
Plays, by Toomer, 27
Poetry, 59, 118
Police, symbolism of, 55–56, 76
Politics, 4, 94, 99
Popular culture: black, 178, 180; racism in, 94, 104

Postmodern novels, 149
Postmodernism, 17, 150, 173, 215
Power: of black women, 201–2; cor-
ruption and, 94, 123; gender and
race in, 137–38; lack of, 178–79;
masculinity and, 95, 100, 134;
means to, 100–101, 127, 164; of
names and naming, 154–55; in
patriarchy, 105–6. *See also*
Dominance
Price, Richard, 166
Progressivism, 66
Prohibition, 51
Prose: in *Cane,* 50; of Harlem
Renaissance, 10–11
Prostitution: in "Karintha" and
"Avey," 53–55; in *Reuben,* 159

Quest of the Silver Fleece, The (Du
Bois), 70
Quicksand (Larsen), 146

Race, 72; in *Cane,* 14, 45, 79–80;
class consciousness and, 9–10,
134; classifications of, 34, 37–38;
and cross-fertilization of cultures,
8–9; gender relations and, 73,
97–99, 119, 130–31, 174; and
guilt, 73–74, 76, 90; heritage of,
79, 84, 90; identity and, 29–30, 71,
80–81, 113–14, 146; importance
of, 2, 5, 32, 174; and lightness of
complexion, 137, 182, 207–8; loyalty to, 2, 7; masculinity and,
84–85, 106–7, 165; mixing, 42,
79–80, 100, 128; as performance,
61–62; self-doubt and, 9–10, 208;
self-hatred of, 160–61; sense of
blackness and, 29–31, 74, 76;
southern codes of, 82, 98;
Toomer's relations with, 12–13,
19, 52, 64; transcendence of, 63,
116; transgression of codes of, 32,
46, 71
Race consciousness: of Du Bois,
120, 174; Hurston's mistrust of,
120, 145
Race difference, 9, 59

Race relations, 84, 96; black subordi-
nation in, 101, 103, 105–6; effects
on black masculinity, 96–97,
115–16; and gender, 115–16; pet
Negroes in, 96–97, 130
Race riots, 52
Racism, 178, 180; effects of, 48, 51,
165; effects on black men, 119,
183–84; Hurston and, 94, 145–46;
in popular culture, 94, 104, 212;
responses to, 147–48, 179
Radano, Ronald, 63
Radical realism, 5
Rage, 5; of black men, 1, 3, 5; of Du
Bois, 148; not expressed by black
men, 3, 7; Toomer's, 55–56
Rape, 51, 97–99, 103, 105
Realism, 8, 28, 149
"Reapers" (Toomer), 26–27
*Reason Why the Colored American Is
Not in the World's Columbian
Exposition, The* (Douglass and
Wells), 213–14
Religion, 124, 130, 157; African,
121, 127, 142; gods of different,
157–59; in *Jonah's Gourd Vine,*
122–23, 128; in Supernature,
117–18
Reuben (Wideman), 17, 149–65, 181
"Rhobert," in *Cane* (Toomer), 53
Romanticism, high modernism undo-
ing, 7–8
Romantics, English, 118, 201
Rosenfeld, Paul, 29
Russell, Irwin, 6
Rydell, Robert, 212

Sacred Factory, The (Toomer), 29
Scarry, Elaine, 191, 194–95
Scruggs, Charles, 29–30, 52, 62, 66,
90, 147
Self, 24, 62, 65, 80, 185, 195, 209;
consciousness of, 49, 120;
embracing, 164, 180; presentation
of, 194, 204; racial, 31, 74; reinvention of, 18, 197–98, 200–201,
203; sense of, 87, 165, 196;
wholeness of, 13–14

Self-doubt, race and, 9–10, 208
Self-hatred, 160–61
Self-reliance, 4
Self-worth, 5, 136, 159, 173, 209
Sent for You Yesterday (Wideman), 150
Seraph on the Suwanee (Hurston), 94–107; duality in, 129–30; motives for writing, 104–5
"Seventh Street," in *Cane* (Toomer), 37–38, 49–53, 55, 159–60
Sexism, 204, 212. *See also* Gender relations
Sexuality, 61, 67, 99, 127, 193; of African Americans, 51, 106; of black men, 52, 98–100, 99, 174; in *Cane,* 41, 43, 52, 54–58, 60; corruption of black men by, 122–23; division with intellect, 59–60; exploitation under slavery, 189–91; in narratives by black males, 3–4; prostitution and, 53–55, 159; in *Seraph on the Suwanee,* 102–3; stereotypes of, 98–100, 106; transgression of codes of, 32
Slave narratives, 5
Slavery, 1, 65, 202; abuses under, 186–92; effects of, 3, 132–33, 194, 195; escapes from, 182–84, 200–201, 205; lack of personhood under, 184–85; legacy of, 24, 45, 101; sexual exploitation under, 189–91; symbolization of, 66–68, 124; as theft of black body, 3, 120, 143; and violence, 184–85
Smith, Valerie, 193
Snakes, symbolism of, 121–24, 130, 135
Snead, James, 105
Song. *See* Music
"Sorrow Songs, The," in *The Souls of Black Folk* (Du Bois), 63–65
Soul music, 178–79
Souls of Black Folk, The (Du Bois), 26, 50, 63–64
South, the, 5, 46, 100, 185; black cultural capital from, 10–11, 14, 63–64; black men as necessary to,

93–94; changes in, 8, 93, 101; Hurston on, 94, 105, 147; influence of, 51, 60; insularity of, 120, 125, 184; relation to North, 77–78, 214; survival in, 81–82, 86; in Toomer's stories, 22–23, 50–51, 53–55, 77–78, 147. *See also* Great Migration
Sparta Industrial and Agricultural School, 21–22
Spectatorial artist, 154; sacrifice of, 70, 78, 90, 210; Toomer as, 17, 31, 33, 41, 48, 77–78, 83, 156
Spencer, Jon Michael, 187
Spillers, Hortense, 64–65, 120, 186
Spirituality, 85, 87–88, 90, 164
Spirituals, in *Cane,* 53, 61
Spivak, Gayatri, 189
Sport of the Gods, The (Dunbar), 146
Stein, Gertrude, 8
Stepto, Robert, 75–76
Stereotypes, of African Americans: in novel of reaction, 6–7; in plantation tradition literature, 5–6; sexuality of, 98–100, 106
Strength, 21, 109, 122–23, 202; of black men, 44–45, 47; as component of manliness, 12, 198–99
Subjectivity, 1, 31, 92–94, 186
Sundquist, Eric, 124–25
Supernature, 117–18, 193, 202; and atonement, 119, 121; retribution by, 123, 125, 128–29, 131, 143
"Sweat" (Hurston), 16, 140

Taft, William Howard, 51
Taney, Roger, 24
Tate, Claudia, 98, 104
Taylor, William, 100
Tell My Horse (Hurston), 114, 121, 141–42
Tempest, The (Shakespeare): in *Philadelphia Fire,* 173–76; Toomer using archetypes from, 66–70, 75
"Theater," in *Cane* (Toomer), 61, 75–76; class in, 58–61, 69
Their Eyes Were Watching God

(Hurston), 16, 92–94, 131–34, 157; authorial narrative opening of, 110–11, 114; gender relations in, 111–14, 135–37; *Moses* compared to, 114–15; race relations in, 96, 113; violence in, 138–43
Thompson, Robert Farris, 161
Thurman, Wallace, 146
Tillman, "Pitchfork" Ben, 99–100
Time, 185, 203; lags in, 194–95; present and past, 197–200, 203, 210
Tocqueville, Alexis de, 100
Toomer, Jean, 26, 31, 50, 62, 66, 68n15, 69; autobiography of, 35, 38–40, 48, 55–56; background interwoven with characters', 11–14, 21, 33, 35–36, 38–40, 83–84; background of, 34, 64, 90; and black culture, 16, 201; in black elite, 52, 69, 79; double consciousness of, 71, 127; effeteness of, 44, 83–84; grandparents and, 20–22, 35–36; influence of South on, 11, 147, 214; as Kabnis, 70, 77–78, 90; as narrator in stories, 33, 35, 38–41, 44, 53–54, 57–58, 70, 79; race and, 19, 33, 64, 79, 90, 207; as spectatorial artist, 17, 156; symbolism by, 31–32, 159–60; temperament of, 33, 55–56, 85; trying to achieve wholeness of self, 13–14; use of oratory in stories, 87–88; using archetypes from *The Tempest,* 66–70, 75; writing of, 13–14, 27–28, 52, 59, 141. *See also Cane; Natalie Mann;* story titles
Toomer, Nathan (father), 12, 34–36
Toomer, Nina Pinchback (mother), 12, 34–40, 48
Torture, in slavery, 190–92
Trains, symbolism of, 31–32, 58, 124–29, 142
Transindividualism, 16, 18, 121, 188
Turner, Darwin T., 31, 34
Twasinta's Seminoles, or The Rape of Florida (Whitman), 200–201
Two Cities (Wideman), 153–54

United States, 8, 120, 212
Universities, 147–48, 170

Vandemarr, Lee, 53, 66
Vardaman, J. K., 99–100
Violence, 24–25, 32, 181, 192; in gender relations, 137–39; in *Reuben,* 164–65; in slavery, 184–85; in *Their Eyes,* 131–32, 141–43; against women, 131, 135, 140, 144
Virility, loss of, 110, 135
Visions, 42, 44, 47–48
Voice, 70, 82; black male, 122; black women's, 92, 112–13, 119, 135; lack/loss of, 74, 177, 189; of oppressed, 67, 69; of suffering, 81, 88–90
Volstead Act (1919), 51

Wagner, Jean, 59
Wahrhaftig, Paul, 168
Walker, Alice, 139–40
Walker, David, 1
Warren, Kenneth, 5
Washington, Booker T., 10–11
Washington, D. C., 51, 52; *Cane* stories set in, 49–50; as New Jerusalem, 159–60
Washington, Mary Helen, 189–90
Watson, Tom, 99–100
Watt, Ian, 10
Weisenburger, Steven, 183
Wells, Ida B., 213–14
White, Walter, 83–85
White City (World's Columbian Exposition), 212–14
White culture, 49
White women, 4, 99. *See also* Women Whites: on African Americans, 1, 8; appropriation of black culture, 129–30; as characters in Hurston's novels, 94, 104; renaming blackness, 30–31
Whitman, Albery Allson, 200–201
Wideman, John Edgar, 17, 176, 178, 196, 215; background and characters',

155–57; works of, 149–50. *See also*
    Philadelphia Fire; Reuben
Wideman, Robert, 155
Williams, Eric, 185
Wilson, Woodrow, 51
Wollen, Peter, 7
Women, 38, 112; in *Cane,* 49,
    54–58; children and, 164, 192;
    men's failure to respond to, 57–58,
    88–90; violence against, 131, 135,
    138–40, 144; white, 4, 99. *See
    also* Black women

Women of Brewster Place, The
    (Naylor), 196
World War I, 51
World's Columbian Exposition
    (1893), 211–14
Wright, Richard, 160

Yarborough, Richard, 1–2, 4
"Young America" (modernist aes-
    thetes), 29–30, 150–51

Zamir, Shamoon, 65